Policing and the Politics of Order-Making

More than half of the world's population lives in cities, and urban centres are expected to absorb almost all population growth in the coming decades. In the process, urban spaces are emerging as sites of intensified insecurity and violence. From the peripheries of megacities such as Mexico City and Metro Manila to densely populated neighbourhoods in Indonesia, Swaziland, Ghana, South Africa, Mexico, Bolivia, Haiti and Sierra Leone, this book explores how cities are policed when the public police is considered inadequate and insecurity is a mainstay of daily life.

In the urban spaces that the book explores, a plurality of order-making practices, norms and actors coexist in an often contested and transient environment. State police and various civilian policing groups are constituted in relation to each other through a mixture of competition, collaboration and interdependence. Collectively, they draw on a variety of both violent and non-violent repertoires of order-making and are animated by a mix of cultural, religious and state-based norms. This compels us to analytically approach policing practices and actors as embedded not only in police networks, but also in the broader social and political relations and networks of urban space. This exploration of the political underpinning of local order-making in contexts of plural policing constitutes the key and original contribution of *Policing and the Politics of Order-Making* to academic literature.

Peter Albrecht is a Project Researcher at the Danish Institute for International Studies.

Helene Maria Kyed is a Senior Researcher at the Danish Institute for International Studies.

Law, Development and Globalization
Series Editor – Julio Faundez
University of Warwick

During the past decades, a substantial transformation of law and legal institutions in developing countries has taken place. Whether prompted by market-based policies or the international human rights movement, by the relentless advance of the process of globalization or the successive waves of democratization, no area of law has been left untouched. The aim of this series is to promote cross-disciplinary dialogue and cooperation among scholars and development practitioners interested in understanding the theoretical and practical implications of the momentous legal changes taking place in developing countries.

Policing and Human Rights
The Meaning of Violence and Justice in the Everyday Policing of Johannesburg
Julia Hornberger

Lawyers and the Construction of Transnational Justice
Yves Dezalay and Bryant Garth (eds)

Gender, Justice and Legal Pluralities
Latin American and African Perspectives
Rachel Sieder and John McNeish

Social Movements, Law and the Politics of Land Reform
George Meszaros

Land Law Reform in Eastern Africa
Traditional or Transformative?
Patrick McAuslan

Justice and Security Reform
Development Agencies and Informal Institutions in Sierra Leone
Lisa Denney

From the Global to the Local
How International Rights Reach Bangladesh's Children
Andrea Schapper

Governing Refugees: Justice, Order and Legal Pluralism
Kirsten McConnachie

Justice Reform and Development
Rethinking Donor Assistance to Developing and Transitional Countries
Linn Hammergren

Law and Society in Latin America
Cesar Rodriguez Garavito

Policing and the Politics of Order-Making
Peter Albrecht and Helene Maria Kyed

Forthcoming titles in the series:

Multinational Integration, Cultural Identity and Regional Self-Government
Roberto Toniatti and Jens Woelk (eds)

Policing and the Politics of Order-Making

Edited by
Peter Albrecht and
Helene Maria Kyed

Routledge
Taylor & Francis Group

LONDON AND NEW YORK

First published 2015
by Routledge

2 Park Square, Milton Park, Abingdon, Oxon OX14 4RN
711 Third Avenue, New York, NY 10017, USA

a GlassHouse Book

Routledge is an imprint of the Taylor & Francis Group, an informa business

First issued in paperback 2016

British Library Cataloguing in Publication Data
A catalogue record for this book is available from the British Library

Library of Congress Cataloging-in-Publication Data
  Policing and the politics of order-making/edited by Peter Albrecht and
  Helene Maria Kyed.
  pages cm. – (Law, development and globalization)
  Includes bibliographical references and index.
  ISBN 978-0-415-74330-3 (hardback) – ISBN 978-1-315-81374-5 (ebk)
  1. Police. 2. Law enforcement – Political aspects. 3. Internal security.
  I. Albrecht, Peter, 1976– II. Kyed, Helene Maria.
  HV7921.P5826 2015
  363.2'3 – dc23
  2014021404

ISBN 978-0-415-74330-3 (hbk)
ISBN 978-1-138-21122-3 (pbk)

Typeset in Galliard and Gill Sans by
Florence Production Ltd, Stoodleigh, Devon, UK

Contents

Notes on contributors

Peter Albrecht is a Project Researcher at the Danish Institute for International Studies. He holds a PhD from Copenhagen Business School, an MSc from London School of Economics and an MA Research Degree from Aarhus University. Peter has co-authored *Reconstructing Security after Conflict – Security Sector Reform in Sierra Leone* (Palgrave-Macmillan 2011) and co-edited *Security Sector Reform in Sierra Leone 1997–2007: Views from the Front Line* (DCAF/LIT Verlag 2010).

Raymond A. Atuguba is a Senior Lecturer at the University of Ghana, Legon. He is currently on leave and working as the Executive Secretary to the President of Ghana. He has previously been the Executive Secretary to the Constitution Review Commission of Ghana and a member of the United Nations High Level Task Force on the Implementation of the Right to Development. He is co-founder of the Legal Resources Centre and the Law and Development Associates, of which two he has been Executive Director. He holds degrees from the University of Ghana and Harvard Law School.

Julie Berg is a member of the Centre of Criminology and a Senior Lecturer in the Public Law Department at the University of Cape Town, South Africa. She has published widely on the functioning and accountability of non-state security governance systems, with a particular focus on the private security industry, as well as on collaborations between state and non-state security nodes.

Louis-Alexandre Berg's research explores the political dimensions of justice and security provision. He has conducted field work on local dynamics of crime and violence and on the development of military, police and justice systems in Haiti, Liberia, Sierra Leone, Bosnia and Herzegovina, Timor Leste and Honduras. He has served as an Adviser to the World Bank, the US Institute of Peace, the US Agency for International Development, and the United Nations Development Program. Dr Berg holds a BA from Brown University, a Masters in Public and International Affairs from Princeton University and a PhD in Government from Georgetown University.

Karl Hapal is a Research Associate of Balay Rehabilitation Center (Balay), a human rights organization in the Philippines. He has published several papers on violence, community politics and prisons. He earned his BA in Community Development at the University of the Philippines and is taking up his Masters studies in Sociology in the same university.

Steffen Jensen is a Senior Researcher at DIGNITY-Danish Institute Against Torture in Copenhagen and an associate of the University of the Philippines. He has published on issues of violence, gangs, vigilante groups, human rights, urban and rural politics, as well as on the relationship between security and development in rural and urban South Africa and in the Philippines. He has published the monograph *Gangs, Politics and Dignity in Cape Town* along with edited volumes on victimhood, policing, human rights and security.

Nathaniel King is the principal of a private college in Freetown, Sierra Leone, and a Research Associate at the Max-Planck Institute for Social Anthropology. He obtained a PhD in Social Anthropology from Martin Luther University, Saxony-Anhalt, Germany. His most recent publication was a United Nations-commissioned report titled 'Citizens' Perceptions of Sierra Leone's Ethno-Political Divide and Diversity Management'.

Helene Maria Kyed is a Senior Researcher at the Danish Institute for International Studies. She holds an MA Honors in Social Anthropology and a PhD in International Development Studies. Kyed has extensive research experience within the fields of legal pluralism and political anthropology, focusing on the politics inherent to state recognition of traditional authorities and the interaction between state and non-state justice and security providers in Southern Africa. Among other publications she has co-edited *State Recognition and Democratization in Sub-Saharan Africa: A New Dawn for Traditional Authorities?* and *The Dynamics of Legal Pluralism in Mozambique*.

Markus-Michael Müller is an Assistant Professor in Latin American politics at the ZI Lateinamerika-Institut, Freie Universität Berlin. His research focuses on policing, transnational security governance and violence, with a regional focus on Latin America. He is the author of *Public Security in the Negotiated State: Policing in Latin America and Beyond* (Palgrave Macmillan 2012). His work has appeared in a number of journals including *Third World Quarterly, Security Dialogue, Journal of Latin American Studies, Government & Opposition, Postcolonial Studies* and *Social & Legal Studies*.

Helene Risør is an anthropologist, PhD. She is Assistant Professor and Researcher at the Interdisciplinary Research Center for Indigenous and Intercultural Studies (ISIIC) at the Anthropology Program at Pontificia Universidad Católica de Chile and Post Doc fellow at the Department of Anthropology at Copenhagen University. Her research focuses on political subjectivity and urban anthropology, in particular issues of civil in/security, violence and post conflict, citizenship, generational politics and migration. Her regional specialization is Latin America, and she has done extensive fieldwork in Bolivia and Chile.

Clifford Shearing is Professor, Institute for Humanities in Africa (HUMA), University of Cape Town; South African National Research Foundation Chair in Security and Justice; Adjunct Professor, School of Criminology and Criminal Justice, Griffith University and Adjunct Professor, School of Criminology, University of Montreal. Prior to 2014 Clifford held the positions of Chair of Criminology and Director, Centre of Criminology, University of Cape Town from 2006–2013. He also held positions at the Australian National University and the University of Toronto. His research and writing focuses on the governance of security.

Emmanuel Addo Sowatey has over fifteen years of research and practical experience in the field of security and development. He specializes in elections security management, security sector reform, international border disputes and natural resource conflicts. He has vast experience in dealing with chieftaincy conflicts in West Africa and has worked with think tanks in Ghana and elsewhere, different government institutions and supranational organizations. He holds an MPhil in African Studies and his current research interest is in understanding the coping mechanism of poor communities in Africa. He currently works as an independent consultant for national and international organizations and media outlets on security issues.

Øyvind Samnøy Tefre completed his Master's in 2010 at the University of Bergen, Department of Administration and Organization Theory, with the thesis 'Persistent Inequalities in Providing Security for People in South Africa: A comparative study of the capacity of three communities in Hout Bay to influence policing'. He is currently a Research Fellow at Bergen University College, pursuing his PhD focusing on private and public responsibility for child protection in Norway and the US, as part of the research project 'The Norwegian Child Welfare System in a Comparative Perspective: Knowledge, decision-making & ethnicity in policy and practice'.

Kari Telle is a social anthropologist and Senior Researcher at the Chr. Michelsen Institute (CMI) in Bergen, Norway. Her research in Indonesia deals with policing and security politics, popular religion, with a focus on Islam and Hinduism, and the anthropology of place and landscape. Together with Jeremy Kingsley she is preparing the book *Performing the State: Religion, Militia and the Legitimation of Violence in Southeast Asia*. She has co-edited the volume *Contemporary Religiosities: Emergent Socialities and the Post-Nation State* (2010).

Acknowledgements

The idea for this volume grew out of our encounters with different policing actors and ordinary residents in urban and rural Africa – both during extensive periods of fieldwork and through involvement in security sector programming. We are deeply indebted to these people for allowing us to follow their everyday work and for sharing with us their views on the kinds of insecurity and uncertainty that they face in their daily lives. These encounters have given us a deeper understanding of how people are actively engaged in trying to make order in even the most violent and disordered neighbourhoods. Bringing together the various contributions of this volume has allowed us to move beyond Africa, exploring the many ways that policing and politics are linked in urban spaces across three continents of the Global South.

The book would never have come to fruition were it not for the privileged position we occupy as researchers in the Danish Institute for International Studies (DIIS). The Institute has provided us with an invaluable research environment for developing and discussing the ideas of this book in a critical, multidisciplinary and constructive manner. We are also grateful to the Ministry of Foreign Affairs of Denmark (MFA) and the International Development and Law Organization (IDLO) that co-hosted and funded a large international conference in 2010 in Copenhagen on 'Access to Justice and Security'. This event brought together all the contributors to this volume, helping us to deepen its regional breadth and empirical depth by assembling new case studies. Particularly we would like to thank Vanessa Vega Saenz (MFA), Tania Schimmel (MFA), Kristoffier Vivike (MFA), Rolf Holmboe (MFA) and Erica Harper (IDLO) for supporting the idea behind the conference and for making funding available.

We would like to express our appreciation to all the academics and practitioners who participated at the conference and who provided constructive input when we first presented our idea about 'the politics of order-making'. Christian Lund, Finn Stepputat, Steffen Jensen, Anne Leander Lars Buur and David Pratten also deserve particular thanks for being great sources of inspiration over the years in developing a critical understanding of policing, politics and order-making.

In getting this book towards publication we extend our special thanks to Julio Faundez, the series editor, for his support of our book proposal, and to Colin Perrin and Rebekah Jenkins from Routledge for their diligence, encouragement and editorial assistance. Likewise, three anonymous reviewers provided very valuable input and constructive criticism.

As editors we would like to thank all the volume's contributors for their inspiring work, patience and endurance, demonstrated both in their fieldwork data and academic writing. Without their invaluable ethnographic case studies on diverse urban contexts of the world this book would not have been possible.

Last, but not least, we are permanently indebted to our families for their patience, support and understanding during our absences as we wrote this book. Thanks to Erik, Mark and Anna Maiya.

Abbreviations

ANC	African National Congress
APC	All People's Congress
ASPEBREK	Asociación de peñas, bares, restaurantes y karaokes
BJS	*Barangay* Justice System
BRA	Bike Riders Association
BRU	Bike Riders Union
CDF	Civil Defence Force
CNDDR	National Commission on Disarmament, Demobilization and Reintegration
COR	Central Obrera Regional/Workers Central
CPF	Community Police Forums
CVR	Community Violence Reduction
DA	Democratic Alliance
DIIS	Danish Institute for International Studies
DILG	Department of the Interior and Local Government
DISEC	District Security Committee
DOCS	Department of Community Safety
FEJUVE	Federación de Juntas Vecinales/Federation of Neighborhood Associations of El Alto
FES	Federation of Secondary Students of El Alto
FPFVI	Popular Front Francisco Villa UNOPI
FYDCA	Firestone Youth Development and Cultural Association
HBCA	Hout Bay Civic Association
HBCPF	Hout Bay Community Police Forum
HBNW	Hout Bay Neighbourhood Watch
HNP	Haitian National Police
HP	hand phone
ID	Improvement District
IDLO	International Development and Law Organization
LPPB	Local Policing Partnership Board
MAS	Movemiento al Socialismo/Movement towards Socialism
MFA	Ministry of Foreign Affairs

MINUSTAH	United Nations Stabilization Force (Haiti)
MPRA	Municipal Property Rates Act
MPS	Metropolitan Police Service or MPS
NACSA	National Commission for Social Action
NDC	National Democratic Congress
NGO	non-governmental organization
NPP	New Patriotic Party
NTB	Nusa Tenggara Barat
PNP	Philippine National Police
PRD	Party of the Democratic Revolution
PUDEMO	People's United Democratic Movement
RSP	Royal Swaziland Police
RUF	Revolutionary United Front
SANCO	South African National Civic Organization
SAPS	South African Police Service
SEDUCA	Servicio Departamental de Educación/State Department of Education
SLP	Sierra Leone Police
SLPP	Sierra Leone People's Party
SLRTA	Sierra Leone Roads and Transportation Authority
UPEA	Public University of El Alto

Chapter 1

Introduction

Policing and the politics of order-making on the urban margins

Helene Maria Kyed and Peter Albrecht

Today, more than half the world's population live in cities. Urban centres are expected to absorb almost all population growth in the coming decades (UN-Habitat 2012; Saatterthwaite and Mitlin 2014). In the process, urban spaces are emerging as sites of intensified insecurity and violence. This is particularly the case in the margins and in the slums of cities in the Global South, which today host more than 800 million people (UN-Habitat 2012). From the peripheries of megacities such as Mexico City and Metro Manila to densely populated neighbourhoods in Swaziland, Sierra Leone, South Africa, Haiti, Ghana, Indonesia and Bolivia, this book explores how urban spaces are policed when the public police is seen as inadequate and insecurity is a mainstay of daily life. How is order enacted in these urban spaces and who de facto engages in policing? How do the people living there respond to situations of insecurity? And how does everyday policing relate to wider political dynamics in the urban space?

These questions are explored empirically in the following ten chapters of this book. A common characteristic across the case study areas is a plurality of order-making practices, norms and actors that remain contested and volatile. State police officers coexist with various 'civilian policing groups', who often dominate everyday order-making. These are groups of ordinary citizens who engage in policing their own areas of residency. In this book such groups range from community policing members, student movements, youth groups, and neighbourhood guards and judges, to militias and secret societies. They draw on a variety of both violent and non-violent repertoires of order-making and are animated by a mix of cultural, religious and state-based norms. Some also exhibit a specific style of sporadic 'direct action' that is cultivated by the particular condition of urban uncertainty. A key characteristic of this urban condition is the prevalence of both collaboration and competition among policing actors and their supporters.

How and by whom a particular order is enacted in urban spaces is contested, and at times violently so. Not one set of actors monopolizes the authority or sovereign position to enact order, entailing renegotiations over the very definition of what *the* order is. This emphasizes order-making as a deeply political matter. Policing is also political in more explicit ways. In the chapters of this book policing actors are co-opted to further the political agenda and power position of other influential actors, including party politicians, public officials, traditional leaders and drug lords. Participating in police work can also be a route to power, resources and clients. Indeed, policing can itself be productive of new political spaces and subjectivities.

Exploring the political underpinning of order-making constitutes this book's key contribution. It adds a more profound political dimension to the growing body of literature on plural policing and security governance that informs most of its chapters (Loader 2000; Bayley and Shearing 2001; Jones and Newburn 2006; Wood and Shearing 2007; Baker 2008; Abrahamsen and Williams 2011). This literature has made a significant contribution to research on policing by moving beyond definitions that centre on the monopoly of the state and its institutions. Rather, policing is defined as a set of practices that can be exercised, and governed, by various state, private and communal actors (Jones and Newburn 2006: 3–4). Moreover, emphasis is on the need for a relational approach to policing. This means that instead of constituting isolated institutions, present day policing actors form part of complex networks or assemblages: they collaborate, compete and enrol each other to make a particular order and to constitute authority (Wood and Shearing 2007; Abrahamsen and Williams 2009). This relational approach opens up to an exploration of order-making 'beyond' the state police, but without substituting a focus on the state with that of the 'non-state' or 'private'.

An omission in much of the literature on plural policing and security governance is a deeper understanding of the links between policing and politics. Politics and power structures are often approached as external to policing practices, as providing the national and global context for how security is governed. The empirical case studies in this book compel us to explore policing practices and actors as embedded not only in 'police networks', but also in the specific social and political relations of the urban space. Political brokerage, patronage and electoral strategies, along with communal, family and ethnic ties shape how policing is organized and performed. Policing actors get involved in and are often productive of local politics. In turn, we suggest that politics is reflective of multiple efforts to concentrate power and enact sovereignty within inherently plural contexts.

While the power to make and define order is indeed dispersed and net-worked, conflicts among actors that seek to consolidate this power around specific institutions, groups and individual positions are equally omnipresent. These articulations of politics are exemplified by different forms of symbolic and physical 'boundary work'. Such boundary work permeates not only how policing is performed, but also how policing actors relate to each other within different networks or assemblages. The result is a 'plurality of power centers' (Bierschenk and de Sardan 2014: 16) and 'partial sovereignties' (Comaroff and Comaroff 2006: 35) that are continuously formed and reformed. It is in this respect that the book adds a more political perspective to the debate about plural policing. In doing so, it draws on a number of recent political anthropological studies that engage in critically rethinking the concepts of authority and sovereignty (Hansen and Stepputat 2005; Lund 2006; Comaroff and Comaroff 2006).

In the remainder of this introductory chapter we first outline the main academic debates within which this book is situated. These debates also lay the foundation for conceptualizing the specific urban contexts that the chapters deal with. We introduce these in the second section. While the ten countries covered in this book have their own specific histories of policing and political cultures, they share a number of features characteristic of 'urban margins' and other high density neighbourhoods that have been affected by a pluralization of governance and neoliberal globalization. In the third section we introduce the main policing actors covered in this book: civilian policing groups. We point to their ambiguous nature and contested relationship with the state, and argue that these characteristics emerge from the urban condition of insecurity. Before concluding with an outline of the chapter contributions, we provide a definition of the key concepts of the book – policing, order-making and politics.

The debates: plural policing, twilight authority and partial sovereignty

Until recently, state-centric theories of policing, sovereignty and authority dominated understandings of alternative order-making actors such as vigilante groups, militias and customary chiefs. They were seen as signs of 'state failure' or simply as filling the void left by an 'inadequate state' (Zartman 1995; Rotberg 2002). In contrast, this book is positioned within a growing body of cross-disciplinary literature that challenges the idea that the state and its institutions hold or ought to hold a monopoly on order enforcement. Sovereignty, authority and policing are approached from an empirical perspective, as a particular set of practices and claims, not as the prerogative of a specific political entity – i.e. the modern state. This reflects an empirically grounded and actor-oriented perspective on how and by whom order is made and remade. It allows the analysis of order-making to include a broad-based set of actors, norms and claims to authority.

To understand the politics of order-making in the urban contexts under scrutiny, the book's approach combines three different bodies of literature that share a critique of state-centric theories. We take our point of departure in the 'plural policing' and 'security governance' literature, which emphasizes networks, assemblages and hybrid governance, but without much consideration of the political contestations and efforts to concentrate power that are defining features of everyday policing. To capture the political dimension of policing, we draw on the one hand on Lund's (2006) work on public authority and local politics, and on the other hand on a number of political anthropological studies of sovereignty and vigilantism (Hansen and Stepputat 2005; Comaroff and Comaroff 2006; Pratten and Sen 2007; Kirsch and Grätz 2010). This latter body of literature allows us to capture the role that violence and moral ambiguity play in the politics of order-making.

Plural policing and hybrid governance

The literature on 'plural policing' (Loader 2000; Bayley and Shearing 2001; Buur and Jensen 2004; Jones and Newburn 2006; Wood and Shearing 2007; Baker 2008) and 'security beyond the state' (Abrahamsen and Williams 2011) challenges previous criminological studies of policing as being equal to the study of the (state) police. This shift is based on a general acceptance that '"policing" is now both authorized and delivered by diverse networks of commercial bodies, voluntary and community groups, individual citizens, national and local governmental regulatory agencies, as well as the public police' (Jones and Newborn 2006: 1). While the emphasis on plurality resonates with earlier socio-legal studies of legal pluralism (Ehrlich 1936; Merry 1988),[1] the shift is not only seen as a theoretical one. It is also a reflection of wider global changes: neoliberal policies of privatization and state deregulation since the 1980s have supported a proliferation of security providers and a fragmentation of security governance away from the state (Abrahamsen and Williams 2011).

A significant contribution of the plural policing literature is the use of a relational approach to policing. Instead of studying one specific institution or discrete system in isolation, the focus is on exploring how a variety of policing providers and auspices relate to, oppose and enrol each other. Concepts such as networks, nodes and assemblages are applied to describe these relationships and the interplay of different practices and rationalities (Wood and Shearing 2007; Abrahamsen and Williams 2009, 2011). This approach is inspired by Bruno Latour's emphasis on knowledge and truth as produced in the encounter between and among people, things and discourse, rather than as pre-existing entities (Latour 1999, 2007). In this perspective, the dichotomies we use to categorize the world – such as public/private, state/non-state – set up false distinctions and separate what are essentially networked or assembled.[2]

A key argument in the literature is that security governance is dispersed among a multitude of actors, and the effect of different intertwined rationalities that cut across the public–private divide. The result is 'hybrid structures' (Abrahamsen and Williams 2009: 8) or polycentric governance arrangements (Berg and Shearing, this volume). Within these structures there are no 'clear-cut hierarchical or vertical relationships' where authority runs in only one direction or from a clearly defined centre (Abrahamsen and Williams 2009: 8, 2011; see also Taussig 1991; Emirbayer 1997: 285; Abrams 2006 [1988], Mitchell 2006 [1999]). This resonates with a Foucauldian understanding of power and governmentality (Foucault 1991), as it challenges a zero-sum conception of power and the notion that power is concentrated in particular institutions or positions.

This rationale is equally captured by the concept of hybridity, which describes the absence of any clear, discrete entities, orders and systems such as state, local and customary.[3] In the urban neighbourhoods analysed in this book, this can be seen in how state police and civilian policing groups draw on each other, and mix a variety of practices, to enact order, even when they have emerged in apparent opposition to each other and at times compete. Indeed, not one particular policing actor assumes the exclusive authority to define and enact order and their operations are in any case dependent on a range of relationships with other significant actors.

In sum, the literature on plural policing helps to explain the diffusion of power away from the state and the emergence of hybrid and assembled relations within the field of security provision. However, little attention is given to the politics at play within these relations at the level of everyday practice. In this book, the different contributions show how policing actors are equally pre-occupied with efforts to *concentrate power* and *consolidate* particular power positions. For instance, this is evident in how they are enrolled in the political projects of powerful others. To insert politics into the sphere of plural policing we draw on two other bodies of literature.

Local politics and twilight institutions

Christian Lund's (2006) study of public authority and local politics opens an analytical space for grasping the politics at play in contexts where power is diffused and the authority of state institutions is contested. He argues that in such contexts a number of actors, who are not *the* state, act state-like not only by performing functions such as policing, but also because they vie for public authority. That is, akin to the state, they seek to 'define and enforce collectively binding decisions on the members of a society in the name of their common interest or general will' (Jessop 1990: 341, quoted in Lund 2006: 675). Lund defines such actors as 'twilight institutions'. Many of the civilian policing groups in this book fit into this category.

By approaching public authority as co-produced by different actors, Lund draws on the reconceptualization of the state as a set of practices and an idea that are not necessarily bound to the institutional frameworks of state agencies (Hansen and Stepputat 2001; Abrams 2006 [1988]; Mitchell 2006; Sharma and Gupta 2006). The state idea revolves around efforts to legitimize the state as *the* centre of authority and as a coherent, transcendent entity, embodying the common will of a territorially defined political community (Abrams 1977: 76–77). A rethinking of stateness allows us to analyse how alternative actors, such as civilian policing groups, frequently contribute to state formation through their everyday order-making practices (see Risør; Jensen and Hapal, this volume). It also brings to our attention how civilian policing groups often act state-like by seeking to establish authority over a territorially defined relative majority, based on the invocation of transcendent qualities such as community, tradition, ethnicity or religion. As such, they constitute a precarious analogue to what is represented and enacted in the name of the state as an idea (Buur and Jensen 2004; Kirsch and Grätz 2010: 16). In short, even if the power to define and make order is de facto defused among a range of actors, such actors are equally preoccupied with efforts to consolidate public authority, and thus to concentrate power.

Lund focuses on the micro-political contestations that infuse such efforts to consolidate public authority within localities where there is a plurality of state and twilight institutions. To be legitimate and effective, public authority needs to be constantly 'vindicated and legitimated through a broad array of political practices' (Lund 2006: 676). This, however, is seldom fully accomplished. Whereas the legitimization of authority is the product of continuous exchanges between providers and users of public goods, such as security and justice, Lund also argues that it is shaped by political negotiations and contestations between different actors who seek to govern specific areas and populations (Lund 2006; see also Bierschenk and de Sardan 1997; Hoffmann and Kirk 2013). This perspective situates policing and policing actors within a wider arena of local politics.

In this book the policing actors do not only compete and negotiate with each other to consolidate authority. Their position and capacity to make order are also shaped and reshaped by how they engage with and are co-opted by local leaders, party politicians, public officials, clandestine big men, powerful businessmen and so forth. Political contestations and negotiations among these actors centre on access to resources, positions of power, and ultimately on who defines and decides *the* order of a given territory and community.

Boundary-work is a central feature of politics. This includes the demarcation of territorial boundaries of a given political community, and the production of separation between insiders and those outsiders who are undeserving of attention. Intrinsic to contestations over public authority are also the articulation of distinctions, hierarchies and vertical encompassment between the institutions that vie for public authority. Like state institutions, other actors also seek to claim superior authority within their field. In such efforts, Lund argues, distinctions such as state/society, public/private, traditional/modern, are often re-articulated by those very actors who in their everyday practices constantly decompose such distinctions (Lund 2006: 673). In this book this paradox is particularly apparent in the relationship between state police and civilian policing groups. They enrol each other and exercise identical practices, but in their claims to authority they just as often define themselves in opposition to one another.

Lund (2006) agrees with the plural policing literature that we should not naturalize distinctions such as public/private and state/non-state. Yet he also argues that our analysis should still pay attention to *how* such distinctions are produced, instrumentalized and contested in practice. They are political resources. This is significant, we suggest, because there is a productive tension in how policing actors enrol, borrow, co-opt and demand from one other, while at the same time firmly distinguish themselves from each other. This tension contributes to enactments of particular tentative orders and forms of authority. In this book these forms of authority are frequently constituted by violent and morally ambiguous practices.

Partial sovereignties: violence and moral ambiguity

A recent body of political anthropological studies of sovereignty and vigilantism add valuable insights to those of Lund (2006), because they help us to understand the violent performances and moral ambiguity of policing actors. These features are intrinsic to the politics of order-making in contexts with plural policing and high levels of insecurity.

Akin to the vigilante groups described in the literature (Buur and Jensen 2004; Pratten and Sen 2007; Kirsch and Grätz 2010), the civilian policing groups in the chapters of this book are agents of security while at the same time regularly contributing to feelings of insecurity. They break the law and transgress moral principles, even as they engage in producing moral and social dichotomies (Kirsch and Grätz 2010: 8–9). Some are also involved in criminal networks and activities (see Müller; Jensen and Hapal, this volume). Acts of violence coexist with a desire for peace and order, and span from excessive, brutal and spectacular displays to minor acts of punishment. This ambiguity produces a fine line between legitimacy and illegitimacy in the eyes of the local populations that the civilian policing groups claim to serve. According to Kirsch and Grätz (2010), it also makes the analogue between civilian policing groups and the state particularly precarious. It helps to explain the shifting ways that state agencies have engaged with civilian policing actors, at times fighting and excluding them and at times including and using them. These shifts are rarely permanent and always ambiguous. Risør (this volume) shows how the illegal acts of order-making by a student movement, which emerged as a clear critique of state legislation, was praised by the local police, who draw on the movement's 'dirty' work to enforce order. In other situations, civilian policing groups come to impersonate the state's Other, e.g., when the state police press charges against community policing groups for using force, even when they draw on their services on a daily basis, as in the case of Swaziland (this volume).

Underlying this ambiguity is, according to Abrahams (1998), that social norms are, or have become, contested. Akin to the vigilantes that Abrahams explores, the civilian policing groups in this book act in frontier zones – that is, in zones of uncertainty and insecurity, marked by 'classificatory vagueness and volatility of social constructions' (Kirsch and Grätz 2010: 6). However, this argument does not adequately explain the specifically violent expressions of order-making in such zones. The debate on sovereignty helps us to fill this gap.

Comaroff and Comaroff (2006: 35) use the concept of partial sovereignties to describe situations where violent enactments of order and its exterior are omnipresent, spectacular and always tentative. This is because not one sovereign body manages to 'exercise autonomous, exclusive control over the lives, deaths, and conditions of existence of those who fall within a given purview' (ibid.: 35). Understanding sovereignty in the plural resonates with a body of literature that has moved from a *de jure* to a *de facto* conceptualization of sovereignty, seeing it as the effect of specific practices that can be exercised by state agencies as well as by a range of 'informal sovereigns' (Hansen and Stepputat 2005; see also Das and Poole 2004; Telle, this volume). Hansen and Stepputat (2005) distinguish sovereign practices from other registers of power. Although the meanings and forms of sovereign performances are 'historically specific, they are however, always constructing their public authority through a capacity for visiting violence on human bodies' (ibid.: 3). Ultimately, sovereign power rests on 'the ability to kill, punish and discipline with impunity' (ibid.: 296–297). This is driven by 'the ideal of uncompromising self-sufficiency and mastership', with indivisibility and exclusive control, which, as Arendt notes, 'is contradictory to the very condition of plurality' (Arendt 1998: 234). Thus, whereas sovereignty requires an order of rules, it is a form of authority grounded in violence. In contexts with 'partial sovereignties' or 'on the margins of the state' (Das and Poole 2004) sovereign power is a particularly unstable project whose efficacy depends on repeated performances of violence (Hansen and Stepputat 2005: 3).

This understanding of sovereign practices allows us to grasp the politics of order-making not only as power games over who punishes criminals, but also as fundamentally concerned with efforts to exercise exclusive control over particular spaces and human bodies. The often very visible role that violence plays in everyday policing across the chapters of this book can be seen as conditioned by partial sovereignties, and thus as sovereign practices. Having said this, we cannot understand the politics of order-making through the lens of sovereignty alone. It is one register of politics that coexists with other more mundane contestations over political positions. Public display of violence and physical punishment are omnipresent potentialities of everyday policing, indeed, in some cases violence has been constitutive of the groups' authority in the first place (see Kyed; Telle, this volume). In other cases, violence or the threat of violence is only one among a number of ways through which policing actors try to establish or maintain power.

The contexts: urban margins

The focus of this book is on densely populated spaces in the Global South where insecurity is a primary experience of everyday life and where ordinary citizens consider public policing and other state services to be inadequate. Most of the spaces dealt with are criminal hotspots, home to violent gangs, sites for drug-dealing, and pools of unemployed and low-paid workers. They resemble what Daniel Goldstein (2012) has defined as 'urban margins' or 'marginal neigh-bourhoods'. A key characteristic of these hoods is the 'absent presence' of the state and its law (ibid.: 77). The state is absent 'in that it does not consistently enforce the law, protect citizen's rights, defend them against threat and harm, or offer them a way to secure justice' (ibid.: 83). It is present through law enforcement by security forces and bureaucracies – or through illicit extortions – in ways that are experienced by residents as repressive, restrictive and often violent. There is a general sense that people are left more or less to fend for themselves in facing problems of crime and violence (Goldstein 2012: 240). How people do so is a key focus of this volume.

The neighbourhoods across the chapters have different historical origins. Some began as government-initiated resettlement areas for urban residents from overcrowded and violent areas of the larger city (e.g. Bagong Silang in Manila and Imizamo Yethu in Cape Town). Others originated as formal housing for low-wage rural migrants to take up jobs in new urban industrial areas, but later expanded into large informal settlements with high unemployment rates (e.g. Mbhuleni in Swaziland, Cité Solei in Haiti and Nima in Accra). El Alto in Bolivia and Foulah Town in Freetown are the result of massive internal migration as rural dwellers seek job opportunities in the city due to economic transformations.

Scholars have situated present-day predicaments of urban marginality within a shared context of increased urbanization and deepened inequalities intensified by neoliberal globalization since the 1980s (Harvey 2007; Bayat 2012; Goldstein 2012). Neoliberal policies of privatization and the partial retreat of the central government as provider of public services have increased unemploy-ment and left an urban population to cater for its own survival or to rely on services provided by national and international charities. In such a system state provision deteriorates due to limited public investments, thereby facilitating further privatization from 'the back-door' (Bayat 2012: 112). The city has primarily become a site for private capital in pursuit of profitability (Harvey 2007), which has fundamentally reconfigured urban space. Public housing schemes are reduced and land markets are subject to large-scale capital invest-ments. Vulnerable households are pushed out of city centres to give way to mega-projects and gated communities for the elite. The result is an expansion of urban slums (Bayat 2012: 112) and a class-based 'zoning' of city spaces (Rodgers 2009).

Harvey (2008) paints a gloomy picture of what he calls the 'neoliberal city'. It is a city with glaring inequality, where capital rules, and the poor and marginalized are entrapped and paralysed. Urban margins through this lens amount to a collapse of social order, where gang violence is the dominant expression of exclusion (Beall 2007; Rodgers 2009). While this perspective enjoys some plausibility across the chapters in this volume, it fails to capture the various, often unspectacular ways in which the residents of urban margins enact citizenship and self-organize to produce order and deal with insecurity. In line with scholars such as Bayat (2012) and Holston (1998), this book challenges the idea that urban margins should be analysed only from the perspective of neoliberal exclusion, inequality and state withdrawal. There are three main reasons for this.

First, the urban margins in this volume depict sprawling activity of new and old forms of order-making and policing groups, however contested and imperfect they may be in producing security and justice. Urban margins are not simply passive or entrapped. Local forms of order-making are politically productive of individual and collective subjectivities and forms of authority, which also influence national politics and contribute to remaking the state. In Indonesia, state policies of decentralization have allowed civilian security groups to exercise forms of informal governance that provide new opportunities for marginalized groups to exercise influence (Telle, this volume). In Bolivia neighbourhood organizations occupy the space of protection left by state regulation, and young students re-engage the state through their order-making practices and in the process emerge as new political actors (Risør, this volume). The capacity of urban residents to organize themselves around security provision varies considerably across the case studies. However, this variety is not simply determined by wider processes of exclusion and state withdrawal. Equally significant are local politics, social and family relations, and notions of community and belonging.

Second, civilian policing has long histories on the urban margins of the Global South and has evolved through ambiguous interaction with state police forces. It is not a phenomenon that results from sudden state withdrawal. As Pratten and Sen (2007) suggest, neoliberal globalization may explain the *increase* in private and community-based security groups, but these groups do not simply 'fill the gap' left by limited or absent state services. The way they operate and legitimize their actions is also shaped by specific cultural and historical notions of justice, security and order that are not identical to those represented by the state. On the urban margins, neoliberal policies have been integrated with existing political entities that were already socio-legally plural and that were never fully-fledged welfare states. Here state police forces operate in a mediated manner, relying on informal negotiations with local power brokers (Mexico City, this volume), traditional secret societies (Sierra Leone, this volume) or young civilian policemen (Swaziland and Ghana, this volume). Neoliberal policies may have challenged the welfare state as an ideal or aspiration, but urban margins were always already spaces with plural forms of governance and partial sovereignties.

Third, under neoliberal transformations urban margins are not simply left to their own devices as isolated uncontaminated spaces. They are also subject to neoliberal policies of decentralization and democratization, which herald civil society participation and citizens' responsibility for their own governance and security. As Bayat (2012: 112) notes, in neoliberalism 'the idea of a diminished role of the state is predicated upon the participation of "civil society" in urban governance through NGOs, local councils, and municipalities to deliver services'. This gives way to new forms of state engagement, rather than simply state withdrawal. The urban margins also constitute significant voter bases for national politicians, resulting in ambiguous forms of engagement and disengagement between the elite and the urban poor (see King and Albrecht, this volume). Intermingled with processes of exclusion, new, often unforeseen, practices emerge that have important implications for social ordering and political mobilization. One example is the privatization and outsourcing of state security provision to private companies and civilians. In South Africa the neo-liberal strategy of Improvement Districts (ID) reshapes urban security as state, company and community actors interact in novel and unexpected ways (Berg and Shearing, this volume). The result is polycentric governance arrangements where authority continuously shifts hands and commercial interests define order-making. Community-policing schemes that mobilize civilians to partner with the state police are another example of neoliberal intervention. Instead of a simple process of state withdrawal, state police officers use community policing to boost their power and rectify their lack of capacity to tackle crime by enrolling new and old civilian policing actors. This relationship is often contested, as the civilian groups become authorities in their own right and engage with national politicians (see Kyed; Tefre; Sowatey and Atuguba, this volume).

Neoliberal globalization helps to explain the causes of urbanization and marginality in the city, but does not account for the multiple ways that people on the urban margins engage in order-making. The various forms of state and political elite engagement with these margins are also ignored. To capture these complexities requires an empirically grounded and historically informed analysis. The ability to organize around the policing of neighbourhoods is not only shaped by political and economic exclusion, but also by context-specific social relations, histories of (re)settlement, and political cultures (Bayat 2012: 118). Urban margins are composite sites with multiple avenues to making order. The policing actors that emerge in these spaces are often ambiguous figures who epitomize the absent present state.

The policing actors: ambiguous and political figures

The chapters in this book deal with the empirical question of who de facto deals with crime and disorder in a given urban space. The most significant type of actor across these spaces is what we call civilian policing groups. It is impossible to arrive at a universal definition of such groups, but some shared features nonetheless justify the label. Their members are citizens who join the group as civilians, not as professionally trained police or commercially hired security officers. They are organized along territorial lines, and their policing activities are in principle confined to specific neighbourhoods or a community. A common *raison d'être* is a desire for peace and order in 'the community', although, as we discuss below, this is frequently not the outcome of local order-making in practice.

The role and idea of the state is typically invoked by the members of the groups to explain their *raison d'être*. The state is presented as ineffective and corrupt. As such, the self-representations of civilian policing groups constitute a direct or indirect critique of state failure to meet the perceived needs of those who resort to them (Abrahams 1996: 44). This does not indicate that civilian policing groups are an exception or extraordinary (Agamben 1995; Hansen and Stepputat 2005). In fact, in these contexts the state police have never been perceived as an adequate provider of justice and security (Albrecht and Buur 2009). Rather, it reflects that civilian policing groups are part of the general evolution of a governance system that assembles mutually constitutive forms of authority (Abrahamsen and Williams 2011: 3). Civilian policing is never just 'a thing in itself', but 'a fundamentally relational phenomenon, which does not make much sense except in connection with and often in contrast to others' (Abrahams 1998: 7). Boundaries between the state and civilian policing groups remain challenged in everyday practice, precisely because they are relationally defined (Vandenberghe 1999; Lamont and Molnár 2002: 167).

The policing groups in this book vary significantly in their origin, size, form of organization, and relationship with the state. Some, like the Amphibi in Indonesia (Telle, this volume), count up to 200,000 members with a strongly bureaucratized organization. Others only have twenty members, such as the community policing group in Swaziland (Kyed, this volume), and although it is institutionalized, its leadership is in constant flux. This, again, is different from loosely organized self-help policing and conflict resolution mechanisms at sub-neighbourhood and family level, such as in Hangberg, Cape Town (Tefre, this volume) and in Iztapalapa, Mexico City (Müller, this volume). Another form of civilian policing is the mobilization of young people around immediate acts of order-making, such as the violent protests by the student federation in El Alto in Bolivia (Risør, this volume) or the Biker Rider Unions in Sierra Leone (Berg, this volume). Finally, some civilian policing groups, such as those in South Africa and the Philippines, are the result of carefully planned state initiatives, but have become partly independent from the state. In Bagong Silang, Manila (Jensen and Kapal, this volume), the *puroks* and *tanods* are part of the justice system that was established by the state to unclog the formal courts. However, in everyday operations these actors are driven more by private interests, family relations and alternative ethics of legality than by a preoccupation with state law and order. Conversely, some of the locally generated self-help groups have become state recognized *post facto* or partly incorporated within state-led community policing schemes. Often, however, they continue to operate outside centrally formulated legal frameworks, and are regulated through patron–client relations and informal brokerage.

Despite this variety, the civilian policing groups in this volume share a number of significant operational logics and repertoires of action. We suggest that these are directly related to the conditions of uncertainty and insecurity facing populations on the urban margins. Four characteristics stand out.

First, civilian policing groups are ambiguous figures, morally and categorically. They embody conventional dichotomies, akin to what has been argued for vigilante groups (Abrahams 1996; Pratten and Sen 2007; Kirsch and Grätz 2010) and 'informal sovereigns' (Hansen and Stepputat 2005). They are both inside and outside the state, performing state police authority as insiders and constituting informal outsiders. They define their *raison d'être* in opposition to ineffectual state-sanctioned policing, but get involved in state-like performances and instrumentalize or are instrumentalized by state officials (Buur and Jensen and 2004; Kirsch and Grätz 2010). They are morally ambiguous, because their efforts to make order often are based on the use of violence, which in the eyes of those who draw on their services is considered both necessary and illegitimate. Similarly, policing actors often serve both private interests and the common good; a strategy to survive personally while at the same time producing specific moral communities (Pratten 2010). Categorically they are ambiguous, because they often switch from being loosely organized self-help groups to becoming formally organized or state-recognized entities. This shift may be part of a group's effort to become established as a local authority and to enter formal electoral politics. However, the transformation is seldom permanent.

Second, policing actors draw on hybrid repertoires of order-making and legitimacy in their everyday practices and claims to authority. The Amphibi and Tigabersatu groups in Indonesia mix 'languages of the state' with customary justice practices and culturally embedded notions of the criminal (Telle, this volume). While dispensing popular forms of justice and providing spiritual insurance through Islam, they also exhibit bureaucratic forms of organization and draw on artefacts of modern state power such as uniforms, titles and membership cards. In Swaziland, the community police mimic state police practices of investigation, arrests and interrogation, and call their court-like set-up 'the station', but they also draw on reconciliatory and compensational justice akin to the courts of traditional leaders (Kyed, this volume).

A third characteristic of a civilian policing group is 'youthfulness'. This does not only signal that their members tend to be young of age or socially young, but also that they are not too strictly tied to any fixed moral register. They are capable of switching quickly between these registers and are less hesitant to act immediately on crime and disorder. This gives way to a specific style of operation, associated with direct action, flexibility, mutability and quick results. In fact, a key source of their legitimacy is their capacity to quickly track down criminals, recuperate stolen goods, and punish law-breakers. This is typically contrasted with the cumbersome process of formal court proceedings, police investigations and the morally rigid proceedings of traditional courts. Youthfulness emerges directly out of the conditions of urban margins. Direct actions with immediate outcomes are attractive in these contexts where there is little access to benefits and security through formal channels and where income, land and material properties are scarce and in any case easily lost (Bayat 2012). Youthfulness also signals the wild, uncontrollable and unstable sides of civilian policing groups. They are never fully reliable and appear erratic. Consequently, they often become part of reproducing the very conditions of insecurity and uncertainty that they have emerged in response to.

A fourth characteristic is the politically transient and transformative nature of civilian policing groups. They are not just security providers, but also ambiguous political actors. Civilian policing actors continuously seek to legitimize their actions and transform themselves into significant authorities in their own right through and beyond their capacity to combat crime and enact order. They are frequently drawn into the political struggles of others, and often enter informal political networks or formal electoral politics. Civilian policing groups may therefore constitute spaces in which politics and political subjectivities are produced. And yet, there is no linear development involved in these political processes across the case studies. This unpredictability is conditioned by the transient and unfixed nature of their authority. Their ambiguous order-making role and their youthfulness are attractive to powerful others and grant them a degree of legitimacy and power. However, these characteristics also make them easily dispensable by those who otherwise support or enrol them, and often groups dissolve and are internally contested.

Civilian policing groups do not overturn the order of partial sovereignties and contested public authority; indeed, they perpetuate it and in the process play a central role in producing politics on the urban margins. This emerges from their immediate capacities to deal with crimes and disorder, and the various, context-specific ways in which these capacities are transformed through networks and assemblages of social relations, political patrons, state agendas and private interests.

The concepts: policing, order-making and politics

The key concepts of this book are policing, politics and order-making. How we define these concepts is informed by the empirical case studies and inspired by process and actor-oriented theories of social life as developed by Michel de Certeau, Chantal Mouffe and Sally Falk Moore. As such, we combine agency and space for the unexpected and unpredictable with the ever-evolving, yet conditioning effects of structures. Thinking in terms of relations and how people, practices and norms combine to establish order through policing brings dynamism to that process.

Policing as relational and boundary-work

In line with the literature on plural policing, we define policing as 'any organized activity . . . that seeks to ensure the maintenance of communal order, security and peace through elements of prevention, deterrence, investigation of breaches, and punishment' (Baker 2008: 5). Thus, *policing* is associated with a set of practices and functions rather than with a particular institution or agency (Jones and Newburn 2006). This definition raises the question not of who ought to police society and of who is in a *de jure* position to do so, but of who actually does it in the everyday (Albrecht and Kyed 2010). Theoretically, the book's focus on everyday practices, rather than normative and legal representations, finds inspiration in the work of de Certeau (1984), and how individual everyday practices are not reducible to the structures in which they occur. In short, the fact that everyday life takes place within institutional systems of norms, practices and actors – for instance, of the state – does not in turn mean that everyday practices are scripted or that there is no room for innovation.

We add two other features to this broader practice-oriented definition of policing in the everyday: policing as relational and as boundary-work. These two concepts inform our political perspective on order-making.

First, policing is fundamentally relational. Those who perform it are not isolated homogenous actors, who represent separate spheres of social life or who enact fixed normative systems in any automatic sense. Rather, policing actors form part of wider socio-political arenas. In these arenas policing actors and their supporters, adversaries and clients take part in often contested articulations of right and wrong, and of who and what constitutes a threat to society. Not any one fixed normative system drives these articulations. Rather they are expressions of context-specific clusters of rules, norms and institutions that have evolved together through *relationships* of interdependence, opposition and appropriation (Kyed 2009). This takes policing beyond the concrete acts of deterrence, punishments and prevention, bringing it into a much wider sphere of order-making and unmaking. At stake is not only security and peace, but also access to resources, entitlements, livelihood and income for the actors involved. Policing actors are for this reason also embedded in wider sets of power relations. Because policing activities provide a route to authority and resources, there are always powerful actors who seek to regulate and control or dismiss and avoid them. There is a technical side to policing, but those who get to provide and control those who do it are deeply political matters. For this reason, the plurality of policing providers and auspices, whether defined as state, commercial or civilian, seldom coexist without competition. They are constituted in relation to each other through a mixture of competition, collaboration and interdependence.

Second, boundary-work is central to policing, and is directly related to its relational dimensions. Policing actors are continuously preoccupied with enacting and negotiating boundaries, not only of particular territorial spaces and populations, but also between order and disorder, right and wrong, and between who is a criminal and who is not (Parnell and Kane 2003). Even if these boundaries are fixed in national laws and moral codes, the category of the criminal shifts in everyday practice and is subject to altering classifications. The boundary-work of policing does not always explicitly challenge any one particular order or body of rules, but it is integral to continuous ways of making and unmaking rules and categories. This is visible in acts of punishment and in who the policing actors decide to apprehend and who they protect. As discussed earlier in relation to the work of Lund (2006), boundary-work is also central to how policing actors define and position themselves in *relation* to each other and to those who support or contest them.

Policing as relational and boundary-work is central to our understanding of *the politics of order-making* and rests on two claims. First, policing actors operate within a wider political arena of overlapping jurisdictions and competing claims to authority, not within one fixed socio-legal order or among peacefully coexisting systems of policing. Second, policing is ultimately concerned with politics in its deepest form. It is about the power to decide who and what constitute a threat to society. Policing and security provision do indeed involve technical acts, but who gets to provide, what is being provided and to whom are deeply political matters. This understanding of the politics of order-making is based on particular conceptualizations of *order* and *politics*.

The meaning of order and order-making

In everyday police parlance notions of order and an order convey different meanings. Order can be a command or direction in the sense of an authoritative act to be obeyed; order is used to describe a condition in which freedom from disorder or disruption is maintained, often as an indication of respect for some established authority. Moreover, order, when paired with law, as in law and order, is commonly associated with the state enforced system of regulations and its security forces. These varied meanings underline notions of order in society and of commands associated with power. That is, power in the Weberian sense of the act of persons to enforce their will upon others' behaviour (Weber 1947). These meanings of the word order are central to policing activities, but they are embedded in deeper processes of regulation associated with the production of *social order*.

We define social order as: a set of linked social institutions and practices that (seek to) conserve, maintain and enforce particular ways of relating and behaving. Order, however, is never fully fixed and complete. Inspired by Sally Falk Moore's (1978) study of legally pluralistic settings, this book adopts a process-oriented understanding of social order as constantly being made and remade through active processes of regulation of social life. Such processes of regulation – what we call order-making – cover enactments and representations of rules, categories, symbols and rituals that give form, order and predictability to social life (Moore 1978: 6). State law is but one example of these processes, coexisting with other forms of order-making.[4]

The view of social order as active processes rests on the assumption that *indeterminacy* is an underlying quality of social life *and* that people are active participants in creating continuity and change (ibid.: 48). Social orders – the regulated, patterned aspects – are omnipresent in social life, but they 'always leave gaps, require adjustments and interpretations to be applicable to particular situations' *and* 'are themselves full of ambiguities, inconsistencies and often contradictions' (ibid.: 39). Social life consists of a variety of situations, and shifting sets of persons, which makes complete regulation of social life impossible. This implies openings and rooms for manoeuvre in social situations, in which rules and categories are the subject of potential negotiations, reinterpretations and remaking. Order therefore is the temporary result of ongoing and sedimented practices to overcome conflict and contradictions, structured and yet constantly morphing as people, practices and norms assemble (and disassemble).

Following Moore's (1978) analysis of *indeterminacy* as a fundamental feature of social life we position ourselves as cautious post-structuralists. Indeterminacy does not rule out order, consistencies and repetition as fundamental features of social life. We do not substitute a study of order, repetition and continuity with a study of inconsistency, contradictions and change and as such depart from privileging either structure/continuity or actor/change. Rather we see indeterminacy and order-making as two implicated forms of behaviour that are played out in social situations. Breaking rules reshapes efforts of partial ordering, and order-making activities frequently produce new forms of disorder and insecurity. This process-oriented understanding of order compels us to study how definitions of order and disorder are negotiated, contested and enacted by different sets of actors through and around policing and security provision. Less explicit in Moore's work is the politics at play in these processes, and thus how contests over power and political positions infuse them.

Politics and the political

Practices that revolve around attempts to establish, define and enact order are expressions of the political, we suggest with Chantal Mouffe (2006) in mind, because such practices always involve the exclusion of other possibilities and alternative forms of order. Order-making is exactly political, because such forms of exclusion underpin particular *power relations* and antagonisms. In police work exclusions are articulated in distinctions between what is *inside* and what is *outside* an order. This is played out in we–they distinctions when it comes to questions of identity and belonging, and in distinctions between right and wrong when it comes to regulating behaviour and punishing violations. Hierarchies of authority and inclusion and exclusion from decision-making and negotiations over order are also frequently produced through policing. This is the kind of boundary-work that we spoke about earlier. In this book physical and symbolic violence play a particularly significant role in such boundary-work, not only in the treatment of criminals or malefactors, but also in the performance of power relations and sovereign claims.

Policing is expressive of *the political* in the deeper sense of the underlying processes through which order is defined and enacted. Yet policing in this book is also frequently implicated in *politics*. It is subservient to more or less explicitly articulated political aims and practices. Overt politics concerns the contestations over power in electoral politics, traditional leadership disputes, and informal big man politics. This includes situations where policing actors themselves become politically organized as a group or run for political office as individuals. Other examples include when policing actors are enlisted by political candidates to mobilize votes, control or exclude particular population groups, or hit down on opposition forces. Relationships between civilian and state police can also enter explicit politics when they openly fight over jurisdictions or accuse each other of illegalities. In Mouffe's (2006) terminology this is the 'Politics' – i.e. the 'practices and institutions through which order is created' – that is the observable expression of the underlying dimension of the political. It is these practices and institutions that we explore empirically in this book. Notions of sovereignty, national and local positions of power as well as personal ambitions and social mobility are important expressions of the political across the chapters of this book. These dimensions of politics define the contested contours of order and order-making on the urban margins.

The contributions: from Metro Manila to Mexico City

The case studies in this volume explore urban spaces across the Americas, Africa and Asia where a plurality of order-making practices, norms and actors coexist in an often contested and volatile environment. State police and various civilian policing groups are constituted in relation to each other through a mixture of competition, collaboration and interdependence. This compels us to explore policing practices and actors as embedded not only in 'police networks', but also in the broader social and political relations and networks of the urban space. This is the key contribution of the book: to explore the political underpinning of local order-making in contexts of plural policing.

In Chapter 2, Jensen and Hapal explore the *Barangay* Justice System (BJS) in the Philippines, introduced in 1978 to alleviate pressure on the formal court system and facilitate locally sensitive arbitration. Focusing on Bagong Silang in northern Metro Manilla, the authors show how policing and order-making through BJS is shaped by family and community relations, and how they are expected to play a central role in electoral politics by the politicians that sponsor them. In Chapter 3, Telle shows how in the case of densely populated areas of Lombok, Indonesia, civilian policing groups emerged in the wake of the decentralization of electoral democracy at the turn of the millennium. These groups have become deeply entangled in electoral politics, and while their formation has enabled marginalized communities to exercise a degree of public authority, they have also reproduced a form of authoritarianism that relies on violence and coercion.

Chapter 4 by Kyed shows that community policing groups comprising young men in Mbhuleni, a criminalized urban neighbourhood in Swaziland, are political in two ways. They constitute an unstable 'new political space' through which their members have the potential to obtain official positions, but they are also a source of power and authority for traditional leaders and elected politicians that seek to further their own agendas. Sowatey and Atuguba show in Chapter 5 how Watch Dog groups in the migrant neighbourhood of Nima, Accra, were set up to make order in areas where public policing has never been prevalent, and how they manoeuvre a context where they are under continuous pressure from politicians and organized criminals.

Adopting a nodal analytical approach, Chapter 6 by Berg and Shearing shows how the establishment of Improvement Districts in Cape Town has led to the emergence of new types of authority constituting hybrid, polycentric security governance arrangements. As the book's only study of an affluent neighbourhood, the authors show how the Improvement Districts are a site in which there are multiple, shifting sites of authority that impact directly on how security is provided in terms of regulation and power.

Through the analytical lens of assemblage theory, Chapter 7 by Müller explores how inhabitants of Iztapalapa, a marginal neighbourhood in Mexico City, deal with insecurity and crime in the everyday. The chapter shows how innovative solutions to urban insecurity are found, which in turn leads to the reproduction of political relations that are shaped by local power brokers, clientelist relations and criminal actors. In Chapter 8, Risør explores the relationship between practices of civil security, state formation and the enactment of citizenship in El Alto, Bolivia. It is shown how popular direct action as a form of instant order-making situated in the space between the legal and illegal appears to defy state authority, yet in the process enhances the political establishment and transforms rather than overturns activities of the state.

Chapter 9 by Tefre explores how crime and insecurity are dealt with by three communities in Hout Bay, Cape Town, which experience widely different socio-economic conditions and racial compositions. He shows that everyday policing and order-making hinges on a group's ability to form a collective identity that can bolster its capacity for action, network with other security actors, and thereby gain access to external resources. Louis-Alexandre Berg in Chapter 10 takes his empirical point of departure in youth groups in Port-au-Prince, Haiti, and the Bike Riders Union of Sierra Leone. The chapter shows the way in which youth organizations engage in local order-making as perpetrators of violence as well as providers of public safety. The role they play depends on the density of social ties in the communities where they operate, and the links between those communities and the state. The final chapter by King and Albrecht explores the role of urban secret societies in making order on Freetown's margins. They argue that people on these margins interact with centres of political power through such institutions, and that the urban secret societies provide the means to engage with the central government from a position of power.

Notes

1   Based on a critique of state-legal centralism, legal anthropologists have for a long time used the concept of legal pluralism to describe the plurality of normative orders and institutions that enforce order within a political organization (Griffiths 1986; Woodman 1998; von Benda Beckmann et al. 2009; Kyed 2009). However, there has been a very meagre focus in this literature on policing and police, with a predominant exploration of courts, disputing forums and, more lately, human rights and other international legal phenomena.

2   The concept of the assemblage originates from Deleuze and Guattari's use of the French terms *agencement* and *dispositif*, which are commonly translated as assemblage. They considered it a site where a 'discursive formation intersects with material practices' (Crary 1992: 31). Latour's combination of actors, discourse and things in his attempt to document the processes and networks through which the world is assembled resembles this line of thinking (Latour 1993: 29–35).

3   The notion of hybridity has long been prevalent in legal anthropological studies, but has focused on courts and dispute resolution, not on the police and policing. More recently, hybridity has become prevalent in peacebuilding studies where notions of 'hybrid political orders' are used to critique the notion of fragile states, focusing not on the absence of state institutions but on how different actors with different kinds of authority, legitimacy and capacity coexist and shape one another (Clements et al. 2007, Boege et al. 2009, Kraushaar and Lambach 2009, Brown et al. 2010, Albrecht and Moe 2014).

4   This point about the coexistence of different modes of rule-generation and order-making within a political organization was a major contribution of Moore (1978) to the development of legal anthropology, which had previously privileged the existence of a single legal field: Western state law.

References

Abrahams, R., 1996. Vigilantism: Order and disorder on the frontiers of the state, in H. Olivia (ed.), *Inside and Outside the Law: Anthropological Studies of Authority and Ambiguity*. London: Routledge, 41–55.

Abrahams, R., 1998. *Vigilante Citizens: Vigilantism and the State*. Cambridge: Polity Press.

Abrahamsen, R. and Williams, M., 2009. Security beyond the state: Global security assemblages in international politics, *International Political Sociology*, 3: 1–17.

Abrahamsen, R. and Williams, M., 2011. *Security Beyond the State: Private Security in International Politics*. Cambridge: Cambridge University Press.

Abrams, P., 1988 [1977]. Notes on the difficulty of studying the state, *Journal of Historical Sociology*, 1:1, 58–89.

Abrams, P., 2006 [1988]. Notes on the difficulty of studying the state, in A. Sharma and A. Gupta (eds), *The Anthropology of the State: A Reader*. Oxford: Blackwell, 112–130.

Agamben, G., 1995. *Homo Sacer: Sovereign Power and Bare Life*. Stanford, CA: Stanford University Press.

Albrecht, P. and Buur, L., 2009. An uneasy marriage: Non-state actors and police reform, *Policing and Society*, 19:4, 390–415.

Albrecht, P. and Kyed, H. M., 2010. Justice and security – when the state isn't the main provider, DIIS Policy Brief based on insights from the conference: Access to justice and security: Non-state actors and the local dynamics of ordering, Copenhagen: Danish Institute for International Studies.

Albrecht, P. and Moe, L. W., 2014. *The simultaneity of authority in hybrid orders, in Peacebuilding*, available at: http://www.tandfonline.com/doi/full/10.1080/21647259.2014.928551 (accessed 15 September 2014).

Arendt, H., 1998 [1958]. *The Human Condition*. 2nd edn. Chicago, IL: University of Chicago Press.

Baker, B., 2008. *Multi-Choice Policing in Africa*. Uppsala: Nordiske Africa Institute.

Bayat, A., 2012. Politics in the city-inside-out. *City and Society*, 24:2, 110–128.

Bayley, D. and Shearing, C., 2001. *The New Structure of Policing: Conceptualization and Research Agenda*. Washington, DC: National Institute of Justice.

Beall, J., 2007. Cities, terrorism and urban wars in the 21st Century. *Working paper 9*, London School of Economics, Crisis States Research Centre.

Bierschenk, T. and de Sardan, J. P. O., 1997. Local powers and a distant state in rural Central African Republic, *Journal of Modern African Studies*, 35:3, 441–468.

Bierschenk, T. and de Sardan, J. P. O., 2014. *States at Work: Dynamics of African Bureaucracies*. Leiden and Boston, MA: Brill.

Boege, V., Brown, A. M., Clements, K. P. and Nolan, A., 2009. Hybrid political orders, not fragile states, *Peace Review*, 2:1, 13–21.

Brown, M. A., Volker, B., Clements, K. P. and Nolan, A., 2010. Challenging statebuilding as peacebuilding: Working with hybrid political orders to build peace, in O. P. Richmond (ed.), *Palgrave Advances in Peacebuilding: Critical Developments and Approaches*, Basingstoke: Palgrave Macmillan.

Buur, L. and Jensen, S., 2004. Introduction: Vigilantism and the policing of everyday life in South Africa, *African Studies*, 63:2, 139–152.

Clements, K. P., Boege, V., Brown, A. M., Foley, W. and Nolan, A., 2007. State building reconsidered: The role of hybridity in the formation of political order, *Political Science* 59:1, 45–56.

Comaroff, J. L. and Comaroff, J. (eds), 2006. *Law and Disorder in the Postcolony*. Chicago, IL and London: University of Chicago Press.

Crary, J., 1992. *Techniques on the Observer: On Vision and Modernity in the Nineteenth Century*. Cambridge, MA: MIT Press.

Das, V. and Poole, D., 2004. The state and its margins, in V. Das and D. Poole (eds), *Anthropology at the Margins of the State*. New Delhi: Oxford University Press, 3–34.

de Certeau, M., 1984. *The Practice of Everyday Life*. Berkeley, CA: University of California Press.

Ehrlich, E., 1936 [1913]. *Fundamental Principles of the Sociology of Law*. Cambridge, MA: Harvard University Press.

Emirbayer, M., 1997. Manifesto for a relational sociology, *American Journal of Sociology*, 103:2, 281–317.

Foucault, M., 1991. Governmentality, in G. Burchell, C. Gordon and P. Miller (eds), *The Foucault Effect: Studies in Governmentality*. London: Harvester Wheatsheaf, 87–104.

Goldstein, D. M., 2012. *Outlawed: Between Security and Rights in a Bolivian City*. Durham and London: Duke University Press.

Griffiths, J., 1986. What is legal pluralism? *Journal of Legal Pluralism and Unofficial Law*, 24, 1–50.

Hansen, T. B. and Stepputat, F., 2001. Introduction: States of imagination, in T. B. Hansen and F. Stepputat (eds), *States of Imagination: Ethnographic Explorations of the Postcolonial State*. Durham and London: Duke University Press, 1–40.

Hansen, T. B. and Stepputat, F. (eds), 2005. Introduction, in T. B. Hansen and F. Stepputat (eds), *Sovereign Bodies: Citizens, Migrants and States in the Postcolonial World*. Princeton, NJ and Oxford: Princeton University Press, 1–36.

Harvey, D., 2007. *A Brief History of Neoliberalism*. Oxford: Oxford University Press.

Harvey, D., 2008. The right to the city, *New Left Review*, 53: 23–40.

Hoffman, K. and Kirk, T., 2013. Public authority and the provision of public goods in conflict-affected and transitioning regions. JSRP Paper 7. Justice and Security Research Programme, International Development Department, London School of Economics and Political Science, London.

Holston, J., 1998. *Insurgent Citizenship: Disjunctions of Democracy and Modernity in Brazil*. Princeton, NJ: Princeton University Press.

Jones, T. and Newburn, T. (eds), 2006. *Plural Policing: A Comparative Perspective*. London and New York: Routledge.

Kirsch, T. G. and Grätz, T., 2010. *Domesticating Vigilantism in Africa*. Woodbridge: James Currey.

Kraushaar, M. and Lambach, D., 2009. Hybrid political orders: The added value of a new concept, ACPACS Occasional Paper no. 14, available at: www.issr.uq.edu.au/acpacs-publications (accessed 5 October 2013).

Kyed, H. M., 2009. The politics of legal pluralism: State policies on legal pluralism and their local dynamics in Mozambique, *Journal of Legal Pluralism and Unofficial Law*, 59, 87–120.

Lamont, M. and Molnár, V., 2002. The study of boundaries in the social sciences, *Annual Review of Sociology*, 28, 167–195.

Latour, B., 1993. *We Have Never Been Modern*, Cambridge: Harvard University Press.

Latour, B., 1999. *Pandora's Hope: Essays on the Reality of Science Studies*, Cambridge: Harvard University Press.

Latour, B., 2007. *Reassembling the Social: An Introduction to Actor–Network-Theory*, New York: Oxford University Press.

Loader, I., 2000. Plural policing and democratic governance. *Social and Legal Studies*, 9:3, 323–45.

Lund, C., 2006. Twilight institutions: Public authority and local politics in Africa, *Development and Change*, 37:4, 685–706.

Merry, S. E., 1988. Legal pluralism, *Law and Society Review*, 22: 5, 869–96.

Mitchell, T., 2006 [1999]. Society, economy, and the state effect, in A. Sharma and A. Gupta (eds), *The Anthropology of the State: A Reader*. Oxford: Blackwell, 169–186.

Moore, S. F., 2000 [1978]. *Law as Process: An Anthropological Approach*. Hamburg: Lit Verlag; Oxford: James Currey.

Mouffe, C., 2006. *On the Political*. London and New York: Routledge.

Parnell, P. C. and Kane, S. C. (eds), 2003. *Crime's Power: Anthropologists and the Ethnography of Crime*. New York: Palgrave Macmillan.

Pratten, D., 2010. Bodies of power, narratives of selfhood and security in Nigeria, in T. G. Kirsch and T. Grätz (eds), *Domesticating Vigilantism in Africa*. Oxford: Bergham Books, 118–138.

Pratten, D. and Sen, A., 2007. *Global Vigilantes*. London: Hurst.

Rodgers, D., 2009. Slum wars of the 21st century: Gangs, *mano dura*, and the new urban geography of conflict in Central America, *Development and Change*, 40:5, 949–976.

Rotberg, R., 2002. The new nature of nation-state failure, *Washington Quarterly*, 25:3, 85–96.

Saatterthwaite, D. and Mitlin, D., 2014. *Reducing Urban Poverty in the Global South*. New York: Routledge.

Sharma, A. and Gupta, A., 2006. Introduction: Rethinking theories of the state in an age of globalization, in A. Sharma and A. Gupta (eds), *The Anthropology of the State: A Reader*. Oxford: Blackwell, 1–42.

Taussig, M., 1991. *The Nervous System*. New York and London: Routledge.

UN-Habitat, 2012. *State of the World's Cities Report 2012/13. Prosperity of Cities*. Nairobi: United Nations Human Resettlement Programme.

Vandenberghe, F., 1999. The real is relational: An inquiry into Pierre Bourdieu's constructivist epistemology, *Sociological Theory*, 17(1), 32–67.

von Benda-Beckman, F., von Benda-Beckman, K. and Griffiths, A. (eds), 2009. *The Power of Law in a Transnational World*. New York and Oxford: Berghahn.

Weber, M., 1947. *Social and Economic Organization*. New York: Free Press.

Wood, J. and Shearing, C., 2007. *Imagining Security*. Portland: Willan.

Woodman, G. R., 1998. Ideological combat and social observation: Recent debate about legal pluralism, *Journal of Legal Pluralism*, 42, 21–59.

Zartman, W., 1995. *Collapsed States*. Boulder, CO: Lynne Rienner.

Chapter 2

Policing Bagong Silang
Intimacy and politics in the Philippines

Steffen Jensen and Karl Hapal

Policing has always been intimately related to political processes and family relations in the Philippines. In this way, it conforms to what we may call the weak states paradigm where accountability is lacking and private interests dominate (Abinales, 2005). While this is also the case, such a fragile state's approach yields few insights into understanding the politics and practices of policing that we explore in this chapter. This feeds into discussions about what Hansen and Stepputat (2001) have referred to as ethnography of the state in which the editors of this volume also frame their introduction. In this perspective we cannot assume much about practices of the state by looking at its formal mandates. Instead, we need to explore how the state is formed and performed through local practices and imaginations along with who actually performs authority and with what legitimacy it is exercised (Lund, 2006). Hence, in our findings, boundaries between what is state and non-state are constitutively blurred. This implies that as the private reaches into the domain that we normally associate with the state, the state and ideas of the state reach into intimate family and community relations. While generally applicable, these remarks are particularly true for policing in the Philippines. Hence, in this chapter, we ask how and to what extent policing has been caught in family and community relations and local politics and what this tells us about the nature of the state and policing in the Philippines.

At the heart of these questions lie concerns about how order-making is part and parcel of local politics and how local politics impact on what we elsewhere have called everyday policing (Buur and Jensen, 2004), that is, the actual forms of policing and order-making that take place on the ground. Our analysis indicates that policing is subsumed under local, electoral politics and family and community relations. However, these relations are inherently complex and they can only be fully grasped if we pay close attention to relations between order-making, policing and politics.

In order to explore these relations, we draw on ethnographic fieldwork, interviews and human rights interventions over a period of four years between 2009 and 2013 in a huge relocation site in the northern part of Metro Manila called Bagong Silang. While we also concern ourselves with the Philippine

National Police (PNP), we primarily focus on a system called *Katarungang Pambarangay* or the *Barangay* Justice System (BJS), because this represents the most accessible and widely used order-making mechanism in everyday policing. This system was first introduced in 1978 during the Marcos regime and further developed by the Local Government code in 1991 after the fall of Marcos' dictatorship in the new government's attempt to decentralize and de-militarize the police. It aimed to unclog the formal court system and to introduce a locally sensitive arbitration system (Asian Development Bank, 2009). We introduce the system in more detail below. Suffice it to say that this chapter will primarily follow the practices of the lowest part of the system comprising *purok* leaders (community leaders) and *tanods* (guards). We follow them as they engage in conflict resolution, are caught in community and family conflicts, including their own, and are expected to play a central role in electoral politics by those political masters that pay and/or recognize them. The terrain set out by these political masters is highly uncertain, temporary and fraught with dilemmas. For some of the *puroks*, the political masters represent their best chance to access networks and resources to realize their political ambitions, while for others they incarnate dangers of disenfranchisement, marginalization and potential violence.

We organize our argument in four parts. In the first section, we explore how policing is structured in Bagong Silang historically and in contemporary terms. In the second section, we explore policing as intimate practices informed by family and communal relations, and show that it is not analytically possible to separate policing practices from the local context. This argument is further pursued in the third section where we analyse how politics and policing are entangled practices. We show this in case studies focusing on electoral politics, political transitions and policing. In the final section, we revisit our argument in order to conclude on the nature of the state and policing in the Philippines.

History of policing and politics

Like other post-colonial societies[1] the Philippines provides an apt illustration of the deeply historically embedded connection between political power and policing. Police and order-making structures aimed at maintaining the elite's position and, in the last century, winning elections (Sidel, 1999). These structures, which had more to do with politics than with crime prevention, were propelled into independence and incarnated in the role of the police in enforcing the law. The Philippines suffered two rounds of colonial experience – a Spanish period that lasted around 300 years and an American period, lasting some fifty years. Both these rounds of colonialism left deep scars in Philippine society and were central in structuring the relations between policing and politics. During the colonial periods, policing vis-à-vis politics was mainly concerned with pacification and criminalization of revolutionaries and other millenarian organizations (Illeto, 1979; Bankoff, 1996).

In 1935, the US allowed the Philippines a measure of autonomy that lasted until the Japanese invasion in 1942. During the late American period (called commonwealth) and into Independence in 1945 after World War II, the main aim of policing was the assertion and preservation of the power of the landed elite (McCoy, 1993; Sidel, 1999). When Marcos declared Martial Law in 1972, policing increasingly became about the suppression of political enemies inside the elite as well as the suppression of the increasingly discontent populace.

The challenge by the Maoist New People's Army (NPA) caused an especially violent politicization and militarization of policing in the form of a counter-insurgency that continued after the fall of Marcos.[2] Although the NPA challenge has largely been defeated (Abinales, 1996), it remains strong in parts of the country. In other parts of the country (Mindanao), different Islamic and Moro separatist groups ensure that politics and (counter-insurgency) policing remain thoroughly entangled.[3]

During most of the twentieth century, the Philippine Constabulary was a central law enforcement agency. It was formed with the 'special duty to suppress and prevent brigandage, insurrection, unlawful assembly and breaches of the peace' (Campos, 1983: 134). Until it was integrated in the Philippine National Police in 1991, its tasks remained unchanged. The post-Marcos reform of the police aimed first and foremost at decentralizing and demili-tarizing the police; to put it under some level of civilian control, as well as to rid the police of the extreme forms of violence perpetuated during the Marcos regime (Quimpo, 2009). In order to achieve this, the 1991 Act (Act 6975) created one national police force, the Philippine National Police (PNP).

PNP was put under a reconfigured Department of the Interior and Local Government (DILG). Furthermore, in order to make the police accountable, its command structures were decentralized so the police would answer to the authority of the municipal mayor (Gutang, 1991). While the left wing and human rights circles lamented the creation of yet another 'militarized monster' through integrating the Constabulary in the police, the Constabulary saw the act as a betrayal and a denigration of the service they had rendered to the nation. However, more importantly for our purpose and in line with John Sidel (1999), the law first and foremost rehabilitated political control of the police to the local political families and strongmen.

Together with the continued politicization of law enforcement inherent, for instance, in counter-insurgency, the localized focus of policing has been a central and enduring trend in Philippine policing. The Spanish had already established municipal and provincial police forces (the *Cuadrilleros* and the *Tercio de Policia*) under the direction of local *principalia* (Philippine landed elite) and local, colonial authorities (Bankoff, 1996). This was continued into independence. As John Sidel notes (1999), the entrenched interests of local *principalia* elites or families were given a national stage to exert their power through the electoral, representative system of the Americans, which was uncontrolled due to a very small state bureaucracy. This created a political system that was enormously localized and based on powerful families using the national state coffers to boost and perpetuate their own power and perpetuate their electoral success. This also involved the use of police and private armies with which to quell resistance. Throughout the first half of the twentieth century this led to constant tension between the interests of the landed elites and national interests, with the former as the perpetual winners (McCoy, 1993), not least because the landed elites and the political families became the national government.

While the intention of the post-Marcos regime allegedly was to institute civilian control over the police, in many municipalities and provinces the police came to serve a reconstituted *cacique* democracy (Anderson, 1988; Sidel 1999), that is, a democracy in which (landed) elites manage to secure their hold on state power through electoral processes. Law enforcement agencies play a central role in this where the Municipal Mayor can assert authority over the PNP and the *Barangay* Captain exerts control over the lowest level of the state law enforcement system, the *Barangay* Justice System. With this, let us move on to Bagong Silang and the *Barangay* Justice System that operates in that area.

Introducing policing in Bagong Silang

Situated at the northern edges of Metro Manila, Bagong Silang was constructed as a resettlement site in the dying days of the Marcos dictatorship as a way of easing Manila's perpetual human overflow (Tadiar, 2005). Between 1985 and 1990 up to 25,000 people a year came to this huge resettlement site next to the Marilao River and the province of Bulaccan. They came from some of the poorest, most overcrowded areas of the huge city: Tondo, Valenzuela, Divisoria, Commonwealth and Payatas. These areas were also perceived as inherently violent places, a reputation that Bagong Silang soon inherited. Apart from a reputation of gang and drug related violence, Bagong Silang also constituted the frontier between the NPA and the military. In other words, it was a highly complex area to police. Responsibility for policing was shared between the Philippine National Police and the *Barangay* Justice System (*Katarungang Pambarangay*) which is the focus of our analysis here.

The concept of the *Barangay* emanates from a distant past where it designated the crew and population of a boat. As such the design is premised on small, intimate groups of people. In many parts of the Philippines, this is still the case and a *Barangay* might comprise a few hundred or maybe a thousand people. However, with urbanization, some of the *Barangays* have become sizable administrative entities often the size of cities. Of all the *Barangays*, Bagong Silang is the largest with about 250,000 inhabitants. Apart from being an important administrative unit, it is also a very large voting block and the politician who commands the votes of Bagong Silang has come far in relation to controlling the municipality of Caloocan.

Bagong Silang has been divided up into phases of which there are nine. Each phase is again divided up into packages, in Tagalog called a *purok* that again is divided into blocks. On these different levels, different political, administrative and order-making tasks are being addressed. For order-making assumed by the *Barangay* Justice System, the block is the central unit.

A package typically covers between 300 and 600 houses with up to 2,500 residents. In Bagong Silang there are 115 packages each with a *purok* leader who has been appointed by the head of the *Barangay*. The *puroks* each nominate ten *tanods* (guards), making the number of *tanods* 1,150. On an everyday level, the *purok* and the *tanods* are charged with maintaining the peace and solving local, neighbourhood disputes. These conflicts may be about debt, public misbehaving, neighbourhood disagreements and conflicts, marital problems, problems with drinking and with the youth, bad language, etc.

If the *purok* leader and his or her *tanods* are not able to solve the conflict or if the parties are not willing to let them mediate, the case is transferred to the next level of the *Barangay* Justice System, the *Lupong Tagapamayapa*, which is a *Barangay*-wide mediation office or directly translated the pacification committee. Together, the *puroks*, *tanods* and *Lupon* constitute the first step in the criminal justice system in the Philippines (Asian Development Bank, 2009). Partly as an attempt to unclog the courts, the *Barangay* Justice System has jurisdiction in less serious criminal cases carrying a penalty of less than one year imprisonment or a fine of less than PHP5,000.[4] Cases that involve children, land and real estate conflicts, corruption cases and cases involving people from different local government structures are also dealt with by other legal entities such as the police and the *Barangay* Council for the Protection of Children.

Between 2008 and 2010 more than 20,000 cases were heard by the Bagong Silang *Barangay* Justice System. Most of the cases were dealt with at the lowest level of the system, that is, the *purok*. In 2008 and 2009, about 3,000 cases (or one in five) were referred from the level of the *purok* to the level of the *Barangay* and the *Lupon*. At both the level of *purok* and *Lupon*, most often conflicts are settled through a *kasunduan* (a pledge or an agreement).[5]

It varies from *purok* to *purok* how many cases are referred up within the system. In one of the blocks that we will explore below, not one case was referred in 2009 from the level of the *purok* to the *Lupon*. In another block some cases were referred upwards in the system. Clearly this had to do with the nature of the conflicts, but also with the different *puroks*. One *purok* that did not refer any cases put much pride in that fact, whereas another *purok*, working in the neighbouring block, emphasized the rules about when to refer, including cases of serious fighting and theft. This *purok* also put emphasis on respecting the wishes of those implicated and not forcing a local solution onto them. Hence, if one party in the dispute wanted to refer the case to the *Lupon*, then the *purok* would follow this wish.

While there are differences between the different *puroks* across Bagong Silang, it is also clear from our material that they share similar complex issues and dilemmas when effecting order. Prominent among those dilemmas and issues are the overlapping spheres of politics, family and community. In the following two sections we first explore policing in the intimate worlds of family and community and second the entangled nature of policing structures and electoral politics. We begin by following one specific *purok* leader, Mr Garcia, to illustrate just how intimate a family affair policing on the ground is.

Policing and the intimacy of family and community

We meet *purok* leader Garcia in 2009 on the first night of our fieldwork in Bagong Silang. It is Maria who has taken us to Garcia. Maria is the *tanod* responsible for the block that we stay in. There are five of these blocks in the area – called a package – that Garcia is in charge of. We have been introduced to Maria as someone who knows everybody in the block. Maria has taken us on a tour, assuring us that everything will be ok: 'Don't worry! Maria will take care of you.' The tour ends in the outpost where Garcia meets us. Garcia is around sixty years old and a very nice man, full of humour and capable of more than a few sexual innuendoes. He shows us his books; in 2009 not one single case from his area had been referred further up the system; he has dealt with all the conflicts, he tells us with pride.

Garcia is in principle a volunteer, appointed by the head of the local government entity, the *Barangay* Captain, to perform an important community service. However, each *tanod* and *purok* leader receives an honorarium from the *Barangay* Captain at the time called Padilla and the then mayor of the larger City of Caloocan, Recom Echeverri. Although the amount is not a lot, it comes with recognition and access to resources as well as the possibility of ascending the political ladder. Both politicians are part of important political families on the levels of *Barangay* and the municipality.

Behind Garcia's chair, a placard indicates the names of Garcia and his ten *tanods*. Four of them are male relatives of Garcia, either his sons or sons-in-law; all of them are middle-aged. Garcia's situation is in no way unique in this regard. If we look at the overall profile of the slightly more than 1,300 *puroks* and *tanods* in Bagong Silang from the period between 2007 and 2010, more than 75 per cent are male and 95 per cent are over thirty in a population with a majority of people below the age of twenty-five (Jensen, Hapal and Modvig, 2013). Although less conclusive, as a proxy for family relations, *tanods* and *puroks* often share the same name or live close to each other. Asked about this, Maria and Garcia explain that the leader must be able to trust the people under him.

Unlike Garcia, Maria was nominated because she allegedly knows her area really well. Hence, Garcia had sought her out to represent 'her' area. In this way, policing is intimate since it appears to be controlled more or less by a small circle of individuals mostly composed of middle-aged men related to each other by blood, kinship ties or common history (*pinagsamahan*). However, intimacy works in more complex ways than through kinship, as notions of neighbour-liness and common history often take precedence. Policing the ones you know requires constant negotiation of such ties. In an adjacent package to Garcia's area, *purok* Ponte was in charge of local security. Ponte was appointed to be *purok* leader due to his close church relations to *Barangay* Captain Padilla. Ponte, in turn, appointed as *tanods* a daughter, a daughter in-law and two of his five sons. The sons have a reputation for rowdiness when they drink – which they do quite often.

One afternoon, one son got into a fight and was stabbed in the arm. The circumstances around the incident were uncertain, with Ponte's family insisting that it was a case of mistaken identity and others claiming that this was part of a conflict over debt. After the fight, the daughter of the house, also a *tanod*, went to the police to file a case, as it was outside the jurisdiction of the *purok* leader (her own father). In the days that followed, the parents of the alleged stabber visited the Ponte family on several occasions to make them drop the case. During these visits they invoked several concepts that all address issues of intimacy: the stabber was a *kababata*, that is, someone the brother who was stabbed grew up with; they had *pinagsamahan*, that is, a common history, and they invoked the notion of *pakikisama*, a kind of neighbourliness. Of these concepts, *pakikisama* is especially central. To see how, we need to visit the *path walk*, a central part of communal life in Bagong Silang.

The path walk is the quintessential public space of Bagong Silang. There are thousands of them across the resettlement site and life is lived more or less within the confines of these narrow streets. People's *kababata* will often come from the same path walk and the history they have will emanate from what has happened here, good or bad. The path walk is densely populated and little of what happens in anybody's house will go unnoticed by the neighbours. This is the space of *pakikisama* – or neighbourliness, the ability to get along. As such, *pakikisama* is highly valued. As Maria said: 'It is deep, deep.' It is what makes it possible for people to be able to survive; it is the ultimate support network.

However, there is a 'darker' side to the concept. As one informant said, 'I can't do anything about it. I need to get along with them [*makisama sa kanila*]. I live in this block; they also live in this block.' Hence, *pakikisama* is ambiguous. On the one hand, it is ultimately virtuous – the ideological rendition of the good community; on the other hand, people are compelled to get along due to the claustrophobic proximity that they live in. To be outside these networks – to be seen not to know how to do *pakikisama* – can be detrimental to one's survival. In this way, we might understand the intimacy involved in *pakikisama* as both compelling and compelled.[6] The Ponte family finally succumbed and dropped the case, specifically because of *pakikisama*, which a *purok* leader, in particular, cannot afford to ignore.

Pakikisama also has other direct effects on what is policed. In Garcia's block, where Maria works as a *tanod*, the local drug dealer and the abortionist are both in blatant violation of the law. However, in both cases Maria evokes *pakikisama* to talk about her relationship to them: they are supportive of people; they do people favours and in spite of Maria's conservative morals, she thinks that the abortionist provides a service that is necessary. She explains:

> I knew that Ken is a distributor of *shabu* (drugs) but it's not just for himself; he is able to help others. Ken helped many people here. People run to him whenever they need help. No difference with the abortionist: we were supposed to target her but then we had an opportunity to know each other. She helped a lot of people so then I stopped.

The drug dealer and the abortionist also know that it is in their best interest to do *pakikisama* because that – at least to some extent – inoculates them from being handed over to the police or to the *tanods*. In this way, compelled intimacy structures policing. It animates who is a criminal, when an act is defined as illegal, and when and how action must be taken – even by those charged with upholding the law. What crimes should be prevented is a moral issue rather than one of legality (Jensen, 2008). However, authorities such as Maria not only exonerate illegality for others. In her own life she ventures into the realm of the illicit as part of a very complex livelihood strategy.

Maria is a *kubrador*, that is, she takes bets in the widespread game of *Jueteng*, which is illegal. Furthermore, her husband earns his income from equally illegal cock fights. This often brings both her and her husband into conflict with the PNP whose members see the cock fights as means of extortion. Maria sometimes rationalizes these activities as her keeping an eye on things (i.e. as an undercover activity), but most of the time she humorously and remorselessly admits her moral 'shortcomings'. Moreover, these activities bring her into the sphere of interest for the PNP as these acts contravene legal codes, not however, as a subject of the law but as a subject of extortionist police corruption.

In conclusion, policing is not just about law and order but also about morality. It seems clear that dichotomies of legality and illegality, state and civil society are constantly blurred through processes that relate to family, community and law enforcement in complex ways. In the words of Judith Butler, they are interdependent and co-produced (Butler, 2004, p. 130). At the same time as people seem to be well aware of the distinctions between the legal and the illegal, they simply ascribe different moral values to different practices akin to Janet Roitman's notion of the ethics of illegality (Roitman, 2006). Hence, abortion can be illegal, amoral *and* the right thing to do. Second, the *Barangay* Justice System relies on politically elected families. To have a conflict with these families might not be very comfortable. However, people, including *puroks* and *tanods*, who are living in these areas, have to negotiate local intimacies that are hard to ignore. There are common histories, a sense of neighbourliness and survival to think about.

As we shall see in the next section, political fortunes change, leaving *puroks* and *tanods* out of a job, meaning that their position of power is temporary. In the blocks in which we did fieldwork, the entanglements and the temporaneity of their positions seemed to make them accountable to the local population. Furthermore, as *tanods* and *puroks* come from the same deprived areas, their livelihood strategies might be in contravention of the very standards they are made to police. Morality is therefore constantly negotiated within the system of policing, allowing law enforcers and residents alike to go on with the business of survival. In this way, the *Barangay* Justice System is intimately entangled with family and communal relations, although not always in the ways intended.

The politics of policing

Besides the fact that policing is always a fundamentally political task, policing structures in Bagong Silang and elsewhere in the Philippines are also part of the political machines of strong families. This is not least because these political families and the state offices they control often hire them and pay their salaries (Sidel, 1999, p. 26). This is particularly important in relation to the *Barangay* Justice System where there are two political masters, the *Barangay* Captain and the Municipal Mayor with the latter often being the patron of the former.[7] In this section, we first show how the *Barangay* Justice System and other policing structures were used for political purposes in the May 2010 election for the municipal mayoral position. In the second part, we present cases around the political transition that took place after the *Barangay* election in October 2010.

A political machine

Purok leaders and *tanods* are supposedly officers of peace. However, they are also, and maybe even primarily, clients of their political patrons. To see how that plays out, let us return to Garcia's outpost. Apart from the placard with the names of the *purok* leader and his *tanods*, the walls are decorated with Garcia's political masters, namely *Barangay* Captain Cesar Padilla who nominated Garcia as *purok* leader and Municipal Mayor Echiverri. Garcia and his colleagues are called upon and expected to take part in political rallies and functions, especially around election time. They are explicitly told that failure to support their patron will mean that the state apparatus will not pay their honorarium that in this way becomes a private donation from the political master even if it is paid for from state coffers.

In all the rallies up to the May 2010 national elections the *puroks* and the *tanods* constituted the bulk of supporters for incumbent Mayor Echiverri, as well as for the Liberal Party on whose ticket the Mayor had decided to run. Echiverri had recently jumped ship from the party of the outgoing president Gloria Arroyo *Lakas ng Tao* (Power of the People) as the times seemed to favour presidential candidate Benigno Aquino III, son of national icon Corazon Aquino to become the next president. Echiverri's senatorial ambitions were known in many quarters. For that to come true, he needed to share a national platform with the stronger candidate when he would reach his three-term limit as Mayor in 2013. At the same time, he tried to pave the way for his son, R. J. Echiverri, to take over as Mayor in the 2013 national elections.[8] In this way, Echiverri incarnates the traditional politician called *trapo*, which in Spanish and Tagalog means dirty rag, identified by a host of commentators as *the* problem in Philippine politics. What defines this politics is: no loyalty to any party or agenda; concern only for one's own fortunes and that of the family; and the mixing of private and public interests (McCoy, 1993; Austin, 1999; Sidel, 1999; Hutchcroft and Rocamora, 2003; Quimpo, 2009).

In Bagong Silang, it was also common knowledge that Padilla and Echiverri were political opponents. Still, because Padilla depended on Echiverri for his fortunes, he had to toe the Echiverri line and organize rally after rally for Echiverri. An insider to Padilla's office said that Echiverri had demanded absolute loyalty. If not, the consequences would be grave for future patronage. Subsequently, Padilla informed all *puroks* and *tanods* that he would not tolerate any absences from the rallies. The daughter of Ponte explained, 'If we don't come, we will not get our honorarium – not from Mayor Echiverri and not from Padilla.'

The discussions about honorarium were constantly present in many conversations with the *puroks* and *tanods*. Honorariums were often late and often smaller than expected. On one occasion, at the Christmas Party of about ten blocks, the Mayor was supposed to come and show his satisfaction with the service of the *puroks*. The excitement was tangible as Echiverri entered the covered court singing his signature song. All joined in. After ten minutes he left again leaving behind the money.

The daughter of *purok* Ponte received the money on behalf of their area. With contempt she looked at the 500 Pesos note (about eight USD) that the ten *tanods* were to split and pretended to step on it. Furthermore, many of the *puroks* supported Padilla or other candidates rather than Echiverri. Maria, for instance, was a staunch supporter of Echiverri's main rival Oca Malapitan whom she hoped would win the 2013 election and allow her to cash in on all her hard work as an organizer for Malapitan. Garcia was originally a protégé of Echiverri. However, at a time of great distress and illness, he had turned to Oca Malapitan for support. Oca helped him and thus incurred what is called an *utang na loob*, a debt of gratitude, with Oca. Hence, Garcia was bound to support Oca, at least discretely. Openly associating himself with Oca would have made him lose his position as *purok*. In the case of *purok* Ponte, there was little doubt. He had a long-standing relationship with Captain Padilla and his wife owed her job in the *Barangay* Hall to Padilla and to Echiverri. To go against this line would have been catastrophic for the financial situation of the family.

Despite the common knowledge that Padilla was not in favour with Echiverri, he supported the Mayor as loyally as he could. Echiverri's election campaign was flawless and he did not even spend much money on it because of the poor opposition. In it he used all the state's resources for his own personal electoral gain. The policing structures, especially, were implicated. *Puroks* and *tanods* constituted the muscle of the campaign and at every rally station, commanders of the Philippine National Police would speak about the heroic deeds of Mayor Echiverri. In the final election showdown, Echiverri used every police vehicle in Caloocan, probably to remind both the police and the general electorate who was in charge. Come election time, Echiverri won a landslide victory over a weak opposition. So did Oca in the congressional election. However, Padilla did not fare well as Echiverri dumped him for his own candidate, Inar Trinidad in the *Barangay* elections some months later. Trinidad, with the support of Echiverri, won the *Barangay* elections. This resulted in a transition, which also affected policing structures and its agents. This will be the subject of the next section.

Policing and electoral transition

When political patrons lose their office at any level in the Philippines, it usually results in a reshuffling of government offices from top to bottom. Posts are being refilled; offices are shut down, new ones are created, and budgets are revamped. All these shifts benefit new political patrons and allow them to repay the many debts incurred while attempting to get elected and prepare them to win the next election. Hence, transitions are moments of great uncertainty for losers and those with weak political connections. In Bagong Silang the Ponte family had much to lose when Captain Padilla lost the *Barangay* elections to Inar Trinidad. Inar was by many seen as Echiverri's favourite candidate in Bagong Silang. Amidst allegations of fraud, Padilla and his supporters were also bitter because of Echiverri's betrayal after Padilla's support during the 2010 national elections.

Bagong Silang is a huge *Barangay*, said to be the biggest in the country, as such it generates the largest revenue through the Internal Revenue Allocation compared to other *Barangays* along with income from a variety of trading permits and issuing of IDs. Needless to say, there are also constant rumours of corruption by officials. In the *Barangay* Hall, there were in Padilla's time more than 250 employees. On top of this number there were about 1,300 *puroks* and *tanods*. While some had to remain because of the jobs they held or because they answered to different political masters, a substantial number of them could not retain their positions. It was a matter of little surprise when *puroks* Ponte and Garcia were told to quit; in fact all 115 *puroks* were told to vacate their office. However, the Ponte family awaited the fate of the mother who worked in the *Barangay* Hall in the *Barangay* Council for the Protection of Children. It was with great relief that Inar informed the mother that she could stay on.

All throughout Bagong Silang, people were sacked from their position, espe-cially if they had been close to Padilla. The official justification was that their loyalty was with the former *Barangay* Captain and not with the *Barangay*. Keeping them in their post would threaten the current administration with too much politicking, which is detrimental to the 'development' of the *Barangay*. However, outgoing employees, such as *puroks* and *tanods*, often see these actions as a purge to the benefit of the incoming *Barangay* Captain rather than an action in the best interest of the *Barangay*.

It was not surprising that the *puroks* were replaced as they almost always play a central role in the political machinery of the Captain. They are in many ways the only representative of the Captain in each block of the huge relocation site. Besides law enforcement, they perform important political tasks of presence and information to and from the *Barangay* Hall. In this way, replacing the supporters of the previous Captain is an ideal opportunity to rid the council of supporters of the previous Captain and to make one's mark. Inar came from the left side (*kaliwa*) of Bagong Silang and knew little of the right side (*kanan*) where Garcia and Ponte resided. As he knew little of the area, he nominated one of the erstwhile *tanods* in Garcia's area who then replaced all of Garcia's kin with her own nominations. In Ponte's area, Inar nominated a political organizer of Echiverri.

After the election there was talk among some of the *puroks* of Padilla. They were certain that the elections were rigged by Echiverri. They claimed to have done a good job in making Bagong Silang peaceful. In response, they formed a new organization, *Samahang ng mga puroks at tanods ng Bagong Silang* (the organization of *puroks* and *tanods* of Bagong Silang) prominently featuring several former *puroks* from the right side of Bagong Silang. The organization tried to convince those replaced to join to make Bagong Silang safe. However, not long after the organization was formed it became part of renewed political struggles between Mayor Echiverri and his deputy-Mayor Erice. Erice had mayoral ambitions and he needed a political machine to fight his battle in Bagong Silang where he was known to be weak. Immediately, he seemed to have seized upon the new organization as a potential cog in his electoral machine.

Shortly after Erice had begun to show an interest in the organization, one of its members was shot dead. Whether or not his death was due to his membership of the organization is uncertain. As the word about the former *purok* had it, he was daring, talkative, sexually aggressive and action-oriented. He frequently punished young people he thought were out of line. He might also have been involved in drugs. However, what spurred the rumour of his death being tied to politics was first that he died immediately after the formation of the organization and second because he was killed in a multi-cab minivan with Echiverri's name on it. Regardless of whether it was politically motivated, it had political consequences. For instance, Ponte's wife forbade him to join the new organization, even to get near any of the ringleaders out of fear for her husband's life and her own livelihood. The death of the former *purok* also laid the organization to rest, along with the hopes of Erice to mount a challenge through it.[9]

While many of the *puroks* did not rely on the income generated from the honorarium, they lost the source of recognition that followed with the post. Some of them had also invested personal resources in the position. Garcia for instance had decorated the room he used as an outpost, a building that had been lent him by one of the central Padilla supporters. However, other, former *puroks* lost much more as the case of Ronel, a former *purok* leader, illustrates. Ronel used to be a *purok* leader in the phase 8 area. During his tenure he managed to construct a *Barangay* outpost. When he was put out of office he wanted to retrieve his materials, including window frames and other building material. He went to the outpost but was met with resistance from the new *purok*. Ronel went on to beat up the new *purok* so badly that he was arrested. However, due to his common history (*pinagsamahan*) with the officials at the *Barangay*, Ronel was released from the police cell and put in an office space at the *Barangay* Hall.

Drawing on his connections again, Ronel managed to be set free the following day. Tragically, Ronel's father suffered a heart attack and died, presumably due to the shock of seeing Ronel taken into custody. But the calamity did not end there. Angry with Ronel and seeking revenge, the new *purok* with his *tanods* sought out Ronel and shot him dead. As a consequence, Ronel's pregnant wife lost their baby. The case illustrates the struggles over territory and resources locally and how they are tied up with state recognition. Ronel had constructed the *Barangay* outpost out of his own pocket, that is, he came to represent, through his own resources, the state in his block. When he was no longer part of the state, he wanted it back.

Concluding remarks

In this chapter, we have explored how and to what extent policing has been caught in family and community relations as well as local electoral politics through an ethnographic analysis of the *Barangay* Justice System represented by the *puroks* and *tanods*. While the justice system is established with a legal, statutory mandate it is clearly not entirely statist. Rather, it is influenced by private interests and logics including family relations, common histories, livelihood and alternative ethics of legality (Roitman, 2006). Furthermore, the *Barangay* Justice System is invariably implicated in electoral processes and political machines to an extent where it often appears as though the political tasks take prominence over policing.

Because the *puroks* and *tanods* are present everywhere in the massive *Barangay* they naturally attract the attention of political players. Hence, when the outgoing *puroks* wanted to establish an alternative justice structure, they were immediately implicated in the political schemes of would-be patrons.

The moment this happened, the organization folded. Hence, we might conclude that it is the structures that are politically interesting for political elites rather than policing and order-making being the point of departure for political careers as it is in other parts of the world described in this volume (see Kyed on Swaziland). At the same time, *purok* leaders clearly have ambitions other than those of electoral politics. This might be to secure themselves and their families and networks privileged access to resources and recognition from patrons and other community members that come with carrying out local policing. It is in this way that joining the policing structures entails both opportunities and dangers that need to be negotiated carefully by *puroks* and *tanods*.

The question is what this tells us about the state and policing in the Philippines. While the analysis points to the importance of private family-based elites working to the detriment of the state in the fragile state literature, this would be an inadequate conclusion. Rather, we should understand the extent to which electoral processes and patronage networks are part of how the state is understood and experienced in the Philippines. It is simply impossible to divorce the campaigning and electoral processes from the idea of the state. In many ways this is how the state is experienced and practised in everyday life in Bagong Silang. Roads are tarred but invariably the name of the patron 'paying' will be engraved in the tar. Water will be provided but the water tank will carry the image of the politician who was able to claim it as his or her accomplishment. While elections are not the only process in which the state is experienced and perceived, they are significant, especially in places such as Bagong Silang that for all intents and purposes is marginalized in terms of public services (Jensen, 2014). In this way, policing in the form of the *Barangay* Justice system performs several tasks. It is one of the central mechanisms for maintaining local order as its mandate dictates. However, it is also one of the most pervasive state presences in marginal spaces such as Bagong Silang and one with clear links to a patrimonial system. While those representatives that we explored seemed to have few political ambitions, every political family and player did, and the *Barangay* Justice System was a key component of electoral processes. Furthermore, the interests of *puroks* and *tanods* were not only altruistic. Through their participation they gained access to resources and networks beyond their local area. Hence, the system became a central and indispensable part of both state formation and the proliferation of private interests to an extent where state and private interests were co-produced and entangled rather than one being dominant at the expense of the other.

Notes

1   See for instance Brogden and Shearing (1993) and Chandavarkar (1998) for South Africa and India respectively.
2   The NPA insurrection came on the back of other peasant rebellions from the 1930s and onwards (Kerkvliet, 1979).

3   Contrary to notions of a weak state, the Philippine state has been remarkably successful in combatting the different insurgencies around the country. For a fuller account of for instance the post-Marcos counter-insurgency targeting the NPA in the late 1980s, see Sidel and Hedman (2000).

4   PHP40 equals approximately USD1.

5   Parallel to the *Barangay* Justice System, in 2007 the *Barangay* Captain in Bagong Silang also instituted the Task Force to be a rapid response team to assist *purok* leaders in cases of violence. The Task Force consists of twenty members that also perform adjudication (as well as enforce bye-laws on traffic and hawking).

6   For elaboration, see Jensen *et al.*, 2013.

7   All policing structures must in some way pay tribute to the political masters. The PNP differs from the *Barangay* Justice System in that they have two masters to serve. Their salary comes from the National Government through the DILG. However, local governments are able to 'command' them too. This happens through the right of the local government to hire and place police officers where they want and to give them support in terms of vehicles, that is, their daily working lives are influenced by local political patrons.

8   As it were, Echiverri did not manage to get his son elected. Rumour has it that he made his peace with his family's main rival Oca Malapitan. In the election in 2013, Oca became Mayor whereas Recom took Oca's place in the Congress as representative for Caloocan First District.

9   Later in 2012 Erice also tried to topple Echiverri through the court system. He warned an official bureau investigating corruption that Echiverri had stolen pension money due to be paid to a fund. Echiverri was suspended for three months pending an investigation. However, the allegation back-fired as Echiverri was exonerated and Erice had to withdraw from his ambitions. He was not even a contender in the 2013 election.

References

Abinales, P., 1996. *The Revolution Falters: The Left in Philippine Politics after 1986.* Attica, NY: Cornell University Press.

Abinales, P., 2005. *State and Society in the Philippines.* New York: Rowman & Littlefield.

Anderson, B., 1988. Casique Democracy and the Philippines: Origins and Dreams. *New Left Review*, 169:3, 3–33.

Asian Development Bank, 2009. *Background Notes on the Philippine Justice System.* Mandalyong City: Asian Development Bank.

Austin, T., 1999. *Banana Justice: Field Notes on Philippine Crime and Custom.* Westport, CT: Praeger.

Bankoff, G., 1996. *Crime, Society and the State in the 19th Century Philippines.* Honolulu, HI: University of Hawaii Press.

Brogden, M. and Shearing, C., 1993. *Policing for a New South Africa.* London: Routledge.

Butler, J., 1993. *Bodies that Matter.* London: Routledge.

Butler, J., 2004. *Precarious Life: The Powers of Mourning and Violence.* New York, NY: Verso.

Buur, L. and Jensen, S., 2004. Introduction: Vigilantism and the policing of everyday life in South Africa, *African Studies*, 63:2, 139–152.

Campos, C., 1983. The role of the police in the Philippines: A study from the Third World. PhD Thesis, Michigan State University.

Chandavarkar, R., 1998. *Imperial Power and Popular Politics: Class, Resistance and the State in India, 1850–1950*. Cambridge: Cambridge University Press.

Gutang, R., 1991. *Pulisya: The Inside Story of the Demilitarization of Law Enforcement in the Philippines*. Quezon City: Daraga Press.

Hansen, T. and Stepputat, F., 2001. *States of Imagination: Ethnographic Explorations of the Postcolonial State*. Durham: Duke University Press.

Hutchcroft, P. and Rocamora, J., 2003. Strong demands, weak institutions: The origins and evolution of the democratic deficit in the Philippines. *Journal of East Asian Studies*, 3, 259–292.

Ileto, R., 1979. *Pasyon and Revolution: Popular Movements in the Philippines, 1840–1910*. Manila: Ateneo University Press.

Jensen, S., 2008. *Gangs, Politics and Dignity in Cape Town*. Chicago. IL: Chicago University Press.

Jensen, S., 2014. Stunted future: *Buryong* among young men in Manila. In A. Dalsgård, M. Frederiksen, S. Højlund and L. Meinert (eds), *Ethnographies of Youth and Temporality: Time Objectified*. Philadelphia, PA: Temple University Press, 41–57.

Jensen, S., Hapal, K. and Modvig, J., 2013. *Violence in Bagong Silang*. Copenhagen. DIGNITY Publication Series on Torture and Organised Violence, no. 2.

Kerkvliet, B., 1979. *The Huk Rebellion: A Study of Peasant Revolt in the Philippines*. Quezon City: New Day.

Lund, C., 2006. Twilight institutions: public Authority and local politics in Africa. *Development and Change*, 37:4, 685–706.

McCoy, A., 1993. *An Anarchy of Families: State and Family in the Philippines*. Madison, WI: University of Wisconsin Press.

Quimpo, N., 2009. The Philippine predatory regime: Growing authoritarian features, *The Pacific Review*, 22:3, 335–353.

Roitman, J., 2006. The ethics of illegality in the Chad Basin. In J. Comaroff and J. Comaroff (eds), *Law and Order in the Postcolony*. Chicago, IL: University of Chicago Press, 247–272.

Sidel, J., 1999. *Capital, Coercion, and Crime: Bossism in the Philippines*. Stanford, CA: Stanford University Press.

Sidel, J. and Hedman, E.-L., 2000. *Philippine Politics and Society in the Twentieth Century*. London: Routledge.

Tadiar, N., 2005. *Fantasy-production: Sexual Economies and Other Philippine Consequences for the New World Order*. Manila: Ateneo de Manila.

Chapter 3

Policing and the politics of protection on Lombok, Indonesia

Kari Telle

Introduction

Security concerns and measures are infiltrating the fabric of everyday life in many parts of Indonesia, giving rise to a plethora of social formations that claim to provide 'protection'. Today, fifteen years after the demise of Suharto's authoritarian New Order regime (1966–1998) and the transition towards decentralization and democratization, this huge archipelago nation is awash with groups whose purported mission is to combat 'crime' and enhance security. What is taking place is not simply a 'privatization of the public order' (Dijk 2001), but also an informalization of security arrangements. Marked by improvisation, flux and short-term alliances, the latter trend is especially apparent among the urban poor and in rural communities with vibrant traditions of self-help and a deep distrust of official authorities.

This chapter contributes to an understanding of contemporary Indonesian political dynamics by addressing the informal authority wielded by civilian security groups. Stressing the political nature of security provision, I draw on examples from the island of Lombok to argue that security groups have emerged as a significant form of informal governance that provides individuals and economically marginalized groups with new opportunities for exercising influence. My analysis centres on Amphibi and Tigabersatu, showing how their hybrid security repertoires have evolved as both groups have become caught up in local-level contestations of power. By focusing on two different groups, I show that the provision of security spans several 'layers of politics' and that acts of policing serve to remake the state.

There is no denying that security groups employ vigilante tactics of intimidation to enforce 'order', sometimes at the expense of ethnic or religious minorities (Telle 2013; Tyson 2013). But violence is only one repertoire of action through which these groups have constituted an informal de facto system of rule, which stands in a dynamic, often uneasy, relationship with the state. Following Klinken and Barker (2009: 7), I regard such repertoires as 'performative templates that can be repeated in different situations and that aim at a theatrical effect on their audience'. These groups have also constituted themselves as forces to be reckoned with by mastering the bureaucratic art of 'speaking like a state', to paraphrase James Scott (1998). While these groups justify their existence by stressing the shortcomings of the official justice apparatus, I suggest that state officials and candidates for political office have become an important audience for many of the order-making practices in which these groups engage.

Drawing on fieldwork in urban and rural Lombok, this chapter makes two interrelated arguments. First, I argue that security groups have invented hybrid repertoires of security.[1] Animated by religiously inflected notions of safety and order, these repertoires bear the imprint of New Order militarism, but also draw on globalized discourses of 'participation'. In accounting for these hybrid repertoires, Bubandt's (2005) ethnographic approach to 'vernacular security' is helpful as it captures the political dimension of security discourses. Stressing the interplay between different but interpenetrating forms of threat management, Bubandt insists that 'complex processes of accommodation and reformulation take place in the interstices between global, national and local representations of the problem of security' (2005: 276). This perspective rejects the universalist pretensions of 'human security' and moves beyond the relativist position that there are multiple cultural constructions of security.

Second, I argue that civilian security groups serve as power brokers between territorially defined communities and the local state as well as the criminal realm. Their in-between position as mediators linking different domains accounts for a key feature of these groups, namely their flexibility, fluidity and pragmatism. This interstitial position contributes to the labile character of these groups, which, as Abrahams has argued for vigilantism more generally, exists 'on the frontiers – structural and/or cultural – of state power' (2007: 423). With the post-98 democratization process in Indonesia, relations between political elites and security groups have changed considerably. Mindful of their numerical strength, these groups articulate claims based on communal or religious identities. No longer content to simply serve as vehicles for elite interests, they have become significant constellations of social power.

The chapter begins with an overview of the shifting dynamics between violence-wielding groups and the state during New Order and in the post-98 era. The next two sections introduce Amphibi and Tigabersatu, with a focus on their organizational features and evolving security repertoires. The section on patronage politics shows how security groups have become involved in local and regional-level contestations of power and how involvement in electoral politics tends to breed tensions. I conclude by suggesting that disillusionment with co-optation may prompt a move from involvement in politics to socio-religious activities and the reinvention of community-based forms of policing.

From 'statist' to decentralized security

An influential stream of scholarship regards the rise of vigilante groups and civilian policing actors as products of globalization and transformations in governance associated with deregulation and the outsourcing of services to the market and to volunteers (Comaroff and Comaroff 2006; Goldstein 2010). According to Comaroff and Comaroff (2006: 16), the effects of neoliberal deregulation imply that government becomes 'less and less an ensemble of bureaucratic institutions, more and more a licensing-and-franchising authority'. While the proliferation of security groups in Indonesia must be understood in relation to the state and to shifts in state power, their formation cannot be reduced to a reflex of neoliberal dynamics. 'The link between vigilantism and globalisation', as Sen and Pratten (2007: 5) note, 'is a powerful argument . . . but only a partial one'. In Indonesia the state has a long history of involving civilians in policing and security management.

The New Order period (1966–1998) in Indonesia represented a period of great centralization. The military-dominated regime turned its version of 'security' into a key societal discourse. The armed forces had a 'dual function' (*dwi fungsi*) to defend the state and a mandate to maintain stability by 'guiding' the development of society. Adapting the late colonial notion of security – *rust en orde* – inherited from the Dutch, the regime 'made "safety and order" (*keamanan dan ketertiban*) the basis of its high-modernist, neo-patrimonial rule' (Bubandt 2005: 281). Benedict Anderson (2001: 13) has characterized the New Order regime as 'a vast machine of state violence'. While the military and the police controlled this machinery, they made extensive and profitable use of state-backed militias and gangs (Lindsey 2001). Such groups were incorporated in ways conducive to the strengthening of state power, but when such groups were perceived to coalesce into forces capable of challenging the regime, the state 'reasserted its power brutally and unambiguously' (Wilson 2012: 296).[2]

A central aspect of New Order rule was the emphasis on involving civilians in security. Apart from reminding people of the ever-present threat posed by internal enemies, be they criminal or political (Siegel 1998), the regime institutionalized forms of community self-policing. In Java the state-sponsored system of neighbourhood watches became an obligatory part of community organization (Barker 1999). This system had, as Barker (2007: 89) has pointed out, several advantages for the regime: it cost the government very little, it facilitated a degree of state control over local security structures, and it 'created a citizenry that thought and acted like police'. With the collapse of the regime in May 1998, the military lost some of its grip on society and both the meaning and practical organization of security was up for grabs.

If New Order militarism made Indonesians inclined to think and act like police, democratization has given further impetus to the creation of a 'vigilant citizenry' (Telle 2013). The assumption that citizens should take responsibility for the creation of safe communities has been fuelled by two interrelated developments: the implementation of a major decentralization reform process and a 'revival of tradition' trend in Indonesian politics. As the impact of the Asian monetary crisis deepened in 1997, demands for political change contributed to bring down the regime. For their part, multilateral donor and development organizations subscribed to the neoliberal doctrine that decentralization would benefit the economy and foster democracy (Robinson and Hadiz 2004). That the discourse of 'participation' and 'local ownership' promoted by these organizations was embraced by diverse actors is hardly surprising given that, under the New Order, local traditions of governance had been emasculated and deemed obstacles to modernization. Now 'local wisdom' (*kearifan lokal*) emerged as the key for remaking the social and political order (Bubandt 2005; Davidson and Henley 2007).

Lombok is one of many places in Indonesia where the re-traditionalization of politics combined with a militant religious politics has translated into a preoccupation with security. Located east of Bali, the island has an ethnically and religiously diverse population of some 3.2 million people. The Sasak, most of whom are Muslims, make up about 92 per cent of the population, with Balinese, Chinese, Arabs, Bugis and Javanese making up the remainder. Civilian crime-fighting initiatives mushroomed in the turbulent period after the New Order collapsed (Colombijn 2002; Telle 2010b). Looking for alternatives to the discredited New Order security apparatus, many politicians and academics welcomed the formation of such groups, which were seen as 'a new form of "people's power" capable of taking care of security concerns' (MacDougall 2007: 287). Despite some fears that such groups could turn violent, state officials and the police have been inclined to extol the virtues of a vigilant citizenry (Telle 2010a, 2013). An aura of masculine prowess surrounded the men who, donning uniforms and mobile phones, signed up and paid membership fees to 'develop' the island by cleaning out crime.

The political landscape emerging on Lombok since 1998 has been characterized by the simultaneous pervasiveness and transformation of the state. While government institutions remain important, the state qualities of governance, which include the ability to enforce collectively binding decisions on members of society, is by no means exclusively nested in those institutions. Rather, multiple groups exercise authority by making decisions of a public, regulatory nature. These include gangs and security groups (*pamswakarsa*) engaged in acts of 'everyday policing' (Jensen 2007). Organized along territorial, religious and/or ethnic lines, the proliferation of such groups has turned the landscape into a 'horizontally woven tapestry of partial sovereignties' (Comaroff and Comaroff 2006: 35) with overlapping and competing logics of violence and territoriality. There is great variety among *pamswakarsa* groups in terms of organizational structure, modes of operation and social legitimacy. Whereas some are little more than village-based neighbourhood watches (*ronda*), others are formal organizations boasting thousands of members spanning sub-districts, districts and provincial boundaries. Some of this variety will become apparent when I now introduce the security repertories of Amphibi and Tigabersatu and their different modes of policing.

Amphibi: a Muslim militia

Nobody knows precisely how many civilian security groups exist on Lombok. By far the most complex and controversial of these is Amphibi, an Islamic militia formed in 1999, whose headquarters is located in the small village of Jerowaru in south east Lombok.[3] From its humble beginnings as a neighbourhood watch, Amphibi quickly developed into a formidable organization whose crime-fighting approach involved drawing up lists of so-called 'operational targets' to be confronted by its elite 'operational team' (MacDougall 2007; Telle 2010b). The terminology of targets (*target*), teams (*tim*) and operations (*operasi*) shows that Amphibi's leadership was conversant with the techniques and 'languages of stateness' (Hansen and Stepputat 2001: 5) employed by the police and the armed forces. Less than a year after its formation, Amphibi boasted more than 200,000 registered members who were putting up the organization's orange command posts (*pos komando*) throughout the island. Although this figure may have been inflated, there is no doubt that Amphibi quickly grew into an organization that inspired terror by staging spectacular violent shows of force.

Targeting criminal networks and middle-men, Amphibi established its reputation as a sovereign force by demonstrating its 'free unconstrained capacity to act' (Kapferer 2004: 6). One telling incident occurred on 17 December 1999 when a convoy of forty Amphibi trucks packed with more than a thousand men forced their way into the village of Sengkongo located on the periphery of Mataram, the provincial capital, looking for 'criminals'. Having killed one elderly man and cut off the hand of another Balinese man, the convoy of trucks entered the large outdoor Baretais market, displaying the severed hand (MacDougall 2007). This incident generated inter-ethnic tensions and my sources in the Balinese community were disappointed by the lack of interest the police took in investigating this attack (Telle 2011).[4]

While this and similar incidents earned Amphibi a reputation for excessive and arbitrary use of violence, it was precisely by demonstrating its 'wild' capacity to act that Amphibi asserted itself as an informal sovereign. This reading would be in line with Hansen and Stepputat's (2005: 3–4) approach to power, in which the focus is on the 'precarious construction and maintenance of localized sovereign power through exercise of actual or spectral violence – transmitted through rumours, tales and reputations.'

Amphibi's authority, while founded on its violent capacity, has also been constructed through non-violent registers of action. Key here is the group's astute ability to communicate in multiple registers, including rumours, open letters and semi-public statements (Telle 2013). 'Would-be-sovereigns,' as Danilyn Rutherford (2012: 13) notes, 'depend on acknowledgment from others for their claims to be effective.' Putting emphasis on processes of recognition, Rutherford's approach to sovereignty stresses how different audiences respond, form and thwart bids for power, thereby capturing sovereignty's internal disturbance. This perspective is important for understanding why Amphibi has cultivated different performative repertoires. Perhaps more successfully than other security groups on Lombok, Amphibi has, to paraphrase James Scott (1998), mastered the art of 'speaking like a state'.

Over time, Amphibi's central leadership appears to have become more reluctant to stage attacks involving large numbers of men. Besides reflecting that crime-fighting has lost some of its symbolic and practical significance for the group, I suggest that Amphibi, in a bid to extend its public authority, has cultivated other forms of communication. This has been done by becoming state-like, not least by fashioning artefacts of modern state power, such as laminated membership cards, ledgers, seals and military-style uniforms. Adopting a territorial form of organization, Amphibi's organizational structure emulates those of state institutions, with departments for security, law, proselytization, economy, welfare and communication. By emulating bureaucratic forms of organization and communication, Amphibi has attempted to garner respectability and to move into the realm of electoral politics.

Although it has proved difficult to keep the sprawling organization together, Amphibi remains an important force on the island. For example, in the run-up to the 2008 gubernatorial elections for the province of Nusa Tenggara Barat (NTB), the small town of Jerowaru where the organization's headquarters is based, hosted several candidates. During the campaign period, the leadership was careful not to publicly declare its support for a particular candidate, but cultivated relations to several candidates. Such alliances and networks of patronage figure centrally in local politics. In the competitive political climate of the post-New Order era, alliances between *pamswakarsa* groups and political elites tend to be transient and unstable, a pattern also seen in other parts of Indonesia (McCarthy 2004; Hadiz 2010; Schulte Nordholt 2012; Wilson 2012).

Tigabersatu: harnessing 'tradition' and toughs

Nobody knows how many security groups exist on Lombok, but my sources agreed that the largest number of groups is found in Central Lombok, a densely populated rural district with relatively high levels of poverty and labour migration to Malaysia and the Gulf states. Here I focus on Tigabersatu, one of the groups active in the district, showing how its hybrid security repertoire evolved as it became entangled in the politics of local level order-making. Formed in response to people's heightened sense of vulnerability to break-ins, Tigabersatu mobilized around discontent with the police, seen as corrupt and mainly serving the well-off. Unlike Amphibi, whose initial ambition was to 'root out' criminal networks, Tigabersatu established mechanisms for recovering stolen goods, thereby alleviating economic insecurity. This approach to tackling crime represented a formalization of informal practices of dealing with criminality. In order to understand this security approach, it is necessary to reflect on the problems of crime and the figure of the thief.

Tigabersatu emerged in an area where people have intimate experience with theft, cattle rustling in particular. It is important to note that thieves often operate according to logic of kidnapping and extortion. This implies that if someone's cow or motorbike is stolen, it does not necessarily mean that the owner has been fully dispossessed. Stolen goods can be recovered, provided that the owner is willing to redeem (*tebus*) the item from middle-men who buy stolen articles, euphemistically known as 'crooked goods' (*barang bengkok*), from criminal gangs. Certain villages are nodes in a thriving black market economy where stolen goods are kept before being resold or redeemed for a ransom payment (MacDougall 2007).

In the area where I have conducted fieldwork since the mid 1990s, people rarely reported theft to the police. This was partly because they feared having to bribe, which would add another economic burden, but also because people generally avoided contact with the police. Instead, people preferred to approach men with access to the criminal realm to recover their goods. Thus, criminal figures, rather than being ostracized or demonized, were a resource for dealing with crime.[5] While men who engaged in criminal activity occupied an ambiguous position in the social landscape, their role as brokers in times of crisis earned them a degree of respect.

On Lombok, people tend to condemn stealing as behaviour that goes against Sasak 'custom' (*adat*) and Islam. The violence meted out to thieves is often held up to illustrate how offensive stealing is perceived to be. At the risk of offending Sasak sensibilities, I nonetheless suggest that thieves (*maling*) have been a source of fascination, if not admiration. My first fieldwork took place in a village with a reputation for fostering generations of potent thieves. The aura of masculine prowess surrounding these men stemmed from the danger they had courted, as anyone who is caught stealing outside their native community risks being beaten to death.[6] Men who raided in distant places were admired for their bravery and shrewdness. By contrast, those who stole from fellow villagers were intensely loathed (see Telle 2003, 2009). Symbolically linked to the witch (*tau selaq*), a malevolent figure who 'eats' people's insides, the neighbourhood thief (*maling gubuk*) embodies a perverted form of masculinity who, rather than protecting the community, destroys communal relations. As a village elder explained: 'As long as those who "like to steal" (*suka maling*) do so in distant places they do not cause trouble to people back home.' This opinion is no longer politically correct. But during times when break-ins occurred in nearby villages and 'crime talk' (Caldeira 2000) became ubiquitous, people hoped that the village's infamous reputation would deter intruders.

Among those who had criminal careers in their youth, some portrayed themselves as driven by poverty, others emphasized the thrill of 'testing' their physical and mental agility as well as their magical knowledge (*ilmu*). This emphasis on magical knowledge and invulnerability deserves comment. Invulnerability figures prominently in the mythology associated with the Javanese strongman (*jago*) of the nineteenth century (Schulte Nordholt 2002), just as it informs the lives of contemporary toughs (*preman*) (Ryter 2009; Wilson 2009). The emphasis on the cultivation and demonstration of magical prowess, what Tony Day (2002) terms a 'culture of security', has implications for how relations of authority are constructed and hence for local dynamics of order-making. Put simply, the possession of magical knowledge is associated with a heightened capacity to act. Moreover, this capacity is not simply an individual asset, but may be harnessed for communal ends.

Tigabersatu's security repertoire incorporates many of the values and practices just described. Established in 1994, when three hamlet-based night patrol groups (*ronda*) merged, Tigabersatu means 'three united'. Under the New Order, it remained a community defence force, but in the early Reformasi era branches were formed across Central and West Lombok. Combining Sasak customary justice and conflict-resolution formats with state derived security discourses, Tigabersatu's expansion was animated by the perception that the state was unable to provide its protective functions (Telle 2009). The unravelling of the New Order state created spaces for the emergence of informal charismatic leaders, who took on the role as self-appointed enforcers of social order.

Since the beginning, Haji Kesumaatmaja, an entrepreneur and tobacco farmer has served as the group's leader. Admired for his outspokenness and the courage to stand up to local authorities, Tigabersatu members stressed his paranormal ability to 'see' things that ordinarily are invisible. When we met in 2006, Haji Kesumaatmaja acknowledged that people who had lost or misplaced possessions often asked for help. Noting that he felt compelled to use this aptitude to aid people, he explained how he simply closed his eyes to meditate and before long an image would manifest itself before his inner eye, allowing him to direct people where to search. Members also emphasized the leader's ability to 'know' events before they manifested themselves in the world. [7] Indeed, claims of supernatural knowledge tend to be important as a source of authority for figures involved in security provision (see Telle 2010a; Telle 2011; Smith 2012).

Tigabersatu's organizational structure is quite similar to many security groups on Lombok. Registered as a community organization (*ormas*), Tigabersatu is a legal entity, with a mission statement, statutes (*anggaran dasar*) and rules of association (*anggaran rumah tangga*). Besides the leader and two deputies, the group has a secretary, treasurer and an advisory team that consists of the heads of the different units. This team meets once every three months to discuss issues affecting the organization, which by 2006 was divided into four sections: organization, security, education and religion. Members belong to units that are supervised by a leader, some of whom belong to the 'special operations team' (*tim operasional khusus*) responsible for carrying out investigations, gathering intelligence and coordinating searches for stolen goods. For much of the post-98 period, Tigabersatu has been supported by the district government, an issue I return to.

Those who want to join Tigabersatu pay a membership fee and it is common for a group of neighbours to register together. A part of this fee remains with the local unit, but most of the money goes to the secretariat. The money is used to make a simple uniform consisting of a T-shirt emblazed with the group's logo. Members also receive stickers to glue on houses or vehicles, serving as a warning that Tigabersatu will take action if the property is broken into or stolen. Membership fees are used on communication equipment, including a hand phone (HP) for every unit leader, police radio and operating licences. Such equipment facilitates the smooth coordination of patrols and searches, and has allowed Tigabersatu to constitute itself as an effective policing network.

Tigabersatu's approach to policing involves disciplinary measures intended to punish and transform criminal suspects, as I learned during my tour of the headquarters. Built by the members, the headquarters consist of a sparsely furnished front room that leads into two small rooms. Plaques above the doors indicate that one is the 'head's office' (*ruang ketua*), while the other serves as an 'interrogation room' (*ruang interogasi*) where suspects are questioned and sometimes locked up during investigations. Though my guide was reluctant to detail how suspects are treated, a unit leader explained that thieves are questioned, beaten and sometimes forced to sign an agreement (*surat perjanjian*) promising to stop their bad behaviour. To which he added, 'You know, we are more sadistic (*lebih sadis*) if we catch one of our own members.' The use of the term *sadis*, which connotes outrageous or monstrous behaviour, suggests that the violence meted out to disloyal members is different from ordinary, disciplinary use of force. Interviews with leaders and lay members confirmed that violence is meant to discipline and transform suspects. The first stage in this process is to confess and to show willingness to repent (*tobat*). Told that they are put under surveillance, suspects are warned that new offences will be punished more severely. Under these circumstances many do repent, and the best proof of being earnest is to join the fight against crime.

Although this recruitment strategy breeds uncertainty as to whether these men have been fully transformed or not, former criminals can be an important asset for groups such as Tigabersatu. Given the focus on retrieving stolen goods, it makes sense to recruit some members with intimate knowledge of the criminal scene. In fact, it is not uncommon for ex-thieves to rise to leadership positions in groups of this kind (MacDougall 2007; Telle 2009). By enlisting former criminals in crime-fighting efforts, Tigabersatu has adapted the informal practice of cultivating ties with criminal figures to overcome insecurity into its security repertoire. This accounts for the moral ambiguity surrounding civilian policing groups whose order-making practices not only put members in contact with the black market economy, but also rely on harnessing the power and knowledge of former thieves and toughs.

Operating in a crowded and competitive landscape made up of a plurality of policing actors, Tigabersatu adapted to the changing circumstance of the Reformasi period by incorporating religious activities into its security repertoire. As one unit leader explained in 2007: 'That we provide assistance when people face death is perhaps the most important thing that we offer. That promise is like an extraordinarily strong magnet.' What he referred to, was the fact that membership entails obligations to carry out religious duties in connection with death. When a member dies, unit leaders are notified and are expected to quickly gather a group of men who will participate in the congregational worship for the deceased. Sasak Muslims place great emphasis on burying the deceased soon after death, preferably within the same or next day (Telle 2000). The collective worship for the deceased often takes place in the afternoon. Hence members like to say that the group's name refers to how members unite (*bersatu*) around 3 pm (*tiga*). Besides the religious merit generated through the recitation of Islamic prayers, the bereaved family receives a small sum of money.

What motivates people to join is not only a desire to safeguard material possessions, but to be part of a religious economy revolving around the generation of Islamic merit, a vital resource for the afterlife (Telle 2000). Hence, Tigabersatu provides a form of spiritual insurance. By safeguarding material resources in 'this world' and ensuring a better existence in the 'next life', membership provides a sense of 'ontological security' (Giddens 2001). While Amphibi takes credit for being the first security group on Lombok to have introduced this practice, many groups have made the provision of religious and monetary assistance in connection with death a key obligation. Although this can interfere with work and family obligations, the prospect of having a large number of men who pray for the deceased is attractive. Membership in a civilian policing group offers the prospect of an impressive turnout that rivals the turnout at funerals of privileged, wealthy members of society. Since 2000, a Muslim preacher (*tuan guru*) who heads an Islamic school has become an honorary member. The sermons are intended to provide moral and religious guidance, not least for those with a criminal past. When members from different units get together, people feel part of an expansive network, with all that this entails of opportunities to make new acquaintances.

Patronage politics: numbers, legibility and political instrumentalization

Having introduced Amphibi and Tigabersatu and their security repertoires, I now discuss how these groups have been drawn into the politics of local and regional contestations over power. The strong interest that leaders of civilian policing groups have in figures and membership records is an apt entry point for understanding contemporary political dynamics. Having worked with several groups, I have come across some startling claims about the scale of these organizations.[8] In 2007, a central figure in Amphibi claimed that the organization was the largest *pamswakarsa* force in Indonesia with close to one million members. Another leader estimated a membership of 357,000 and stressed the importance of updating the membership lists in order to know how many counted as 'true' members. That the discourse of 'genuine' and 'fake' members emerged at this time was related to the upcoming gubernatorial election in July 2008. Prior to this election, leaders in Jerowaru grew concerned that they were losing control over the sprawling organization. Suspecting that membership fees were being 'eaten' at the sub-district and district levels, they also worried that some members would try to enrich themselves by selling 'fake' membership lists to prospective candidates and their campaign teams.

This preoccupation with figures is shared by many security groups.[9] Tigabersatu leaders were also keen to portray their organization as having a large membership. When I interviewed the secretary in 2007, he stated that Tigabersatu had a total of 23,396 members divided into sixty-three units. It turned out that this figure included 6,044 'full' male members and their dependants. This group keeps two sets of records: a list of 'full' members, essentially male household heads, and a second list of household members. Besides the need to collect fees and coordinate activities, this meticulous record-keeping is informed by the desire to be recognized as a sizeable, well-coordinated crime-fighting force.

In the post-Suharto period, numbers have become an important commodity for security groups. Leaders have learned that numbers are a key resource in the era of democracy with direct elections for the positions of village head, mayor, district head and governor. Scott (1998: 101) writes that 'legibility is a condition for manipulation', as it is only through the invention of units that are visible that states can intervene effectively in society. For Tigabersatu and similar groups, 'legibility' has been a strategy for gaining respectability and access to security-related projects. By producing neat membership lists and ledgers, Tigabersatu has made itself 'legible' to members of the state and figures aspiring for public office. Groups boasting large numbers and whose records seem credible can bargain more effectively with candidates for political office who are more inclined to invest in groups that appear well organized.

I mentioned earlier that Tigabersatu has enjoyed the support of senior members of the government in Central Lombok, including the district head. Although the leaders initially were eager to tell me that the organization enjoyed the protection of 'big people' (*orang gde*), it turned out that this alliance was not unproblematic. While these patrons have provided welcome funds and moral support, their donations also generated suspicion that these funds had been 'eaten' by some members while others had been unfairly left out. These issues became acute in connection with the run-up to the gubernatorial election in 2008.

On Lombok, the level of cynicism regarding electoral politics is such that people say that since political candidates always 'forget' their promises once they have secured office, it is best to demand that they pay upfront. In connection with the gubernatorial election, it was rumoured that some Tibabersatu leaders had accepted a significant sum of money from one of the candidates. The suspicion that some leaders had enriched themselves generated anger. Tensions grew more intense when this candidate failed to win the election and disappointed supporters blamed other members for having voted for other candidates. The conflict escalated from blackmail and verbal assault to vengeful raids of fellow members' cattle (Telle 2009). Despite efforts to put an end to this and to rebuild trust, these efforts failed. Some months after the election Tigabersatu split and several units formed a group named Beriuk Sadar, a Sasak expression meaning 'conscious together'.

While the backing of senior government officials brings funds and can be of help if members get into trouble with the police, such protection has a price. Besides the expectation to vote for the patron in the next election, groups may be asked to take part in demonstrations or provide security services. Let me illustrate this with reference to Tunjung Tilah, a security group in Central Lombok that was formed in 2000. Shortly after this group celebrated the inauguration of its new headquarters in 2006, an event attended by many senior officials and to which both the district head and his deputy made donations, Tunjung Tilah was asked to provide security in Kawo, the site of a protracted conflict related to the construction of an international airport. Echoing the 'official' argumentation that the airport would bring new jobs and development to a depressed region, Tunjung Tilah's leader explained that they had provided security at the site on at least three occasions.[10] To this he added that, under no circumstances, would he permit Tunjung Tilah to take part in a demonstration just for the sake of getting cigarette money and petrol. Insisting that Tunjung Tilah was not a mob for rent, Amaq Satum claimed that his group would only mobilize for causes that members, mainly farmers of humble means, would endorse. Though I remained doubtful, I was impressed by the fact that Tunjung Tilah's leader, a farmer reputed to have had a criminal career in his youth, insisted that they would not compromise their political vision for pecuniary rewards.

What I believe Tunjung Tilah's leader was saying, was that in this era of democracy, 'small people' (*orang kecil*) like himself, who have hardly tasted the fruits of Indonesia's economic development, have finally learned to protect their own interests. The case of Tunjung Tilah illustrates that security provision has become an important route, if not to formal positions of power, then certainly to positions of informal authority with all that entails in terms of bargaining power in relation to state officials and political elites. However, Tunjung Tilah has also faced problems involving allegations of mismanagement of funds, which eventually led it to splinter into smaller groups.

Conclusion

Developments in post-1998 Indonesia illustrate the political nature of 'everyday policing' (Jensen 2007) as groups across the archipelago seek to enforce and consolidate particular notions of 'order'. This chapter has examined some of the ways in which security has been configured by civilian policing groups on the island Lombok in their engagement with other local actors, bureaucrats and aspiring politicians. Broader shifts in state power, including decentralization and the introduction of electoral democracy, have provided the conditions in which a plethora of civilian security groups have emerged and thrived. The proliferation of security groups, each with its distinct vision of security and ways of enforcing order, reveals that security provision has become the basis for 'new' local politics in which new actors are asserting themselves and advancing their interests. The introduction of regional autonomy and a competitive electoral climate has opened opportunities for the exercise of authority by individuals and groups, who previously were largely excluded from the political process.

While the formation of civilian security groups has become a route to power and authority for a new set of actors, it is worth asking whether these groups represent a 'new' form of politics? In some ways security groups are reproducing a local level form of authoritarianism similar to that of the New Order state. Conducted behind a façade of respectability, security provision has in some cases become a lucrative intersection of criminal and political interests. But there are also significant differences to the situation under the military-dominated New Order regime. Abidin Kusno (2004: 2385) captures this shift by noting that, 'In contrast to the New Order state which used to be the centre of authority constantly controlling and watching the behaviour of its subjects, the post-Suharto state is under the gaze of the public.' This means, for example, that security groups assert themselves in public, using vigilante tactics of intimidation and violence to convey their dislike of particular officials or initiatives.

Heads of civilian security groups, especially groups boasting large memberships, are often courted by aspiring politicians hoping to secure positions in district or regional government or to enlist such groups in their projects. Mindful of their numerical strength, heads of civilian security groups make deals with those who seem inclined to recognize the interests of the social and economic underclass to which most of their members belong. However, as I have shown, such alliances tend to be highly unstable. Furthermore, the expectation that such alliances have been lubricated with hefty amounts of money tends to erode social cohesion and trust among members, in some cases leading to internal conflicts and violence. Such conflicts may also result from disagreements among members over how leaders, who have brokered such alliances, expect members to intervene in political disputes as paid muscle or to provide security in connection with controversial projects.

Over the past few years, it has become apparent that security groups are growing dissatisfied with being vehicles for elite interests. The changed political dynamics has boosted the confidence of heads of security groups, who sometimes aspire to political office and a seat in parliament. Some *pamswakarsa* groups, notably Amphibi, have succeeded in getting their members into the provincial-level parliament.[11] This is a development also seen in other parts of Indonesia, including Jakarta, where the Betawi Brotherhood Forum (FBR), a citizen militia that claims to represent the native population of Jakarta, is 'no longer content to serve as merely the disposable foot soldiers of political or economic elites' (Wilson 2012: 298). Similarly, Ryter (2009) has shown how members of New Order paramilitary youth groups (OKP) have become parliamentarians in North Sumatra since 1998.

Disillusionment with political co-optation is also prompting some groups to emphasize the value of social and religious activities, stressing their independence from 'corrupt' politics. Besides safeguarding property and generating Islamic merit for the afterlife, membership provides access to extensive social networks that offer protection and a degree of security.

Operating with complex, hybrid security repertoires, I have argued that these groups tend to be flexible in terms of how they operate and what aspect of security provision they choose to stress. This implies that their activities easily span several layers of politics, from the localized level of order-making to the politics of national sovereignty. Their hybrid conception of security also implies a degree of resilience, despite the fact that groups splinter and reform. Casting themselves as vigilant citizens, members draw on long-standing cultural frameworks that hold men responsible for protecting their homes and neighbourhoods from harmful intruders, a masculine responsibility that also entails the right to discipline and punish. The assertion of this form of masculine prowess and autonomy has been boosted in the context of democratization and the re-traditionalism of politics in post-New Order Indonesia.

Acknowledgements

I would like to thank Helene Kyed and Peter Albrecht for their helpful comments and suggestions.

Notes

1 I have carried out fifteen months of fieldwork in Sasak communities in Central Lombok since 1994. Another eleven months of fieldwork have been carried out in urban Lombok, mainly among the Hindu Balinese minority.
2 A case in point is the campaign known as the 'Mysterious Shootings' in the late 1980s, when several thousand petty criminals and gangsters were summarily executed across the island of Java, see Wilson 2012.

3 Amphibi's founder and leader is Tuan Guru Hajji Sibawahi, an Islamic cleric whose father, Tuan Guru Hajji Mutawalli was also a well-known preacher.
4 When this incident was reported in Lombok Post (18 December), it was estimated that 2,000 armed men took part but the paper did not name the group involved. This editorial practice is partly motivated by a desire to avoid intimidation and vandalism.
5 Arrangements of collaboration between police and people engaged in illicit business are ubiquitous in Indonesia, see Nooteboom 2010.
6 The lynching of suspected criminals is quite common in many parts of Indonesia, see Colombijn 2001; Herriman 2012.
7 The Sasak term for people possessing this paranormal ability is *biguq*. Some assumed that the leader also had the ability to know long in advance the time of somebody's death (*ilmu tilik*). People who are reputed to possess such knowledge are both feared and admired, and they often work as healers.
8 I have discussed (Telle 2011) the significance of inflated numbers with reference to Dharma Wisesa, a security group organized by Hindu Balinese minority on Lombok.
9 In the lead-up to this election, local authorities were concerned that security groups (*pamswakarsa*) would fan conflict. For an in-depth analysis of these conflict-avoidance strategies, see Kingsley 2012.
10 Reports have been made that other *pamswakarsa* groups, including Bujak and Sekujung, were involved during some of the occasions that turned ugly in Kawo, the site of the international airport, see Tyson 2013.
11 See Smith 2012 for a discussion of how Nahdlatul Wathan (NW), Lombok's largest Islamic organization, split into two rival factions in 1998, each faction developing their own militias. Many Nahdlatul Wathan cadres hold high positions in local and regional government. The current governor of West Nusa Tenggara, popularly known as Tuan Guru Bajang, has come out of this mass-based 'traditionalist' organization.

References

Abrahams, R., 2007. 'Some thoughts on the comparative study of vigilantism', in: David Pratten and Atreyee Sen (eds), *Global vigilantes*. London: Hurst, 419–442.
Anderson, B. O'G., 2001. 'Introduction', in: Benedict Anderson (ed.), *Violence and the state in Suharto's Indonesia*. Ithaca, NY: Cornell Southeast Asia Program, 9–19.
Barker, J., 1999. 'Surveillance and territoriality in Bandung', in: Vincente Rafael (ed.), *Figures of criminality in Indonesia, the Philippines, and colonial Vietnam*. Ithaca, NY: Cornell Southeast Asia Program Publications, 95–127.
Barker, J., 2007. 'Vigilantes and the state', in: Tony Day (ed.), *Identifying with freedom: Indonesia after Suharto*. New York and Oxford: Berghahn Books [Critical Interventions 9], 1–18.
Bubandt, N., 2005. 'Vernacular security: The politics of feeling safe in global, national and local worlds', *Security Dialogue* 36:3, 275–296.
Caldeira, T. P. R., 2000. *City of walls: Crime, segregation, and citizenship in Sao Paulo.* Berkeley, CA: University of California Press.
Colombijn, F., 2002. 'Maling, maling! The lynching of petty criminals', in: Freek Colombijn and J. T. Lindblad (eds), *Roots of Violence in Indonesia*. Leiden: KITLV Press, 299–329.
Comaroff, J. and Comaroff. J. L., 2006. 'Law and disorder in the postcolony, an introduction', in: Jean Comaroff and John L. Comaroff (eds), *Law and order in the postcolony*. Chicago, IL: Chicago University Press, 1–56.

Davidson, J. S. and Henley, D. (eds), 2007. *The revival of tradition in Indonesian politics: The deployment of adat from colonialism to indigenism*. London: Routledge.

Day, T., 2002. *Fluid iron: State formation in Southeast Asia*. Honolulu, HI: University of Hawai'i Press.

Dijk, K. van, 2001. 'The privatization of the public order: Relying on the Satgas', in: Ingrid Wessel and Georgia Wimhöfer (eds), *Violence in Indonesia*. Hamburg: Abera, 152–167.

Giddens, A., 2001. *Modernity and self-identity: Self and society in the late modern age*. Cambridge: Polity Press.

Goldstein, D. M., 2010. 'Toward a critical anthropology of security', *Current Anthropology* 51:4, 487–517.

Hadiz, V. R., 2010. *Localizing power in post-authoritarian Indonesia: A Southeast Asia perspective*. Paolo Alto, CA: Stanford University Press.

Hansen, T. B. and Stepputat, F., 2001. 'Introduction', in: Thomas Blom Hansen and Finn Stepputat (eds), *States of imagination: Ethnographic explorations of the postcolonial state*. Durham and London: Duke University Press, 1–38.

Hansen, T. B. and Stepputat, F., 2005. 'Introduction', in: Thomas Blom Hansen and Finn Stepputat (eds), *Sovereign bodies: Citizens, migrants and states in the postcolonial world*. Princeton, NJ: Princeton University Press, 1–36.

Herriman, N., 2012. *The entangled state: Sorcery, state control and violence in Indonesia*. New Haven, CT: Monograph 62/Yale Southeast Asia Studies.

Jensen, S., 2007. 'Policing Nkomazi: Crime, masculinity and generational conflicts', in: David Pratten and Atreyee Sen (eds), *Global vigilantes*. London: Hurst, 47–68.

Kapferer, B., 2004. 'Introduction: Old permutations, new formations? War, state, and global transgression', in: Bruce Kapferer (ed.), *State, sovereignty, war: Civil violence in emerging global realities*. New York and London: Berghahn Books [Critical Interventions No. 5].

Kingsley, J. J., 2012. 'Peacemakers or peace-breakers? Provincial elections and religious leadership in Lombok, Indonesia', *Indonesia* 93 (April), 53–82.

Klinken, G. van and Barker, J., 2009. *State of authority: The state in society in Indonesia*. Ithaca, NY: Southeast Asia Program.

Kusno, A., 2004. 'Whither nationalist urbanism? Public life in Governor Sutiyoso's Jakarta', *Urban Studies* 41:12, 2377–2394.

Lindsey, T., 2001. 'The criminal state: *Premanisme* and the New Indonesia', in: Grayson J. Lloyd and Shannon L. Smith (eds), *Indonesia today: Challenges of history*. Lanham: Rowman & Littlefield, 283–297.

MacCarthy, J. F., 2004. 'Changing to grey: Decentralization and the emergence of volatile socio-legal configurations in Central Kalimantan, Indonesia', *World Development* 32:7, 1199–1223.

MacDougall, J. M., 2007. 'Criminality and the political economy of security in Lombok', in: Schulte Nordholt and Gerry van Klinken (eds), *Renegotiating boundaries: Local politics in post-Suharto Indonesia*, Leiden: KITLV Press, 281–306.

Noteboom, G., 2010. 'The mutual dependence of Madurese migrants and police officers in illegal businesses in Samarinda', Indonesian Studies Working Papers, No. 11. University of Sydney.

Robinson, R. and Hadiz, V. R. (eds), 2004. 'Neo-liberal reforms and illiberal consolidations: The Indonesian paradox'. Hong Kong: City University of Hong Kong [Southeast Asia Research Centre, Working Paper Series 53.]

Rutherford, D., 2012. *Laughing at Leviathan: Sovereignty and audience in West Papua*. Chicago, IL: The University of Chicago Press.

Ryter, L., 2009. 'Their moment in the sun: The new Indonesian parliamentarians', in: Gerry van Klinken and Joshua Barker (eds), *State of authority: The state in society in Indonesia*. Ithaca, NY: Cornell Southeast Asia Program, 181–218.

Schulte Nordholt, H., 2002. 'A genealogy of violence', in: Freek Colombijn and J. Thomas Lindblad (eds), *Roots of violence in Indonesia*. Leiden: KITLV Press, 2–61.

Schulte Nordholt, H., 2012. 'Decentralization and democracy in Indonesia: Strengthening citizenship or regional elites?' in: Richard Robison (ed.), *Routledge Handbook of Southeast Asian Politics*. London and New York: Routledge, 229–241.

Scott, J. C., 1998. *Seeing like a state: How certain schemes to improve the human condition have failed*. New Haven, CT: Yale University Press.

Sen, A. and Pratten, D., 2007. 'Global vigilantes: Perspectives on justice and violence', in: David Pratten and Atreyee Sen (eds), *Global vigilantes*. London: Hurst, 1–24.

Siegel, J. T., 1998. *A new criminal type in Jakarta: Counter-revolution today*. Durham and London: Duke University Press.

Smith, B. J., 2012. 'Reorienting female spiritual power in Islam: Narrating conflict between warriors, witches and militias in Lombok', *Indonesia and the Malay World* 40:118, 249–271.

Telle, K., 2000. 'Feeding the dead: Reformulating Sasak mortuary practices', *Bijdragen Tot de Taal-, Land- en Volkenkunde* 156:4, 771–805.

Telle, K., 2003. 'The smell of death: Theft, disgust and ritual practice in Central Lombok, Indonesia', in: Bruce Kapferer (ed.), *Beyond rationalism: Rethinking magic, witchcraft and sorcery*. New York and Oxford: Berghahn Books, 75–104.

Telle, K., 2009. 'Swearing innocence: Performing justice and "reconciliation" in post-Suharto Lombok', in: Birgit Bräuchler (ed.), *Reconciling Indonesia: Grassroots agency for peace*. London: Routledge, 55–76.

Telle, K., 2010a. 'Dharma power: Searching for security in post-New Order Indonesia', in: Bruce Kapferer, Kari Telle, Annelin Eriksen (eds), *Contemporary religiosities: Emergent socialities and the post-nation state*. New York and Oxford: Berghahn Books, 141–156.

Telle, K., 2010b. 'Seduced by security: The politics of (in) security on Lombok, Indonesia', in: John-Andrew McNeish and Jon-Harald Sande Lie (eds), *Security and development*. New York and Oxford: Berghahn Books, 130–142 [Critical Interventions 11].

Telle, K., 2011. 'Spirited warriors: Conspiracy and protection on Lombok', in: Kirsten Endres and Andrea Lauser (eds), *Spirited modernities in Southeast Asia*. New York and Oxford: Berghahn Books, 42–61.

Telle, K., 2013. 'Vigilante citizenship: Sovereign practices and the politics of insult in Indonesia', *Bijdragen tot de Taal-, Land-en Volkenkunde* 169:2–3, 183–212.

Tyson, A., 2013. 'Vigilantism and violence in decentralized Indonesia: The case of Lombok', *Critical Asian Studies*, 45, 201–230.

Wilson, I. D., 2009. 'As long as it's *halal*: Islamic *preman* in Jakarta', in: Greg Fealey and Sally White (eds), *Expressing Islam: Religious life and politics in Indonesia*. Singapore: ISEAS, 192–210.

Wilson, I. D., 2012. 'Testing the boundaries of the state: Gangs, militias, vigilantes and violent entrepreneurs in Southeast Asia', in: Richard Robison (ed.), *Routledge Handbook of Southeast Asian Politics*. London and New York: Routledge, 288–301.

Chapter 4

Rival forms of policing and politics in urban Swaziland

Helene Maria Kyed

Swaziland is the last Kingdom of Africa. Internationally it has earned the repu-tation as an authoritarian regime that prohibits political parties and freedom of expression and that puts down protestors with brutal police force. By the royalists and those in power, Swaziland is by contrast portrayed as a homo-genous order with shared cultural traditions, peaceful coexistence and no ethnic divisions. Sovereignty is unquestionably vested in the King, who himself is the High Commissioner of Police. The King vies for absolute power by appointing all senators and ten out of sixty-five Assembly members who make up the country's modern political institutions. He also governs through the traditional institution of chiefs who are custodians of the land.

These images portray only one side of 'political society' in Swaziland (Chatterjee, 2004; Mouffe, 2005; Nuijten, 2013). In the shadow of official repressive politics and parallel to the public performance of organised protest, there is a wider 'force field of antagonistic relationships, contesting groups, and opposing interests' (Nuijten, 2013: 11). Such alternative politics are played out in different spheres that are not necessarily defined as political – such as policing – and they feed into official politics in rather unexpected ways. This takes place within a context where the King's *de jure* claim to unquestionable sovereignty is challenged by the de facto coexistence of partial sovereignties (Comaroff and Comaroff, 2006).

In this chapter I explore everyday policing as an alternative space of politics in urban Swaziland. I focus on a civilian community policing group that emerged in 2004 in the low-income neighbourhood of Mbhuleni.[1] By success-fully combating crime the members of the group have managed to transform themselves from being unrecognised, unemployed, young men to becoming politically significant. Their capacity for direct action and use of force has brought down crime and given them status as a kind of 'informal sovereign' (Hansen and Stepputat, 2005): i.e. they both aid and challenge the *de jure* superior authority of the state police. Their public order-making activities simultaneously make them a significant asset in the political contestations of traditional leaders, elected politicians, and local government councillors. As such, the community police group constitutes a 'new political space' through which its members can transform themselves and to which others can turn as a source of power to advance their political agendas. This has emerged in the context of rising crime and unemployment in Mbhuleni and has been supported by a wider national movement for community policing.

A core argument of this chapter is that community policing in urban Swaziland is not only subject to the different political strategies of others, but is also a space where political dreams and alternative politics develop as its members gain recognition from order-making activities. However, the authority of the community police is always uncertain. This is because it exerts a style of politics that is characterised by 'ambiguity', 'youthfulness' and 'momentariness', which are ultimately founded on the capacity to use force in resolving problems of urban disorder. These characteristics give the community police group a comparative advantage in relation to official authorities, but they also inhibit the development of a well-organised, enduring institution. Without any legal recognition, community policing is rather a 'transformative' space for individuals to move forward in life. Before turning to how this was played out in the neighbourhood of Mbhuleni, I first provide a short national political background to community policing in Swaziland.

The origins and national politics behind community policing

Most Swazis date community policing back to the time when the former King Sobhuza II introduced the slogan of *nawe uliphoyisa* (you too are the police). Although police-like functions had been performed by civilians in the past, the word *uliphoyisa*, which is the SiSwati translation of the English word police, was mainly associated with the foreign police force that existed during the British Protectorate, and which was substituted by Swazi state police at independence in 1968. Citizen involvement in policing became a significant issue again in the late 1980s, due to a crime wave that was caused by rising unemployment and the influx of refugees from warring Mozambique and apartheid South Africa.[2] Since then different state and popular initiatives have taken place and now all districts and neighbourhoods have some version of community policing.

The King's slogan continues to grant legitimacy to the community police, but the origin of the 'real' community police is politically disputed. There are two conflicting stories: one is represented by Senator Robert Zwane, who argues that it is a popular initiative (see also Khumalo, 2004; Hamilton, 2005, 2007); the other by Headquarter officials of the Royal Swaziland Police (RSP) who argue that the police created it.

In Zwane's version community policing began in the rural areas in the early 1990s when cattle owners organised themselves to deal with the increase in cross-border cattle raiding. The state lacked the capacity to deal with the problem and it was even suspected that police and military were involved in the criminal networks. Based on the popular actions, Zwane proposed the new concept of *Emphoyisa Emmango* (community police) to his chief, who along with ten other chiefs endorsed it and allowed the civilian policing groups to operate. At that time the relationship to the RSP was tense, because 'the police were afraid that the community police would take over their job'.[3] To Zwane it is politically important to present community policing as an institution independent of the state police. His national political career took off when he sponsored a national radio programme to spread the concept of community policing to the rest of the country. In 2006 he founded the Swazi Community Police Association to unite the different groups that existed and campaigned for a law that would grant them official independent status. In 2008 Zwane was appointed Senator by the King, which he claims was because of his involvement in developing Swaziland's version of community policing.

Police Headquarter officials by contrast claim that the 'real' community police were created in 1991 by the former Commissioner of Police, who was assisted by a UK government advisor. In 1993 the Prime Minister called on all chiefs to mobilise people to select community policing members, who then received training and were organised according to RSP criteria.[4] Whatever else existed of self-help policing and whoever claimed not to be under the RSP initiative were portrayed as unlawful vigilantes. Zwane was seen as among the latter. He was accused of having illegally brought the community police over on his side with uniforms and ID cards, enabled by his excessive wealth, which, rumours had it, he had partly acquired through cattle raiding.

This criminalisation of the Senator points to the politically ambiguous relationship between state and community police. While Zwane's community police work was blessed by the King he was despised by those below the King in the police force. At stake was the authority of the police as an institution. Claiming ownership of community policing, and subordinating it to the police, was seen as a way to regain some of the confidence that the RSP had lost as crime escalated in the 1990s. The independent success of the civilian community policing groups was a threat to the state police, none more so than Zwane who even managed to consolidate a position in Government. In this light, a law that would bring community policing under state regulation was important to the RSP. Yet this has been a contentious affair.

In early 2014, there was still no legislation on community policing. Several attempts to include the concept into a new Crime Prevention Bill have failed due to political contestations over ownership, status and benefits (salaries, uniforms, instruments). The main protagonists in this fight have been Zwane and the former Police Commissioner, who is now also a Senator. The new Police Commissioner is more supportive of the community police concept, but to him independence of the community policing groups from the police, as proposed by Zwane, is still not an option.

The contentious legal process and the fights over its origin reflects how 'community policing' – as both a policy concept and as the name used by civilian policing actors – has become a politically significant matter in Swaziland. This intertwinement of policing and politics, I suggest, ultimately boils down to contestations over sovereign power. The latter is understood here as the exercise of exclusive control over particular territories and populations, which is founded on enactments of violence that mark out the boundaries of a specific order and those who manage to define it (Hansen and Stepputat, 2005; Comaroff and Comaroff, 2006). The civilian community police in Mbhuleni, to which I now turn, came to constitute a kind of 'informal sovereign' (Hansen and Stepputat, 2005: 32), contesting the RSP's, and ultimately the state and the King's, *de jure* sovereign power. With this position the community police members also became significant to the power games between various local leaders and politicians, often linking local to national politics.

Mbhuleni – from street to station

Mbhuleni is part of the Kwaluseni Constituency, which today is one of the most densely populated areas of the country due to its proximity to the industrial capital of Matsapha with an estimated population of 50,000. The population consists mainly of a large number of young labour migrants from the rural areas. Originally, Kwaluzeni was one of the King's grazing areas. This means that it only had cattle herders and no traditional chief, who otherwise administer land at the local level across Swaziland. Today the area has elected local government structures and two disputing traditional leaders, but because of its history as a grazing area it is still spoken of as an informal settlement.

In early 1990s Mbhuleni became notorious for very high levels of crime and violence, as many factories closed. Unemployment steadily increased as migrants continued to come. Apart from theft and prostitution, armed criminal gangs were housing the area, and random violence in the streets during broad daylight was common. When I began fieldwork in 2011 crime had markedly reduced although livelihood uncertainty and unemployment were still high. The change in level of crime was accredited to the work of a community policing group.

Just as in Zwane's version of 'community policing', the group that became famous for its successful 'war on crime' in Mbhuleni was the result of a popular initiative taken by civilians in 2004. The RSP did set up an official community police group in the mid 1990s, but it quickly fell apart. Also the RSP hardly ever entered the area, and a leadership dispute meant that the traditional structures were weak in enforcing order. Effectively, there was no policing in Mbhuleni. In late 2004, a number of male residents between twenty and thirty-five years old literally seized the streets in what initially were spontaneous actions by small, scattered groups. The majority were non-natives who had lost their jobs in the factories or who had never had employment in the first place. They were fed up with the fact that no one was doing anything about the crime in their area. They began by attacking the criminals in the streets when they heard screams from people being assaulted. Some accompanied people to work to protect them from attacks.

In early 2005 the young men began to unite into an actual group, which the members called the community police (*Emphoyisa Emmango*) – a concept already known from the police and the media. Then more young men joined. Within a few months there were around twenty members. There was no organised recruitment or leadership at this point. In fact, retrospectively, there were different claims to who really founded the community policing group, reflecting how it emerged in an ad hoc fashion. Chris, one of the founding members, remembered the first period as a forceful 'war on crime', adding that: 'In the beginning we were just operating on our own [without the police and local leaders].' Operations were characterised by direct physical actions, in the form of attacks, capture and beatings of criminals in the streets. Some used *shamboks* (a kind of baton) and carried bush knives. Others just used their bare hands. Soon they also began to target the gangs at their hangouts. Occasionally, criminals were handed over to the police, but only after punishment.

The community police's success in combating the criminals slowly transformed the group into an authority of its own. The real turning point was when they were awarded an outdoor venue by an old lady, in fact a daughter of the former King. Here they began to receive cases, essentially forming a court-like set-up, which they called 'ma-station'. They also kept criminal suspects here until the police fetched them, at times tied to the tree if they made trouble. But many cases were also resolved here. The community police members became clever at recuperating stolen goods and in dealing with con-men. Their main 'investigative method' was physical force or a threat thereof. They earned the reputation for prompt, immediate action against the 'thugs'. They became sophisticated in information gathering and case resolution. Gradually, residents of Mbhuleni began to approach their 'station' even with social and labour-related cases, ranging from family quarrels to landlord–tenant disputes. These were resolved using reconciliatory and compensational justice procedures, akin to the local traditional courts.[5]

In short, the community police's 'station' had become an alternative space for resolving disputes and crimes. This was an alternative that in the eyes of many residents was desperately needed in light of police absence and weak traditional leadership. Due to its success in crime fighting, the community police group was at the end of 2005 officially recognised by the local King's Council – one of the traditional leadership structures. This was supported by the Matsapha Police Station Commander. Recognition marked the beginning of the political significance of the community police group, also in more negative terms.

Shortly after their recognition the group was met with political opposition as the then Member of Parliament (MP) of Kwaluseni organised a demonstration of around 500 people to end community policing. The main message was that the community police of Mbhuleni 'beat them [the criminals] too much'[6] and that 'it's for the RSP to decide on somebody who was found stealing, not the community police'.[7] After this event some members resigned, but overall the community police group came out stronger. They also began to collaborate more with the RSP and to receive training. In 2006 the King's Council, based on a RSP model, required the community police to organise themselves, and elections for chairperson and other positions were held. In 2007, a system of financial community contributions was introduced (Emalangeni 5.00 per household per month), so that the members could cover mobile phone and food expenses while on duty. Along with these forms of institutionalisation, the community police group continued to be externally as well as internally contested. The media displayed terrifying pictures of wounded victims of community police violence in Mbhuleni. This ignited opposition among human rights groups against community policing at national level.

Within the Kwaluseni area, contestations between the RSP and the community police group over the local control of crime and violence began to emerge. Simultaneously, local politicians and traditional power holders began to engage the community police members in their own political agendas and to play them out against each other. Due to these different forms of political contestation, the kind of authority that the community policing group had carved out for itself remained precarious. This was reflected in a range of ambiguous relations and power games. I begin with the relationship to the state police.

The state police and sovereign power

To the state police, the community police came to be seen as both 'their extended arm' and as their biggest competitor. On the one hand, it was only after the community police had taken over the streets from criminal gangs that the police began to enter the neighbourhood, mostly by picking up criminals caught by community policing members. The then coordinator of crime prevention at the Matsapha police station explained to me: 'we need those [community police] to reach particular areas where they live, because we cannot always be there. So the community police are there on our behalf. It has worked wonders for us.' Work for the police involved locating suspects, aiding investigations, patrolling, and witnessing in police hearings. Officers also occasionally transferred petty crimes to the community police group. Indeed, community police work was part of (re)constituting state police authority in Mbhuleni. But this was ambiguous.

The *de jure* superior authority of the police, ultimately embedded in the sovereign power of the King, was constantly challenged in practice. This was exemplified by how the RSP officers constantly failed to control the violence meted out by the community police members as an element of enforcing their version of order in the public spaces of the neighbourhood. This violence, as in the understanding of sovereign power provided by Hansen and Stepputat (2005), is not only constitutive of the particular power position assumed by the community police members over order in Mbhuleni and over the criminals. It also directly opposes the fundamental and *de jure* claim to state monopoly on legitimate violence, as in the Weberian understanding of sovereignty.

In this light a too autonomous civilian community police was a problem to state police authority. The efforts by the RSP to subordinate the community police group under their command were challenged in ways that were very visible to any observer: community police operations were played out in the streets and therefore always publicly visible. This made the question of who controls public order an open one: it was clear to everyone that *de facto* the state police was seldom in control. The visible performance of violence outside police control illustrated how the community police group competed over the sovereign power that for both the RSP and the community police was the primary source of their authority. In the everyday this tension translated into 'playful power games', straddling friendship-like relationships and outright condemnation.

While police officers had the advantage of professionalism and officialdom, community police members bragged about being much stronger in dealing with local (dis)order because 'we know where all the criminals are and we're not afraid to punish them'.[8] They mocked the law for being unreliable, as Jabulani told me: 'Law is like a game. Even when you catch someone stealing a cell [phone] there needs to be so much evidence to be punished by law.' Playful complaints as well as stark criticism coexisted with personal exchange of experiences and favours between individual officers and community police members. Despite some individual differences the relationship was, however, always ambiguous. The police officers could never fully count on the loyalty and good behaviour of community police members, which in turn meant that the community police members could not always rely on RSP protection. At the heart of this ambiguous relationship was not only the fact that community police operations at times broke with the law. More importantly was the incapacity of the RSP to (appear to) control the violence applied by the community police group. This became clear in how the police handled the legal charges that began to appear against community police members in 2009.

All the Mbhuleni community police members that I knew had been charged at least once for using excessive force. They firmly believed that the new Station Commander in 2009 was the one who had instigated the official complaints by telling his officers to encourage people – even those guilty of crime – to press charges against the community police. This was to manifest his authority in the area under his command. According to Lukhele, one of the Mbhuleni community police members, the police did this 'because they are envious that we are doing their job better than them. And that we are stronger than them'. In court, the community police members in turn defended themselves by arguing that they used force in self-defence when the criminals resisted arrest.

The intriguing thing is that hardly any of the complaints went to court and that those that did ended up with only short-term imprisonment and payment of fines (even in a case where the victim of a community police beating died!). When I asked RSP officers why this was the case, it became clear that it was because the court cases against the community police would obstruct the work of police station level officers, and, worse still, make them look unable to control their 'extended arm'. An officer told me:

> It is not good that the public knows of them [cases against community police], because we need the good work of the community police [. . .] in any case, you find that in most cases, we see that it is the criminals who lie and want to see the community police charged, so we arrest that criminal instead.[9]

This kind of state police protection coexisted with regular arrests of community police members, who were sometimes put in the cells, until the case was negotiated. At the Matsapha police station community police complaints were handled rather informally inside the 'Petty Department' for common assaults. Here officers facilitated a negotiated settlement between community police and complainant, which typically involved monetary compensation.

The complaints over the community policing members were used, I suggest, to (re)perform police control and superiority, at least momentarily. Yet, this was only effective when cases were resolved by the RSP *outside* of the official legal system and away from public view. Court cases set precedence for the behaviour of the unregulated community police and manifested the superiority of state law. They did not have the effect of (re)constituting the authority of the local state police in the everyday control of public order. This reflected how community police work, including their beatings of criminals, had – according to many officers that I spoke with – become intrinsic to state police achieve-ments in places such as Mbhuleni. Inside the walls of the Station the officers could enact their *de jure* sovereignty by both punishing and protecting the community police members, thereby regulating their behaviour, yet without obstructing their hard work on the streets. The legally ambiguous nature of community police groups in places such as Mbhuleni made them difficult to tame by the police, yet also easy to dispose of if things got out of hand.

Conversely, to the community policing group the complaints were costly in fines, seen as unjust and made them vulnerable – to RSP and criminals alike. Their capacity to use violence outside police control was central to their position as 'the authority of the street' – not only in relation to the police, but also to the criminals. As a kind of 'informal sovereign', the Mbhuleni group existed in an ambiguous relationship with the RSP and the state more broadly.

As Hansen and Stepputat (2005: 32) argue: 'the informal sovereign who has become 'a law onto himself' are [. . .] central to the endeavours of governments and police forces to produce legitimacy and to perform the sovereignty of the state.' Simultaneously they are 'wild' or uncontrollable figures in the eyes of the RSP. They resemble what Adelkhah (1999: 33) has defined as the 'playful and defiant masculine sovereignty', embodied by young, mobile, unattached men who are morally ambiguous, at the edge of respectable society, but also 'heroic and in the forefront of rebellions against injustice'. Such figures arouse recognition and admiration as much as they incite fear and aversion. These characteristics also made the community police members significant figures to engage with by those who had a stake in local politics in Mbhuleni, as I will address next.

Contestations over local leadership and competitive politics

In Mbhuleni there are four official political structures, supported by state law. First, the King's Council, which is approved by the King. Second, there is the *Umphakatsi*, which is led by an appointed *Ndvuna* (headman) and supported by the regional Chief TV, but which is contested by the King's Council. Third, there is the *Inkhundla* local government structure, which is led by an elected *Ndvuna*, and three elected councillors. Finally, there is the Kwaluseni Member of Parliament. The first two are considered traditional structures, and the latter two are modern institutions in Swazi dualistic political terminology. The 'traditional' are appointed within the chieftaincy and royal set-up, according to 'blood', and are in charge of the land and residency taxation, whereas the 'modern' are elected and in charge of development (school, infrastructure, health care etc.). The former acquire resources from land allocations and dispute resolution. The latter get salaries from national government. Their authority is therefore based on quite different sources, but in practice there are many overlaps and shifting alliances between them.

The community police group in Mbhuleni was politically significant to the above official authorities in two related ways. First, as they set up the 'station' they challenged the areas of jurisdiction of the different official authorities. The community police group laid claim to development benefits by having brought 'peace and security' to the area. By policing law breakers they assumed a visible form of territorial control. The community police also challenged the traditional structures when they resolved neighbour quarrels and family disputes and worse still when they dealt with irregular land allocations. Lots of money is involved in land transactions, not least in high density areas such as Kwaluseni, so this was a dangerous field to enter for the community police. It went to the core of traditional authority, which primarily is based on land administration in Swaziland.

Second, because they competed with the traditional structures in local level order-making, the community police group was subjected to contesting official claims to lead and represent them. This in turn was influenced by the traditional and elected authorities' strategies to boost and maintain their positions of power. The *Inkhundla* (local government) *Ndvuna*, Mrs Bhembe, insisted on a hierarchy where the traditional structure of the King's Council approved the members, yet where they ultimately reported to her. She considered herself as the representative of the community police group when it came to government matters outside Kwaluseni. Mrs Bhembe had the advantage that her husband was the coordinator of the Crime Prevention Unit at the Matsapha police station, so larger community police meetings and trainings in the constituency were convened by the Inkundla. The Ndvuna of the Umphakatsi likewise proclaimed that he was the superior authority, and that he was the one that the RSP called when there were problems. This was disputed by the King's Council, which had officially approved the community police group in 2005. It claimed that the Umphakatsi was an entirely false set-up. This was embedded in a fierce dispute over authentic traditional leadership, which culminated in the early 2000s when a self-proclaimed chief, Chief TV, installed the current Umphakatsi to challenge the King's Council.

Although there is no doubt that the Mbhuleni community police received more clients in dispute resolution due to the traditional leadership dispute, the dispute also influenced them in other ways. They were drawn into the conflict to boost the power of each side. In 2008 the Ndvuna unsuccessfully tried to bring the community police under his authority by establishing a parallel group in the area where the Umphakatsi is located. One of the founding members, Mabuza, and a few other recruits, left the group to join the other side. Mabuza was rewarded with a seat in the Umphakatsi. The then chairman of the Mbhuleni community police, Mtunzi, was strongly against this. He had been a member of the King's Council since 2004. Conflicts erupted now and then between the main protagonists, Mtunzi and the Umphakatsi allies. The Ndvuna himself pursued contradictory strategies. At times he tried to 'buy' the community police with protection in court cases – the Ndvuna himself being a Staff member in the National Swazi Court. At other times he tried to weaken the Mbhuleni group by reporting their beatings to the police.

In November 2012 the Ndvuna also initiated a project of what he called 'community police zoning' where new members were elected in the sub-zones of the area. He did this entirely on his own without the involvement of existing community police groups and the RSP. In this way he could better control the groupings, and (re)claim authority over community policing, which would boost his power more generally. Yet the initiative was unsuccessful. New recruits were either inactive or ended up joining the Mbhuleni group. Meanwhile, due to the traditional leadership dispute, the King's Council proved ineffective in asserting any strong leadership over the community police. Mtunzi had been their 'eyes' in the community police group, and played the role of policing the extent to which the community police members pledged allegiance to the Council. But as I return to below, he also used this position as a personal political strategy.

The Ndvuna of the Inkhundla, Mrs Bhembe, did not openly oppose the Umphakatsi's efforts to assert authority over the community police. Yet in her own tacit ways she tried to ensure political alliances to win the next elections by sponsoring t-shirts for the community police members. In 2012 she began to help resolve some of the complaints against the community police members. This was widely believed to form part of her political campaign for the 2013 elections. The MP elected in 2008, Mr Dhlamini, also had support from some of the community police members in Mbhuleni. He promised to represent their interests in parliament. In 2011 he gave them mobile phones, but only in January 2013 did he resume contact, presumably to prepare for his re-elections.

The use of the community police members in competitive politics was ambiguous. Not only was it risky because of their legal ambiguity and street-level style operations, which always made alliances unpredictable, politicians also feared opposition from within the community police group. Although they were not a real threat in 2008, there were community police members who ran for elections both as councillors and as MPs. In October 2012 the Mbhuleni group chased away a new member, because he was suspected of being an 'infiltrator' sent by Mrs Bhembe (the Indkundla Ndvuna) as a strategy to reduce the chances of aspiring candidates to the MP and the Ndvuna positions from within the community police group. Elections for these positions were held in 2013, and indeed one community police member, Mtunzi, ran for the position of Ndvuna and won it.

The political instrumentalisation of the community police members strengthened the political significance and independence of the community police in Mbhuleni as an emerging authority in its own right. It also nurtured political aspirations among some members, such as Mtunzi. Yet, at the same time politicisation fed into constant leadership disputes *inside* the community policing group, as people allied with different external fractions. This was especially the case after the chairman position was left vacant in late 2010. There were no re-elections, because the King's Council was too fragmented to authorise it, and the community policing members refused to be led by the Umphakatsi. Jabulani took over de facto leadership. He was one of the founders of the Mbhuleni group and a very active member, who was also recognised by Senator Zwane. However, Mtunzi disputed Jabulani, because he wanted the position for himself so as to heighten his own political chances in the national elections.

What these issues point to is that 'community policing' had become a 'new political space' for furthering its members' personal ambitions (Pratten, 2010). While not everyone aspired to political positions, all the members viewed 'community policing' not as a way of life per se but as a transformational space that could potentially further their personal ambitions. I discuss this aspect next, thus moving to the level of individual politics and aspirations *inside* the community police group.

Personal political ambitions and mobility

The majority of the Mbhuleni community police members were unemployed, poorly educated, non-native younger men, and had families to support. They struggled to improve their life and had many aspirations for the future. Although not all of them had political ambitions, they shared a desire for some form of recognition. They wanted to become somebody who did something in the community, which could then be converted into different forms of personal gain and maybe even a self-transformation. Most hoped that community police work could help build up experiences and expand connections so as to get a salaried job that eventually would finance a piece of land and property for their family. A number of former members had already had success in achieving these attributes of becoming 'an elder', especially through jobs in the private security sector.

Community policing represented a 'transformational space' that could bring those involved from a state of uncertainty and insignificance to becoming somebody *inside* community policing and potentially also *outside* of it. It was not a space to remain in or a place to grow old. This was because there was no licit, stable income and no officially recognised authority that could give members the status of 'Elder'. Of those who aspired to political positions and indeed excelled in politics, Mtunzi and Jabulani stood out as particularly illustrative, and yet also very different examples. They are the focus of the next two sections.

Mtunzi – the 'bad boy'

To Mtunzi, community policing had facilitated a complete transformation: from being a bad boy, living among the criminals when he was a young teenager, to becoming a good person before God, with a strong standing in society and with high political ambitions. Despite his criminal background, Mtunzi was a son of one of the older families in Mbhuleni. This status as native increased his possibilities to enter local leadership positions. He was appointed to the King's Council not because he was an active community policing member, but because he had been a youth member of the Umpakatsi. Thus, the King's Council saw his appointment as a way to gain supporters from its competitor in the traditional leadership dispute. Mtunzi's strength was his alliances across the traditional structures. No one dared to challenge him openly. In the internal disputes over community police leadership Jabulani tried to reason with him, but never challenged him directly.

To the advantage of Jabulani, Mtunzi hardly ever engaged in everyday policing. He mostly came by when important decisions were to be taken or when there were public meetings. It was clear to all community policing members that 'Mtunzi is only here [at community police] to become MP'.[10] He campaigned in 2003, and again in 2008 where he used his position in community policing to boost his chances to win. His defeat both years, he claimed, was because the former MP had paid some of the other community policing members, including Jabulani, to undermine him.

Mtunzi was always on the lookout for alliances, and suspicious of enemies. He was known for using 'dirty tricks' to achieve his goals, and in doing so to split the community police group. At some point he was accused of having used the Emalangeni 5.00 community contributions to distribute to those community police members who supported him, but he lost this support when it appeared that he put most of it in his own pocket. In 2011 Mtunzi recruited new members to create havoc inside the group so as to question the authority of Jabulani. They were not interested in policing, but mostly just hung out, harassing the other members. Later it turned out that they were part of an organised group of criminals, specialising in ATM machine scams. However, this new criminal fraction did not last long, as Mtunzi realised that it tattered the groups' reputation to such an extent that it threatened its survival. He depended on the groups' legitimacy for his own political agenda.

Mtunzi was a real player and a well-known womanizer. No one that I spoke to really believed in his political ambitions. Rumours said that he switched between alliances. At some point he had supposedly supported the outlawed political party, PUDEMO (People's United Democratic Movement), which allegedly had split up the King's Council. In late 2012 he apparently admitted his political defeat to Jabulani as he changed his political strategy for the 2013 elections. He now wanted to campaign with Jabulani, who would run for the MP post, whereas he would go for the more inferior position as Ndvuna of the Inkhundla. Mtunzi's idea was to make a 'community police political team', as he called it. He believed it could work 'because we know the community best. We just get so close to the community'.[11] However, behind his back Jabulani admitted that he would never agree to such a team. So Mtunzi ended up being nominated for the Ndvuna post on his own. To everyone's surprise he won.

Mtunzi's attempt to transform the community police into an actual collective political actor accentuates the emergence of community policing as a new political space that has potentially opened a window for the young, un-employed, men to excel in life. Yet it was an idea that was fraught with tensions and ambiguities. The internal splits, the entanglement of legality and illegality, and the fact that community police authority was founded, ultimately, on their capacity for violence, made it hard to achieve any stable political position, as a group.

Jabulani – the 'pastor'

Jabulani joined the community police as a 'calling from God'. He strongly believed that his hard work in bringing down crime would eventually be rewarded by God, in this life. He had many years of schooling and had been to Bible college, but lost his job in 2004 and never found a new one. His big idol was Robert Zwane. He wished to end up as a national political figure, endorsed by the King. He was a strong royalist, in contrast to the oppositional attitude of Mtunzi.

Jabulani had a very different approach to politics than Mtunzi. He worked his way slowly towards his political goals, accumulating alliances and recognition, using also the national political arena. In everyday policing he was known as the less violent deliberator and as a good investigator, although he did indeed use force in certain situations. He often used the Bible and his passion was to turn the bad boys into good, God fearing, persons. Among the population he was popular, and when asked who the leader of community police in Mbhuleni was, people would give his name. Jabulani's dream to achieve a Royal appointment to the Senate was related to his wish to represent community police interests at the national level. This would also give him a salary to realise his other dream: to get land and build a house for his family.

When I first met him in 2011 he had no intentions of entering competitive politics. His problem was that he was no native to Kwaluseni, but had moved there in the mid 1980s. This was also reflected in his apparent incapacity to mobilise enough authority to control the group internally. He did not have the connections to the local leadership networks that Mtunzi had. Nonetheless, when I returned in 2012, Jabulani had changed his mind. Because of community policing, 'people love me here', and 'I have received people, even two churches, who say I should go for the elections [to parliament]'.[12] On the national scene Jabulani had excelled. He had been appointed by Zwane to take over the national radio programme and in 2012 he was also asked to chair Zwane's national association for community policing in Swaziland.

In competitive politics Jabulani was very careful: 'I will see a big number that is convincing, that I can take my chances with [to get elected], because this thing of politics, I don't want to hurt myself.'[13] In fact, Jabulani faced a dilemma. He really wanted to make a career within community policing, but with the stalemate in legislation there was no official recognition and authority to rely on. As he noted to me, people also expected of him, after so many years with the community police, that he 'moved on' and 'moved upwards' to something else, because one could not grow old in the community police in Mbhuleni. Even so, he ended up not standing for the 2013 nominations, presumably awaiting instead a royal appointment.

Conclusion

Community policing in urban Swaziland illustrates the intimate intertwinement of politics and policing in the context of de facto partial sovereignties (Comaroff and Comaroff, 2006), local leadership disputes and livelihood uncertainties. From taking over those streets that no one else could order, community policing has become not only an alternative police, but also a new 'political space' for young men who otherwise had little access to recognition, official jobs and political office. This is a space within and over which contestations of power, resources and clients take place, and that implicates the national political arena.

Community policing in Mbhuleni is also a space where political and job careers can be made, akin to what Pratten (2010: 120) has shown for vigilante groups in Nigeria. It is a space that can aid the careers of community police members themselves as well as those other politically ambitious persons who use alliances with the community police as a source of power to further their political goals. These forms of politics are silenced in the bigger picture of what in the eyes of external observers constitutes politics in the Kingdom: i.e. sovereignty as exclusively vested in the King and competitive politics as undermined by Royal appointments and the outlawing of opposition movements. While these elements certainly also reflect the current political landscape in Swaziland, the micro-politics of community policing illustrates another side of 'political society' (Chatterjee, 2004) that differs from official politics. The politics of community policing is based directly on the capacity for immediate order-making. This politics has three main characteristics that ultimately reflect the livelihood uncertainties and distrust of official politics that predominate in urban margins (see Introduction to this volume) such as Mbhuleni.

First, the politics emerging from community policing is characterised by 'ambiguity'. It embodies conventional dichotomies, much in line with what has been argued for vigilante groups (Abrahams, 1996; Pratten and Sen, 2007; Kirsch and Grätz, 2010) and 'informal sovereigns' (Hansen and Stepputat, 2005). They are both inside and outside of the state, as 'insider' performers of state police authority and as unruly, informal outsiders. They both embrace legality and illegality, legitimacy and illegitimacy: they bring order, recuperate goods and correct criminals, yet continuously also produce disorder and transgress the law through favours, extractions and excessive violence.

The second characteristic is 'youthfulness'. Not only are the members young of age or socially young, they are also known for their capacity for 'direct actions' without hesitation and for shifting positions. Youthfulness in this sense signals 'not being tied too strictly' to any fixed moral registers or traditions as is the case with the 'Elders' and with the 'State'. Although the community police use such registers, in fact draw on them to resolve cases, their strength lies in being able to mix and switch quickly between them. This makes community policing attractive in dealing with immediate problems of crime, getting stolen goods back right away, and making sure criminals are punished. Yet it also means you can never fully rely on them.

Third, the politics of community policing is characterised by 'momentariness' in the sense of being temporary and quick. Community policing in Mbhuleni very rapidly turned into an authority in its own right, with its own court-like set up or 'Station'. This has become a source of status to its members. Yet it is a temporary form of 'street authority' that is not stable and consolidated. Community policing as a political space is a transient one. It is only really valuable if it takes you somewhere else, somewhere more certain. 'Momentariness' is attractive to those powerful outsiders who enlist community police in their political projects. This is because they are always expendable, with no formal rights or recognition specific to the status of community police. You can use them as a resource for protection or to boost your status, and then you don't need to take responsibility for their actions if something goes wrong. To the community police, protection by the state or the 'Big Man' can quickly switch to punishment.

Taken together, these three characteristics represent a style of politics where especially the capacities for direct action and quick results are very central, but also where the risks are high and where there is a lot of uncertainty for the actors involved. This kind of politics emerges, I suggest, in line with Asef Bayat (1997; 2012), in contexts where people by and large do not have access to state benefits through formal channels and where elections and political movements have failed to improve livelihoods. In these contexts there is a preference for mutability and immediate outcomes in improving livelihood uncertainty and a sense of security, rather than stringent rules and regulations. The latter are experienced as exclusionary, not as a route to socio-economic benefits and justice. Direct actions are important in situations of uncertain livelihoods, because you can always lose your job, your plot of land, your market stall, and insecurity from crime is high. The paradox of course is, as Lindell and Utas (2012) highlight for youth in cities more generally, that the main actors in producing momentariness strive for stability and have long-term aspirations towards fixed positions and trajectories – e.g. for becoming an 'Elder'. It is unlikely that community policing in Mbhuleni will ever turn into a collective political movement in its own right, despite efforts at the national level to make this happen. Yet in the process some individuals, such as Mtunzi, will succeed.

Notes

1   The chapter is based on ethnographic fieldwork from January to March 2011 and from October 2012 to January 2013.
2   Written speech by Crime Prevention Councilor, A. K. Dhlamini, 08.06.2004.
3   Interview, Robert Zwane, 01.03.2011.
4   Written speech by Crime Prevention Councilor, A. K. Dhlamini, 08.06.2004.

5   The purpose of this chapter is not to discuss how the community police members resolved disputes and crimes, but it suffices to say that they did so in a hybrid manner, drawing on a mixture of traditional Swazi, Biblical and state police procedures and norms.
6   Interview, Lukhele, 09.02.2011.
7   Interview, Chris, 13.02.2011.
8   Interview, Chris, 13.02.2011.
9   Interview, Dlamini, Petty Department, 17.01.2013.
10 Interview, Chris, 13.02.2011.
11 Interview, Mtunzi, 14.10.2012.
12 Interview, Jabulani, 15.01.2013.
13 Interview, Jabulani, 15.01.2013.

References

Abrahams, R., 1996. Vigilantism: Order and disorder on the frontiers of the state, in H. Olivia (ed.), *Inside and outside the Law: Anthropological Studies of Authority and Ambiguity*. London: Routledge, 41–55.

Adelkhah, F., 1999. *Being Modern in Iran*. London: Hurst.

Bayat, A., 1997. Un-civil society: The politics of the 'informal people', *Third World Quarterly*, 18:1, 53–72.

Bayat, A., 2012. Politics in the city-inside-out, *City and Society*, 24:2, 110–128.

Chatterjee, P., 2004. *The Politics of the Governed: Reflections on Popular Politics in Most of the World*. New York: Columbia University Press.

Comaroff, J. L. and Comaroff, J. (eds), 2006. *Law and Disorder in the Postcolony*. Chicago, IL and London: University of Chicago Press.

Hamilton, S. S., 2005. Cross-border cattle rustling and its socio-economic impact on rural southern Swaziland, 1990–2004, *Journal of Contemporary African Studies*, 23:2, 37–41.

Hamilton, S. S., 2007. *The State, the Security Dilemma, and the Development of the Private Security Sector in Swaziland*. Pretoria: Institute for Security Studies (ISS).

Hansen T. B. and Stepputat, F. (eds), 2005. *Sovereign Bodies: Citizens, Migrants and States in the Postcolonial World*. Princeton, NJ and Oxford: Princeton University Press.

Khumalo, C., 2004. Community police men and the elimination of crime in Swazi communities, 1996–2003. BA Dissertation.

Kirsch, T. G. and Grätz, T. (eds), 2010. *Domesticating Vigilantes in Africa*. Woodbridge: James Currey.

Lindell, I. and Utas, M., 2012. Networked city life in Africa: Introduction, *Urban Forum*, 23, 409–414.

Mouffe, C., 2005. *On the Political*. London and New York: Routledge.

Nuijten, M., 2013. The perversity of the 'Citizenship Game': Slum-upgrading in the urban periphery of Recife, Brazil, *Critique of Anthropology*, 33:1, 8–25.

Pratten, D., 2010. Bodies of power: Narratives of selfhood and security in Nigeria, in T. G. Kirsch and T. Grätz (eds), *Domesticating Vigilantes in Africa*. Woodbridge: James Currey, 118–138.

Pratten, D. and Sen, A. (eds), 2007. *Global Vigilantes*. London and New York: Hurst and Columbia University Press.

Chapter 5

Community policing in Accra

The complexities of local notions of (in)security and (in)justice

Emmanuel Addo Sowatey and
Raymond A. Atuguba

In low-income neighbourhoods of Accra, Ghana's capital, civilian policing groups known as 'Watch Dogs', have been formed by local residents to deal with their own security and justice needs. In contrast, residents in high-income areas hire private security companies or guards. Moreover, this latter group uses their connections to politicians in the ruling party to lobby the state police to attach greater importance to the security of their area, including, if possible, more public police visibility. It is within this security architecture in general, and public policing in particular that the chapter examines how the poor and densely populated community in Accra called Nima has responded to its security and justice needs.[1]

That most people in a place such as Nima depend on multiple policing actors to meet their security needs is not peculiar to Ghana. Baker (2006) shows that in urban communities across Uganda and Sierra Leone, residents have resorted to a wide range of policing groups to meet their security needs. The inability of the state-sanctioned police to provide security has created a security vacuum (Baker 2006: 56), and as a result, an array of policing actors has arisen that constitute a plural policing landscape (see Adu-Mireku 2002; Anderson 2002; Baker 2002, 2004, 2009; Aning 2006).

A number of reasons underpin this reality. First, in a number of African states, public policing has never fully displaced other forms of indigenous policing systems throughout the post-colonial era (Turner 1955). The endurance of some of these indigenous policing groups has been driven partly by internal dynamics, including the flexibility of civilian policing groups, the way these groups understand and address security concerns, and their sensitivity to local justice and security needs, which involve metaphysical and socio-cultural matters. Externally, the continued endurance of some civilian policing groups has in part been sustained by the rolling back of the state through structural adjustment programmes.

This chapter argues that the establishment of a Watch Dog group in the poor urban neighbourhood of Nima in Accra was a self-initiated rather than police-driven response to appropriately address local security needs. It has created the space and opportunity for ordinary people to address their own security and justice needs. The chapter brings an additional argument to existing literature on civilian policing actors by showing not only the changing dynamics and phases that such groups inevitably undergo, but also, importantly, the space that the Watch Dog group creates to incorporate local views of what security and justice mean to different people and how these can be properly addressed.

The chapter begins with an outline of Nima's demography and a brief explanation of local notions of security and justice. This is followed by a description of the Watch Dog, its *raison d'être*, operations, recruitment processes, motivations, and its engagement with the public police and other state institutions. The last section discusses the two key challenges that confront the Watch Dog: The interference of politicians and drug barons into its affairs. The chapter concludes by making a short comparison with high-income areas of Accra, arguing that closer relations to politicians and greater wealth allow them to use a wider range of security options. This also means that in such well-off neighbourhoods, Watch Dogs have not been as successful.

Security and justice in Nima

Nima is an adulterated word of *Nee Mann* that means Nee's Town in the Ga language. It is a low income and densely populated suburb of Accra and lies about 5 kilometres from the Central Business District. According to informal discussions with senior police officers, Nima Police Division has one of the highest rates of crime in Ghana, and most residents of Accra consider this to be the case.

Nima started building its own identity as a migrant community in the 1940s as a result of the fast urbanization of Accra. Some of its earliest settlers were families of soldiers from the Royal West African Frontier Force in Accra who were asked by the British Colonial authorities to leave the military camp due to security concerns during the Second World War. Interestingly, in the immediate aftermath of the Second World War, residents of Nima took up part of their own security. In an interview with the father of the President of the Watch Dog under scrutiny in this study, Imam Amadu Ibrahim, it was thus pointed out that community policing in Nima was no novelty.

Ibrahim revealed that after the war, the youth of Nima constituted a self-policing group that patrolled the community at night. Again, in the late 1990s and early 2000s, another sub-state policing group emerged in Nima called *Isakaba*. This group was named after a group in Nigeria that had been popularized in certain communities in Ghana through a film called *Isakaba*. In Nigeria and Nima, *Isakaba* was seen as an advocate for the poor against the powerful in society, corruption and other perceived antisocial behaviour. Whereas one group thinks the group has Islamic inspirations, others regard it as a purely social movement for the poor.

Nima is a predominantly Muslim community, but most Ghanaian ethnic groups are represented. A substantial number of its residents are from the three northern regions of Ghana: Northern, Upper East and Upper West. In addition, other West African nationalities are represented in Nima. A notable aspect of identity and nationality in the neighbourhood is that a number of residents claim that they are both Ghanaians and citizens of other West African states. This proclamation of dual nationality allows these residents to stay connected to their ancestral heritage as part of their identity.

Local notions of security and justice among most of Nima's residents incorporate spiritual and physical dimensions and emphasize the connection between them. To a large extent, the spiritual world influences and shapes the physical. As a result, one needs to be spiritually sensitive and fortified in order to respond appropriately to physical security and justice needs. This view is not unique to Nima residents. It resonates with the belief among many Africans that there is a causal relationship between the metaphysical and physical world, which shapes how crime and justice can be addressed. In the case of Nima, it is clear that there is a widely held view among residents that criminals, particularly armed robbers, have strong spiritual support and to successfully arrest and prosecute them demands spiritual buy-in.

The origin and changes of the Watch Dog

In the words of a resident of Nima: 'We don't have anywhere to go; Nima is like our home land.'[2] This quote describes one of the key motivations of creating, maintaining and sustaining the Watch Dog group that operates in Nima West. It is a sub-state policing group and the community policing unit of the Ghana Police Service has for a long time considered it to be the best Watch Dog in the country.[3]

By most standards, Watch Dog is a vigilante group, known for being brutal, untrained, on the boundary of criminality, and of having a myopic vision (Abraham 1987; Buur and Jensen 2004; Sen and Pratten 2007). These notions are common stereotypes for low-income communities that are suspected to nurture and harbour criminals. However, for groups such as the Watch Dog there are practical reasons why they exist as providers of security and justice. As one member of the group indicated, before it was established 'there was no night or day in Nima: crimes that could only be committed at night elsewhere were carried out in the day'. Criminals acted with total disregard for the police.

The Watch Dog was formed by locals with no input from the public police in 2003. This was due to a heightened state of insecurity and the inability of the public police to appreciate and incorporate local security concerns into their operational plans. A sense of belonging is often shaped by and through state institutions (Loader 2006). However, the way that the public police has engaged in Nima sends a message about how the police is 'often systematically oriented to maintaining dominant societal interest and values in ways that foster and reproduce insecurity among economically and socially disadvantaged groups' (Loader 2006: 211).

Following from the above, the search for security and justice alternatives resulted in the creation of the Watch Dog, which was not necessarily intended to take over the role of the state police, but rather to respond more appropriately to local security and justice needs and concerns. These responses were designed to be sensitive to local notions of what security is and how it can be provided. Moreover, the initiative of forming the group was achieved by a strong sense of communal belonging and interdependence among Nima residents, with additional support from the diaspora outside Ghana.

In order to provide security based on local notions of security and justice, the first step of establishing the Watch Dog was to put together a trusted body of indigenes. These people were chosen on the basis of having deep knowledge of the various criminal networks that operate in Nima. These are also people who act in the spirit of voluntarism and who articulate a desire to contribute to the safety and security of the community.

The group initially met with the public police and outlined their objectives, which were to provide security for members of its community. The police then granted them the licence to operate as part of its community policing scheme. Next, the group sought moral authority and legitimacy from the community's members and leadership. To this end, they met prominent chiefs, pastors, imams and other opinion leaders who gave their backing and support by signing the objectives of the group in a public ceremony. This was a public show of their approval, however, without legal effect. The Nima diaspora, particularly in the United States, later gave their strong support to the group by providing them with some logistical support.

The support and buy-in from various constituencies within and outside Nima gave the group the moral authority to begin their operations. By going to the police and the chiefs the Watch Dog wanted to gain legitimacy at both state and community level. As such, they avoided ending up in the same situation as the public police, which had state legitimacy, but limited local approval and credibility.

The name of the group has undergone three major changes since its establishment in 2003. These changes reflect lessons of the group that have shaped and influenced its response to local security needs. The group was first known as the Nima West Neighbourhood Watch Dog Group, but was changed to the Nima Maamobi Neighbourhood Watch Dog Group. The reason for the name change was that, although the initial focus and scope of the group's work was to protect lives and property in Nima West, the group soon realized that the networks of a number of criminals reached into other parts of Nima and Maamobi. To be more effective, the group therefore started to conduct some of its community policing duties in other parts of Nima and subsequently in Maamobi.

Later, the group changed its name again to Nima West Counselling, Rehabilitation and Neighbourhood Watch Group. This change stemmed from the experience and desire of the group to prevent, reduce and tackle crime from a holistic perspective. According to the Watch Dog leadership, it became obvious during their operations that a large number of the criminals that they apprehended were minors who they considered to be victims rather than criminals. The group found that most of these minors were being exploited by criminals and lacked proper parental care.

The group therefore decided to help rehabilitate and counsel some of these minors on the dangers of drugs and crime. They also made efforts to rehabilitate those who were already on drugs and/or had been released from prison. These additional responsibilities were assumed by the group without regard to the fact that none of its members were trained to do social work. Instead, they used their local knowledge of how to rehabilitate drug addicts through, for example, counselling minors to stop and focus on personal development that could help them break out of poverty. Formal education was regarded as key to this process and numerous activities were carried out to this end.

The different names of the Watch Dog reflect the phases that the civilian policing group has gone through. Over time, it came to see criminal behaviour as a symptom of deep-seated socio-economic and historical factors that had to be addressed accordingly. Indeed, the metamorphosis in name and responsibilities of the Nima Watch Dog confirms the point that policing, as it is currently practised globally, is too reactionary in its institutional responses and routines.

Recruitment procedure and the role of community members

There are two ways to join the ranks of the Watch Dog: There are those who join voluntarily and those who are identified by the group itself as well as by chiefs and other community leaders. Those encouraged to join the Watch Dog are mostly young adults who are rehabilitated by the group or for whom the group provides an escape from criminal activity. The Watch Dog leaders rely heavily on their in-depth knowledge of residents in Nima and their familiarity with the area to undertake background checks of prospective members. In order to feel a sense of representation in the decision-making process within the group, some families also encourage young adult relatives to volunteer to join the group.

The recruitment process is rigorous and detailed attention is paid to each applicant. The recruitment process has evolved over time based on previous experiences. Generally, there is a slight difference in the recruitment process for those who are born, raised and live in Nima and Maamobi versus those who have lived most of their lives outside these communities.

If the applicant is born, raised and lives in one of the two areas, doing a background check takes approximately a week. The leadership of the group will ask Watch Dog members who are peers of the applicant to do the background check in the home of the applicant, ask about his or her behaviour at home, in school or madrasa/makaranta, etc. They will also seek the views of community members and elders regarding the applicant's respect for parents, elders, companions and other social and religious indicators and criteria to judge whether the person is well behaved. In a closely knit community such as Nima, community members are reliable sources for gathering information and intelligence about a person.

As such, the involvement of residents in their own security begins at the stage of recruitment. This is not the case regarding the public police. In addition to engaging community members, the zonal commander of the Watch Dog in the area where the applicant lives also carries out a background check. Then, when the youth of the Watch Dog and the zonal commander submit their reports, the whole leadership cross-checks for consistency and difference. This strategy makes room for intergenerational differences in assessing an applicant, given that the leaders are mostly in their late forties or early fiftiess while other members commonly are under thirty-five.

The reports on the applicant are then reconciled and a decision taken by the group on his or her eligibility. If the potential member goes through this first vetting process, the person is accompanied to the public police for their finger print to be taken and to be cross-checked against police records. After clearance from the police, the group places the applicant on probation for three months before s/he is confirmed or rejected. On the other hand, where the potential member is new in the community, it takes between three and five weeks to conduct the background checks on the person (it is important to note here that it was the group who took the initiative to establish and maintain a relationship with the public police).

After the background checks the applicant is put on probation for three months, and then given an identity card. The identity card is a proof of the individual's membership of the group. So far, over twenty potential members out of about 100 members (at its peak) have been rejected after the background check and two have been sacked after indulging in crime and deviant behaviour such as disrespect or stealing. Still others have been identified as infiltrators for drug dealers and sacked.

A number of direct and indirect participatory processes involved in forming the Watch Dog are not only pathways to enhancing community oversight. They also make the group democratic and strengthen trust between the residents of Nima and the group, making it easier for people to volunteer information about criminals without fear of being exposed. In addition, the phase of conducting background checks constitutes an entry point and platform of collaboration between the Watch Dog and the police and prevents criminals from joining the group.

Command structure and the spiritual foundation of policing

The Watch Dog is designed to maximize efficient use of its resources and relationship with the public police. They have accomplished their set objectives through strong strategic, operational and tactical coordination as well as reliance on local knowledge of members and moral authority from prominent and ordinary Nima residents. The leadership generally consists of elected members, although their deputies and two other officers are appointed. At the top is an Executive Council that is headed by a President who also leads general operations. Other members of the Executive Council include a Vice-President, Operations Coordinator/Commander, Assistant Coordinator/Commander and Secretary.

The leadership, especially the very top, is chosen/elected based on local concepts of security. These people are believed to have strong spiritual powers to rally members and to protect them. The President of the Nima Watch Dog is the son of a former Imam of Nima (aforementioned Imam Amadu Ibrahim) who was the chief Imam of a prominent mosque (Kardo Mosque) for seventy years. Consequently, it is believed that the Imam who had deep knowledge of the Qur'an, spiritually fortified his sons, including the President of the group. Fighting them would equal fighting strong spiritual powers. Furthermore, the President belongs to a very large family known as Kardo, which provides him with a wide social network that gives him legitimacy, perceived spiritual powers and support. Thus, even though elections are held to form the group, what informs and influences that process involves local views on how security can be provided and maintained, and by whom.

The elected officials get to choose their own deputies on the basis of whom they trust. In addition, the porter and treasurer are also not elected. Together, these groups are the core of the Watch Dog and liaise with the state security apparatus to discuss issues of cooperation and coordination. The next tier is made up of the field or zonal commanders. The rationale for the creation of the zones is primarily to ensure operational and tactical efficiency. At the bottom of the organizational structure are field operatives and administrative support staff.

At one point of the Watch Dog's activities, the field operatives numbered over 100. This made it one of the biggest sub-state policing groups in terms of numbers and influence in Ghana. One striking characteristic of Watch Dog members is their contextual knowledge of criminal psychology in the Nima context, which they use to prevent and detect crime. As noted above, the link between the spiritual and physical world is strong in this regard. The President of the Watch Dog explained that some criminals perform spiritual rituals at midnight, prior to embarking on criminal activities. For instance, some criminals slaughter ducks, dogs, chickens and drain the blood unto their deities and smear the rest of the blood on their body before going out to execute their criminal plans. Others wear rings and spiritual ornaments such as talismans for the same purpose.

These rituals and ornaments are believed to hold strong spiritual powers that protect criminals from arrests, gunshots, bladed weapons, successful prosecution and conviction. Furthermore, it is believed among members of the Watch Dog and most residents in Nima that some of the charms can make one disappear. Indeed, in some instances, they have the ability to keep the distance between a criminal and his or her pursuers, regardless of whether the latter are faster than the former. In other words, criminals will always elude arrest and successful prosecution with the aid of spiritual powers.

Against this background, members of the group and some residents believe that when a suspected criminal has been arrested, it is necessary to pay special attention to finding and destroying any charms, amulets or deities that the suspects may hide. If not, the suspect will be released from police custody without proper investigation and state prosecutors will not be interested in pursuing the case due to spiritual manipulation. In other instances, the criminal may be sent to court but, as long as his or her spiritual ornaments are intact, they can be activated and directed to free the suspect.

The leadership of the group used the arrest of a notorious armed robber to point to the reality of direct links between the spiritual and physical world. The criminal, who had been wanted by the public police, but remained on the loose, was finally arrested in a joint operation between the Watch Dog group and the public police. When the robber was arrested he showed no sign of remorse, fear or concern. However, he screamed when he saw that members of the Watch Dog found and destroyed his charms and other spiritual ornaments. For the members of the group, the criminal screamed because he knew that his conviction had been secured (and freedom lost) once the charms were destroyed. The armed robber was convicted a few weeks later.

The leadership of the group argues that their success in the arrest and conviction of criminals is due to a number of reasons. First, the Watch Dog holds deep local knowledge of how criminals operate, particularly how they obtain spiritual support. Second, the ability to use their spiritual understanding complements efforts of the public police to detect the criminal. Third, most residents of Nima have confidence in the group partly because they trust that the group fully understands all dimensions of insecurity. How to appropriately deal with this insecurity accounts for their success. In this respect, Nima residents believe they share a common view on how security and justice should be organized and provided, which in turn helps to build trust and confidence among Watch Dog members and residents.

Furthermore, the leadership of the group indicates that some of them are also spiritually fortified against the charms of the criminals. They have charms and amulets that are more powerful than those of the criminals and that make it relatively easier for them to fight the criminals. One of the leaders pointed out that, during most of their dangerous operations to arrest armed robbers, those among them who are spiritually fortified transfer some of their spiritual powers to other members of the group. They transfer the powers by holding hands in a circle while reciting certain words. At times the transfer is done in silence.

The role of the Watch Dog in providing security and justice, including their use of spiritual power, challenges the Western understanding that a supreme constitution is one of the main features of a state. Nima points to the existence of plural legal regimes and justice systems, which operate even in stable democracies such as Ghana. The partly spiritual approach that the Watch Dog adopts as it combats crime in Nima has contributed to the legitimacy and acceptance of the group among its residents and beyond. This makes the group more sensitive to local notions of justice and security, which in part contributes to its wide acceptance and credibility.

The Watch Dog creates a space that enhances local participation in security and justice sector governance at the micro level. They make room for often marginalized citizens to have a say in how their security is prioritized and addressed. In turn, this space creates the possibility of strong oversight by Nima residents over how security at the local level is governed, a role that can hardly be accomplished with respect to the public police.

Operations and tactical discipline of the Watch Dog

To understand the practical discipline of the Watch Dog and its effectiveness as compared to the public police one has to understand the architectural layout of Nima. The housing and road layout is complex and confusing to non-residents. The houses are located very closely to one another and most of them do not have the high residential fences or walls that are found in middle-income housing areas. As such, the area is closely knit by virtue of its geographical and architectural layout, which in turn facilitates interaction among the people who live there.

Foot patrol is the best way to provide security at night in Nima, and the Watch Dog embarks on patrols by foot and motor bikes to acess the (potential) hideout of criminals. This way of operating is part of the strength of the Watch Dog as the group knows the terrain in which it operates. It has been adapted to ease and facilitate their operations and to make optimal use of individual expertise of the group's members. So, when they embark on an operation based generally on tip-offs from locals, the initial standard operation procedure is to call the zonal commander or leader in charge of the area where the crime is taking place or is about to take place to do a reconnaissance and report to the operating centre of the Watch Dog. If the problem can be solved by the zonal commander and his team, they deal with it and then report to the operating centre. When the situation proves too challenging to handle for the team in that zone, it requests backup from other zones. If a suspect is arrested, the person is sent to the group's headquarters, which is an office rented and paid for by the leader of the group, and then to the police station. The time between when a suspected criminal is arrested and handed over to the police varies between thirty minutes and two hours, depending on the nature of the crime and the attitude of the suspect.

When a suspect is interrogated by members of the group, the kinds of techniques used depend on whether the suspect is considered to cooperate or not. At their headquarters a combination of techniques are used that include verbal questioning, at times slaps and corporal punishment, pleads and appeals for the criminal to cooperate, e.g. by pointing out other members of the gang. Interrogation techniques often reflect local notions of how security and justice might be accessed. In such cases, the use of reasonable force against suspects, and at what stage of the interrogation process, the kind and intensity of force that may be used, is evident to group members and members of the community, but may be uncomfortable to outsiders.

It appears that as the Watch Dog has increased engagement with the public police, their views on some aspects of their operations have changed, for instance, regarding who has the right to use force and what the limitations of their powers are. In other words, notions of security and justice are not static, but evolve and are negotiable, although some areas, such as Watch Dog beliefs in the supernatural, remain fairly constant.

The availability of mobile phones has become critical in Watch Dog operations as it enhances their ability to communicate vital information and also to mobilize quickly. In interviews, various members of the Watch Dog attested to the fact that without the availability of relatively cheap mobile phones they would be less successful in their operations. For the Watch Dog, communication has been key in their planning and execution of operations. Accordingly, members have more than one phone number in order to take advantage of the cheaper rates and easy communications between numbers operated by the same network (telephone company).

Regarding justice, the Watch Dog has settled numerous cases such as debt collection, marital problems and disagreements, deviant behaviour of minors, and so forth. The group is able to carry out these services because, first, its members are easily approachable by locals and use a combination of local languages, dialogue, persuasion and force when needed. Second, they understand local notions of justice and security, and, third, unlike fees and bribes charged by some chiefs and public police officers, their services are free of charge. Fourth, cases are not unnecessarily adjourned and, fifth, the Watch Dog is widely respected and therefore has substantial legitimacy and moral authority in Nima.

Finally, unlike the state-sanctioned courts, the Watch Dog does not use intimidating procedures and legal jargon, which frustrate ordinary citizens who have their cases tried in the formal justice sector. In one instance, the Watch Dogs settled a case of debt of about $10,000 between two business partners and after the case had been settled no money was paid to the Watch Dog. They also punish, including corporal punishment, what the community sees as deviant behaviour, such as children who do not go home for days but stay at internet cafés to commit advance fee fraud (known as 419), premarital sex, disrespect of elders, not going to school and similar social and civil matters.

Motivation and survival of the Watch Dog: Community ties

The services offered by the Watch Dog are purely voluntary and members do not get any financial remuneration despite the high risk involved in their operations. Criminals who have been convicted and return to Nima pose a threat to members who helped in their arrest and conviction. In two extreme cases, wives of some of the field commanders were physically assaulted or threatened. The members of the Watch Dog had no insurance and relied on members' voluntary contributions to cater for injuries sustained during the course of their work. At the time of writing, there have not been any direct work-related deaths, although the Watch Dog has confronted armed robbers on countless occasions. The leadership of the Watch Dog believes that they are spiritually fortified, which protects them and other members who go on foot patrols against armed robberies. The Watch Dog has also received major moral and logistical support from the Nima diaspora, particularly those living in New York, United States.

However, to fully understand the rationale and motives that drive the Watch Dog, it is important to know a bit more about the residents of Nima. Nima is a migrant community and predominantly Muslim. Muslims are the second largest religious group after Christians. This is not unique to Ghana but a general characteristic of West Africa. There are hardly any conflicts between Muslims and Christians in Nima. The President of the group traces his descent directly to the first settlers of Nima, but the exact date of its establishment is not known. As indicated above, his father was a prominent Imam who held the first Islamic Gum'ah prayers in Nima. These Gum'ah prayers were the second to be held in Accra altogether. Although the President of the Watch Dog traces his ancestors to Mali, he sees himself as a Ghanaian and Nima as his home town. But to the average Ghanaian, no one comes from Nima, since it is just an urban settlement.

For the Watch Dog President, and many others, this feeling of being a descendant of a migrant who was a chief Imam of the community, and a person whose forefathers co-founded Nima, creates a deep sense of 'patriotism' and duty towards Nima. In addition, this background is a source of legitimacy that allows the Watch Dog President to head the group that provides security and justice within the community. It appears that outsiders marvel at the degree of bonding between members of Nima Watch Dog and the community. However, for members of the group, Nima is their homeland and they will protect it with all their resources, even if their lives are at stake.

Apart from being a migrant community, almost seven out of every ten residents are born in Nima and live there, and speak Hausa no matter their religious and ethnic background. Hausa is the *Lingua Franca*. Consequently, anybody who speaks Hausa becomes part of that community, and as such the local worldview of belonging is also based on the language that one speaks. Within the Watch Dog group, Hausa is the main means of communication, solidarity and bonding. Despite the strong influence of Hausa in the socio-economic lives of most residents of Nima, Hausa is not a Ghanaian language but originates from Northern Nigeria and Southeastern Niger. However, it is widely spoken within Muslim communities in Ghana. The ability of the group to speak Hausa gives them an added advantage over the public police in fighting crime in Nima and Maamobi.

Relations with the public police and other state institutions

The relationship between the Community Policing Unit of the Ghana Police Service and the Nima Watch Dog has over the years been cordial, which could be attributed to the attitude of the personnel of this unit. In fact, the Watch Dog has been a flagship of the Ghana Police Service Community Policing Scheme.

The relationship between the Watch Dog and the Nima police division has largely been shaped by the attitude, understanding and appreciation of the role of the Watch Dog by the Divisional Police Commanders. This has resulted in shifting periods of smooth and strained engagement, respectively. The leadership of the Watch Dog emphasizes that the relationship has gone through two major phases. The first was characterized by strong cooperation, which peaked around December 2008, followed by a period of tension, mistrust, low morale among members and the Watch Dog's subsequent near collapse (since mid 2010).

From its inception in 2003 until December 2008, the then Divisional Police Commander appeared to understand the practical challenges and the limitations of the police as the prime provider of security. The Watch Dog was thus actively encouraged to operate in Nima and to complement the efforts of the public police. This seems to have been a win–win situation, where the police hardly ever interfered with the work of the Watch Dog.

This phase saw strong cooperation and joint operations between the police and the Watch Dog. Several hardened criminals who had earlier eluded the police were arrested and no-go-zones created by the criminals were dismantled. Security was established, which was not the case before the Watch Dog existed. Indeed, the National Headquarters of the Ghana Police Service gave two awards to the Watch Dog for fighting crime effectively and working with the police to this end. For the police, there was no conflict between their notions of security and those of the Watch Dog as long as crime was tackled and the media, public and police were not worried about the *modus operandi* of the Watch Dog.

Relations during the second phase (June 2010 until the time of writing) have been characterized by tension, mistrust and virtually no cooperation between the Watch Dog and the police. The fractured relationship undermined the effectiveness and enthusiasm of members of the Watch Dog to combat crime. What is not clear is whether the low morale within the Watch Dog and the mistrust that has developed between the Watch Dog and the police is a result of the curtailment of the Watch Dog's power and authority by the new Divisional Policing Commander or something else (e.g. lack of funds). From the perspective of Watch Dog members, the new Divisional Policing Commander made it clear that while the Watch Dog could embark on operations without prior police consent under the former Divisional Police Commander, this was no longer tolerated. This directive, in the view of the members, was designed to undermine their enthusiasm to combat crime and in so doing please some politicians who wanted to stop the growing influence of the group.

As noted above, another reason why the relationship between the police and the group was strained was because a new police directive was introduced that requires permission from the police whenever the Watch Dog wishes to undertake operations. However, the element of surprise was one of the Watch Dog's vital strategies, which underpinned their success during the first phase. Having to wait for permission from the police to begin an operation slows down their ability to respond to criminal activity efficiently. For the group's members the slow response of the police to crime is a major contributing factor to the credibility crisis that the Ghana Police Service is currently experiencing. The Watch Dog does not want to undermine the trust that the locals have in them by delays in responding to crimes. They assert that, all too often, they have been able to prevent and arrest suspected criminals because of their surprise and swift response to (potentially) criminal activities.

In addition, they are also able to identify and destroy spiritual powers of criminals. Because of the trust that community members have in them, they have easy access to vital information, which has been extremely helpful in their operations. Their response time is far better and swifter than the police and this partly explains why, in most cases, they have dealt with crime effectively before the police arrives.

Some residents even suspect that some police personnel collude with the criminals and, if prior permission is needed, individual police officers could jeopardize Watch Dog operations by tipping off suspected criminals. When the Watch Dog started arresting drug peddlers, some drug dealers sent a delegation to them to negotiate the terms for peaceful co-habitation. This would have meant that the Watch Dog would not operate where the drug peddlers operate and, in return, the dealers were prepared to pay a monthly fee to the Watch Dog. The Watch Dog members refused the offer. With this and other cases where suspects had been released by the police under suspicious circumstances, some locals suspect that the police can even tip off criminals when the group seeks its prior approval before operations. This kind of police protection of criminals happens at the same time as the police, on other occasions, try to take credit for the arrest of tough criminals that have in fact been apprehended by the Watch Dog alone. What this points to more broadly is that the relationship between the police and the Watch Dog is characterized by both collaboration and competition.

Given the strained relationship between the Watch Dog and the police, the group has decided not to confront the police. Instead, they have withdrawn their services, expecting that criminal activity will rise significantly, which in turn will force the state police to call upon the Watch Dog. Under these circumstances, the Watch Dog will negotiate with the police from a position of authority. However, in discussions with junior and senior police personnel, it became apparent that different police officers have different views on what the roles, responsibilities and powers of such groups should be. This lack of clarity affects the different types of relationship that police personnel have with groups such as the Watch Dog, and also creates the space for politicians to manipulate and define such relationships based on the politicians' overt and covert political interests. The lack of clarity regarding the nature of the relationship between the public police and such groups on the one hand and the boundaries of the powers of community policing groups on the other hand have been explored elsewhere (Ruteere and Pommerolle 2003; Benit-Gbaffou 2008). For instance, Benit-Gbaffou (2008: 95) notes that in post-apartheid South Africa: 'The line between what communities are entitled to do and what they should hand over to the police is very blurred, even more so if norms of social order vary in space and time.'

Apart from the state police, other state institutions also make use of the Watch Dog. For instance, the East Ayawaso Sub-Metropolitan Assembly has requested the Watch Dog to provide its staff with security when serving summons. Prior to this request, the Metropolitan workers could hardly serve summons to those who were violating the Metro Laws regarding unauthorized buildings, rearing cattle and livestock in urban areas, etc. Government workers were often assaulted physically and verbally when they attempted to carry out their lawful duties. The Watch Dog has also helped the Ghana Water Company to identify and arrest those who install illegal water pumps in their homes to avoid paying water bills. The critical role that the Watch Dog has played for these state institutions seems to indicate a reversal of roles or positions of authority in the sense that the statutory bodies and the police rely on the service of a sub-state policing group for security and protection.

Core challenges: politicians and drug barons

Key challenges, apart from low morale because of the attitudes of the public police, come from politicians and drug dealers or barons.

Politicians seem to either want to manipulate the group or undermine their operations. Indeed, in the run-up to the last two general elections in 2008 and 2012, the leadership of the Watch Dog claims that the two major political parties, the National Democratic Congress (NDC) and the New Patriotic Party (NPP), sought to convince them to be affiliated with them, but the Watch Dog declined. What is not entirely clear is why the group flourished and expanded during the era of the NPP, while its powers waned under the NDC. What is instructive is that just after the NDC was declared as winners of the 2008 elections some youth in Nima, regarded by some residents as criminals and deviant youths, celebrated in the streets of Nima and said that the election result meant the end of the Watch Dog (with respect to the leadership of the group, their membership cuts across the various political parties, religious groups and ethnic groups).

During elections, power disputes between the Watch Dog and the state also intensified as politicians from the incumbent party often tried to use the police to stop the Watch Dog from clamping down on hawkers. This is ambivalent, however, because at the same time the politicians want the Watch Dog to fight criminals so that the politicians can take credit for dealing with crimes. Thus, the relationship between the Watch Dog, the state, and national politicians is not static, but changes according to major national events and political changes, particularly evident during general elections.

The strong role played by drug barons in Nima also challenges the work of the Watch Dog. At times this merges with the actions of the police and the interests of politicians. For instance, there were numerous occasions where it appeared that politicians had pressured the police to refrain from prosecuting suspects of drug dealing (in Ghanaian parlance 'make the case die'). This became apparent when the Watch Dog arrested peddlers, who the police had not arrested for a very long time at particular locations in Maamobi. In the words of one of the Watch Dog leaders: 'My friend, we have fought armed robbers and other criminals but none of them are as dangerous as drug barons. They have a very extensive network that reaches the top of society and power.'

The drug dealers – or barons – seem to have instilled some fear in the leadership of the Watch Dog. A leader of the group hinted that some drug dealers, whose peddlers they had arrested, have started to make up lies about the Watch Dog, and link some of its members to acts of armed robbery. Also, the Watch Dog has not been immune to attacks. In fact one of the greatest challenges to the Watch Dog happened on 15 November 2011 when its President was injured by suspected criminals. This attack demystified him and his spiritual charisma and questioned his spiritual fortification. The matter severely tested the Watch Dog's strength and position vis-à-vis criminal networks.

Conclusion

This chapter examines the strategies that a low income and densely populated migrant community such as Nima adopts to provide for their own security and justice needs. By setting up the Watch Dog, Nima has designed a strategy that is sensitive to local views on security and justice. They incorporate spiritual and physical elements into the service they deliver, and emphasize the connection between the two. As such, when the Watch Dog engages with the state, their strategy and sensitivity to local notions of security and justice is not necessarily changed. In sum, a densely populated community such as Nima relies heavily on its own initiative, including local residents and resources as well as a strong sense of community and innovations in addressing its security and justice needs.

If we look at Accra in general there is a wide variety of security arrangements, and not all areas have successful Watch Dog groups. Political connections play a significant role in this regard. In high-income areas such as North Legon, residents are strongly connected to political parties and other socio-economic networks. This makes it relatively easier to access state resources, including services by the public police. Private security is also prevalent, which includes the employment of young men from poor communities to undertake physically dangerous night patrols. Thus, in North Legon not a single person who goes on foot patrol is a resident of the neighbourhood.

In short, where members of a community have strong links with a political party or the public police they, and the communities they represent, are likely to be regarded as a priority area of the Ghana Police Service. Because this is not the case for the low-income neighbourhood of Nima, its residents have had to rely on local proactiveness and self-designed and sensitive methods to meet their justice and security needs. In Nima, one is therefore tempted to conclude that there is an inverse relationship between the wealth of a community or the lack of it and the strength and success of its Watch Dog. The lack of presence and sensitivity of the public police offers a space for low income communities to create other platforms to address their wider security and justice needs based on local perceptions and beliefs.

Notes

1   The data for this paper was mainly gathered over a period of three years in Nima through ethnographic fieldwork. In addition, one of the authors spent time as a volunteer administrative assistant with the Nima Watch Dog and the other spent time working with *Isakaba* during his doctoral research on policing. These experiences exposed them to the structure and modus operandi of the groups.

2   This quote and all other quotes in the text are the authors' own translations from Ga.

3   Interview with a police officer at the headquarters of the Community Policing Section of the Ghana Police Service, 30 August 2013, Accra, Ghana. The officer had worked in this section since its inception.

References

Abraham, R., 1987. 'Sungusungu village vigilante groups in Tanzania', *African Affairs*, 66:343, 179–196.

Adu-Mireku, S., 2002. 'Fear of crime among residents of three communities in Accra, Ghana, *International Journal of Comparative Sociology*, 43:2, 153–168.

Anderson, D. M., 2002. 'Vigilantes, violence and politics of public order in Kenya', *African Affairs*, 101, 531–555.

Aning, K., 2006. 'An overview of the Ghana Police Service', *Journal of Security Sector Management*, 4:2, 1–37.

Baker, B., 2002. 'When the Bakassi Boys came: Eastern Nigeria confronts vigilantism', *Journal of Contemporary African Studies*, 20:2, 1–22.

Baker, B., 2004. 'Protection from crime: What is on offer for Africans', *Journal of Contemporary African Studies*, 22:2, 165–188.

Baker, B., 2006. 'Beyond the state police in urban Uganda and Sierra Leone', *African Spectrum*, 41:1, 55–76.

Baker, B., 2009. 'A policing partnership for post-War Africa? Lessons from Liberia and Southern Sudan', *Policing and Society*, 19:4, 372–389.

Benit-Gbaffou, C., 2008. 'Community policing and disputed norms for local social control in post-apartheid Johannesburg', *Journal of Southern African Studies*, 34, 93–109.

Buur, L. and Jensen, S., 2004. 'Introduction: Vigilantism and the policing of everyday life in South Africa', *African Studies*, 63:2, 139–152.

Loader, I., 2006. 'Policing, recognition, and belonging', *Annals of the American Academy of Political and Social Science*, 605, 202–221.

Ruteere, M. and Pommerolle, M., 2003. 'Democratization security or decentralizing repression? The ambiguities of community policing in Kenya', *African Affairs*, 102, 587–604.

Sen, A. and Pratten, D., 2007. 'Global vigilantism: Perspectives on justice and violence', in David Pratten and Atreyee Sen (eds), *Global Vigilantism*, London: Hurst, 1–24.

Turner, R., 1955. 'Law enforcement by communal action in Sukumaland, Tanganyika territory', *Journal of African Administration*, 7:4, 159–165.

Chapter 6

New authorities

Relating state and non-state security auspices in South African Improvement Districts

Julie Berg with Clifford Shearing

Drawing on the work of the Ostroms (Ostrom, 1987; Ostrom, 1991; Ostrom, 1999a; Ostrom, 1999b; Ostrom, 2001; Ostrom, 2005) and utilising a nodal analysis, research was conducted on an experiment in polycentric governance – that is Improvement Districts in South Africa. The research sought to explore the practices and implications, for security provision or policing, of collaborative governance arrangements with multiple authorities.

The creation of Improvement Districts (IDs) in South Africa has been a deliberate governance strategy aimed at mobilising and integrating state and non-state[1] resources (Shearing and Berg, 2006, p. 191). They have for the most part been pitched in the rhetoric of neoliberalism – through responsibilising citizens and drawing in the corporate sector to streamline government services (Clough and Vanderbeck, 2006). However, empirical studies have found that this is not necessarily how IDs function. Although they were originally developed as a neoliberal strategy employed by the state, they have in some instances developed into something more nuanced and complex, where the state and non-state have intermingling authorities and functions (Berg, 2004; Caruso and Weber, 2006; Morçöl and Patrick, 2006; Morçöl and Zimmermann, 2006a). In other words, as the IDs have become more established the day-to-day practices and decision-making, especially with relation to the provision of security and policing services, have come to push at the boundaries of neoliberal agendas.

In light of this, the aim of the chapter is threefold. First, the chapter seeks to understand how the emergence of new authorities of governance has impacted on security by exploring the nature and operation of policing within the IDs, utilising nodal and polycentric governance theory as analytic and conceptual tools to do so. Second, it makes the argument that IDs constitute a site in which policing authorities are *shifting*, rather than static, thus having implications for order-making in light of effectiveness, regulation and power. Third, it discusses the normative implications of shifting sites of authority that the establishment of IDs entails.

Nodal and polycentric governance theory is associated with the work of Vincent and Elinor Ostrom (see for instance Ostrom, 1999b; Ostrom, 2001) and it is closely aligned to the nodal governance theorists, who focus their work predominantly on the study of security governance. Nodal governance is a conceptual tool used as a framing device to understand the distribution of power of polycentric governance arrangements through exploring the 'mentalities, institutions, technologies and practices' of 'nodes'' (Wood and Shearing, 2007, p. 27). The Ostroms and the nodal theorists argue that no conceptual priority should be given to one node or type of system (monocentric or polycentric), but that this is largely an empirical question depending on the context and considering the empirical reality of governance developments.

Using these analytical and conceptual framings, which do not favour particular nodes, was considered appropriate to allow the empirical realities of ID functioning to speak for themselves. This is in light of the fact that international research is divided in terms of how IDs operate. Some claim that they are merely a part of government or 'nested' in them and function like public administration systems (Caruso and Weber, 2006, p. 189; Morçöl and Zimmermann, 2006b; Wolf, 2006). Others have described IDs as 'neo-liberalism personified' (Ward, 2006, p. 68). Others again argue that IDs are in fact more nuanced than this. As such, they represent complex sites of 'active networked governance' and that they are active 'participants in metropolitan governance' (Morçöl and Patrick, 2006, p. 162).

It was in fact found through research conducted on the IDs by one of the authors that IDs are polycentric formations with multiple sites of authority. Polycentric governance formations are defined as 'self-organizing and self-governing' (Ostrom, 1991, p. 18). They are 'adaptive' systems where there is a multiplicity of autonomous rule-enforcing auspices (which can be state or non-state) (Ostrom, 1999a, p. 493). These auspices may operate at different scales, they may be of different sizes, and of different degrees of specialisation but their jurisdictions overlap (Ostrom, 1999a; Ostrom, 2001; Ostrom, 2005). They are, in other words, sites of multiple, independent authorities that take account of each other (Ostrom, 1991).

However, it was also found that not only are there multiple independent authorities within the IDs but that authorities within the IDs are constantly shifting from node to node – whether state or non-state. What follows is a closer look at what IDs are through a focus on the rationale for their formation, the process of their establishment and how they operate. The purpose of which is to explore how and why they are polycentric formations constituted by shifting sites of authority, and furthermore to discuss the implications of this, especially in terms of their impact on order-making and security governance practices.

New authorities: the emergence and operation of Improvement Districts

IDs are non-profit, public–private corporations that have been created by (local) government as a supplement to local government services through the collection from property owners of additional or 'top-up' taxes (Briffault, 1999). There is also usually a petition process involved in their formation and they operate in localised, demarcated urban spaces (Wolf, 2006). These spaces may be relatively small, usually only a few city blocks and may be commercial–industrial areas or a mix of commercial–residential areas (Briffault, 1999; Wolf, 2006). However, an important characteristic of IDs is that they alone manage their budgets and, furthermore, their budgets are ring-fenced for ID use and spaces only (Vindevogel, 2005).

The types of services IDs may provide as a top-up to what local government is already providing may include, for instance: consumer marketing; advocacy; maintenance (cleansing and lighting); parking control; social services; public safety and security; and/or 'streetscaping' – making public spaces more access-ible and attractive (Morçöl and Zimmermann, 2006a; Wolf, 2006; Lippert, 2007, p. 37). In order to achieve these functions, they may hire their own personnel (such as private security companies and/or cleaning staff) and they are responsible for the day-to-day management of the ID space (Vindevogel, 2005). IDs are generally held accountable to local government through having to report on activities and spending, however, the nature of this relationship is dependent on context (Caruso and Weber, 2006; Meek and Hubler, 2006; Wolf, 2006). IDs are attractive because their localism and relatively small size have been seen as advantageous as they can provide 'efficient, innovative and responsive' service delivery (Garodnick, 2000; Caruso and Weber, 2006, p. 189; Ward, 2006).

IDs are seen to be more effective, since they avoid the 'free rider' problem.[2] This is because, once the majority of ratepayers in the proposed ID vote for its establishment, it is compulsory for *all* in that ID to pay the top-up rates whether or not they opposed its establishment (Briffault, 1999; Lippert, 2007). Thus, the main motivation for their establishment seems to be due to the economic, and subsequent political benefits they provide, as local government, which is constrained fiscally and capacity-wise, can draw in the private sector to contribute towards the revitalisation of urban spaces (Clough and Vanderbeck 2006; Ward 2006). In other words, the non-state sector is brought in to provide extra services, whereas the state (in theory) indirectly maintains its role as auspice or meta-regulator (Loader and Walker, 2006).

South African developments: national and local legislation[3]

In South Africa there were a range of immediate drivers that resulted in the ID initiative being adopted at a local level. One of the main reasons was the problems faced in the central cities – that is, declining property values, high crime and grime, fiscal constraints and so forth (Didier *et al.*, 2012). This, too, impacted on the adoption of the IDs with the main impetus for the adoption of the ID initiative largely coming from the private sector in collaboration with what Didier *et al.* (2012, p. 8) call 'technopoliticians' – public officials who straddle the public–private divide. As a result of collaboration between these public officials and the private sector, South Africa's first ID was established in the city of Pretoria in 1999, with many cities following suit in 2000 and 2001.

South African IDs are mandated by national legislation in the form of the Local Government Municipal Property Rates Act or MPRA (2004). What follows is a brief synopsis of what this Act entails as it pertains to IDs; this is followed by a case study of Cape Town legislation.

The MPRA makes provision for local government to establish IDs or ' special rating areas' and so to levy and collect additional rates in those areas.[4] Before doing this, however, the MPRA stipulates that the municipality first has to 'consult the local community' securing the consent of the majority of the members of the community who reside in the proposed ID and who would have to pay the additional rates.[5] Thus, consultations would have to take place with respect to proposed ID boundaries and the intended means to improve or upgrade the area.[6] Once these decisions have been approved and confirmed with the community, local government is then mandated to 'establish separate accounting and other record-keeping systems' with regards to collecting the top-up rates from the ratepayers in that area.[7] The MPRA also makes provision for the establishment of 'a consultative and advisory forum' – the purpose of which is to enable representatives from the ID to give input with respect to the proposed improvements for the area.[8]

The facilitating legislation above is applicable to all local governments/ municipalities in South Africa of which there are approximately 290 (Cooperative Governance and Traditional Affairs, 2009). Each municipality is entitled to establish its own by-law with regards to the setting up of IDs or special rating areas. In light of this, rather than outline the by-laws of all the municipalities in South Africa that have adopted the ID initiative, the normative framework that enables the establishment of special rating areas in the City of Cape Town will serve as a case study:

There have been a number of amended by-laws in Cape Town for the establishment of IDs. The latest version is the 2012 *Special Rating Area By-Law* and *Special Rating Area Policy 2012/13*. According to the *Special Rating Area Policy 2012/13* the main purpose of the IDs is to top up municipal services for the purposes of 'improving or upgrading the area'.[9] The *Special Ratings Area By-law 2012* outlines the procedure for the establishment of an ID and is akin to the MPRA mentioned above in that it creates a process of consultation (public meetings for instance) in the establishment of an ID. This process may be lengthy, with international research indicating that it can take anywhere from sixteen months to five years, depending on context (Briffault, 1999).

In order for an ID to be established, a property owner within an area has to make an application to the City.[10] The application has to be in writing and include a five-year business plan (which includes a motivation report, implementation plan and term budget) as well as the written consent of the majority of property owners in the proposed ID.[11] In order to obtain this written consent, a notice must be sent out to inform all property owners (within the proposed ID) of the intention to apply for an ID and the fact that they would be liable for extra payment for the ID, as well as invite property owners to a public meeting.[12] The purpose of the public meeting is to allow for a consultative process, thus giving an opportunity for property owners to voice dissatisfaction with the proposal.[13] If there is general agreement for their establishment, then the public meeting can provide the opportunity for property owners within the proposed ID area to decide on the boundaries of the ID.[14] An application is made to the City and the applicant then has to publish a notice of the application as well as a written notice of application to all the property owners within the proposed ID.[15] Those opposing the application have a period of time in which to submit written objections to the establishment of an ID.[16] The City, after receiving all written objections, makes a decision with respect to approving or denying the application.[17]

If approved, the ID would have to elect a management body to carry out the business plan – the management body is essentially a not-for-profit company.[18] Depending on the size of the ID, its needs and the resources at its disposal (how much income per annum it retrieves from the ratepayers in its area) this 'company' may consist of, for instance, a general manager, a security manager, a marketing consultant and/or a manager in charge of cleansing if this is separated from the security manager role. In most cases a service level agreement is signed with the City, in which the City agrees to provide its usual services in the ID with the ID management body allocating staff to top up these services using the additional levies paid by the ratepayers.

It is the duty of the City to act as meta-regulator through ensuring that the management body of the ID complies with the provisions of the City by-law and policy.[19] A city councillor must also be elected to sit on the ID management meetings, but does not have voting rights.[20] At the end of each financial year, the management body of the ID is required to submit audited financial statements and an annual report to the City as well as to the sub-council of the city in their area.[21] It is also up to the City to levy the additional rates on owners of rateable property in the ID which the City is then responsible for collecting 'in the same manner as other property rates imposed by the City'.[22] The City then pays this amount over to the management body of the ID to carry out its implementation plans.[23] This is, however, subject to a finance agreement between the two entities.

The by-law does not stipulate the time period of the ID's existence. But by implication, allowing an ID to extend the time period of its implementation every fifth year, suggests that the ID is established for a five-year term, subject to possibly limitless renewals. In the case of Cape Town, it seems that an ID comes to an end through mutual decision as an ID can be dissolved 'for any good cause' as prompted by an application from the ID property owners or by the City *on consultation* with the management body of the ID for it to be 'wound up'.[24] However, according to Briffault (1999), there are few IDs that are dissolved before their time period is up or otherwise, since, it may be difficult to disband it, as Garodnick (2000) has suggested – for a variety of reasons, both practical and political. For instance, a fiscally constrained state may become economically dependent on IDs to provide service delivery and be unable to replace ID services should they be disbanded. Similarly, because of the financial gain of business (and other powerful groups) within the ID spaces, the state may face undue political pressure from lobbyists if they were to attempt to disband them.

In practice, the main emphasis for the majority of IDs in South Africa is on security provision due to the fact that crime rates are high and it is therefore a focal concern of many of the IDs. What follows is a description of how policing is undertaken within ID spaces.

Policing in the IDs: whose authority?

A direct engagement with security in their spaces necessarily means that for IDs to succeed they have to network with other security bodies, both directly or indirectly, contributing to safety (or unsafety) in their areas. What is also apparent is that by introducing private security into public spaces, the IDs have changed the dynamics of public ordering in those spaces and defined an order that sometimes complements, sometimes conflicts with these other security agencies. The IDs gain legal authority from the normative framework, as discussed, and at a local level, the private security companies contracted by them exhibit both a symbolic authority as well as legal authority in terms of the fact that they may act on the rights granted to every citizen to protect him/herself through the Criminal Procedure Act.[25]

The real power of the IDs, however, comes from their ability to enrol others (Braithwaite and Drahos, 2000). It is the very fact that they have limited policing powers compared to the state that has forced them to engage with, and enrol, state agencies in order to conduct their own business. Their security focus may be at once very narrowly engaged with criminal activity in their spaces or very broad in the sense that all things taking place in their spaces are potentially linked to safety issues.

In support of this approach, private security in many IDs has been tasked and paid by the IDs to conduct visible patrols and monitor any signs of disorder – whether physical or social. These are reported to the ID security manager who then takes it further with the relevant authorities (usually the City). Private security guards patrolling IDs in many respects have become the 'eyes and ears' of the ID through their record-keeping of security risks and signs of disorder. Those responsible for ensuring that the reported incidences are attended to (whether it is the City or one of the state police agencies) are then held accountable by the ID and follow-up is constantly done to ensure that the incidences are in fact attended to. For example, one of the IDs indicated that the City has a week to respond to its complaint, after which the ID security will again monitor what has and has not been done and follow up with the City again. The City is consequently enrolled in the intricacies of local level ID security.

Private security plays a monitoring and crime prevention role within the IDs with a strong emphasis on visible patrolling. They – both IDs and the private security they hire – tend to be very proactive and may sponsor equipment to the state police and/or community organisations involved in patrolling. Unlike in other neighbourhoods, private security companies contracted by the ID do not engage in armed reaction because it is not considered part of the ID's responsibility. Their duties are heavily focused on issues around urban management – by-law enforcement, parking infringements, petty crime and grime issues. Serious crimes and specialist policing activities are not part of their mandate although they may play a peripheral supportive role to the South African Police Service (SAPS), as a force-multiplier to high-level operations and events.

There is also the acknowledgement that private security companies working in the IDs have taken on a special role in that they work in public spaces whereas other private security companies are usually responsible for private spaces (such as private buildings for instance). The management of one ID involved in the research acknowledged that it has 'made it [their] business' to liaise with 'private space' security and so ensure open communication (by means of radio communication) with them as 'public space' security providers.[26] The IDs and contracted security may also play a consultative role in light of the fact that they spend a lot of time on the streets getting to know the needs of the ID 'community' (ID ratepayers and those entering the ID spaces).

There appears to be a good level of cooperation among the various security and policing role-players in many ID areas and many of those interviewed agreed that the introduction of the ID initiative has been a positive development particularly in terms of the improvement of relationships among those involved in security provision and security-related services. It is also clear that relationships between private security and SAPS are particularly well-functioning in these areas – some describing their relationship with SAPS as excellent. The private security companies contracted by the IDs acknowledge that they are merely a 'top-up' service to SAPS and that they cannot conduct their affairs properly (or legally) without the support from the primary security service providers (Metropolitan Police Service or MPS, and SAPS) – the IDs do not and cannot function in isolation from, or outside of, state policing if they are to engage with law enforcement related activities.

This ties in with their emphasis on crime prevention – due to limited powers it is much easier for private security to prevent crime than to try and react to crime. Similarly, private security guards on patrol rely on the presence of City law enforcement personnel or MPS to assist in the enforcement of by-laws, since private security companies do not have the authority to issue fines or deal with by-law offences on their own. They may hold the suspect or evidence until SAPS or the MPS arrives but cannot take the matter further than this.[27] However, this is only when their duties overlap into the duties of others, since as mentioned, they have a much broader mandate than simply law enforcement.

They have therefore shaped enrolment practices because of the fact that they require the support of state agencies to fulfil their mandate. In other words, it is necessary for the IDs to shape the behaviour of these institutions to get them to cooperate and improve their service delivery within ID areas. In this way enrolment of the state is taking place in terms of behaviour modification but it cannot be thought of as a top-down, centralised, authoritative enrolment as conventionally understood. At times it is subtle, collaborative and networked but nevertheless effective in many instances – effective, in terms of the success of the IDs (in comparison to non-IDs) in getting the state to address its needs. For example, by providing resources the private security companies may engage in joint operations with SAPS and MPS (such as raids and road blocks), engage in regular meetings and joint forums, share radio communications and may also play other types of supportive roles, such as filling in paperwork for SAPS.

Because of the adaptability and dependability of private security it is usually the case that SAPS will respond immediately to calls from private security – knowing that the call will be legitimate and that private security would have possibly eased the burden by filling in the relevant paperwork. This development of good relations with SAPS is a conscious enrolment strategy deployed by private security to get SAPS to respond to their needs, making them in turn more responsive to their client needs. For instance, according to one private security company interviewed, donating radios to SAPS was a method of enrolment as it was seen as a way 'to keep the police'.[28]

What is clear is that SAPS do not and cannot embody all the knowledges and capacities needed to ensure the levels of safety and security desired in the IDs.[29] Private security has extended the knowledge base of the state police, with the ID increasing the number of sources and sites of knowledge as well as linking nodes to each other and to particular problems. Some of the IDs make use of, not only private security to monitor and prevent, but also cleaners and parking marshals to act as further 'eyes and ears'. Thus, security can come from everywhere, through private security guards, parking marshals or cleaning staff.[30]

The IDs have thus actively created local linkages between various nodes where there were possibly none before and may coordinate the activities of a range of different players dependent on the particular issue or need. It may be argued therefore that IDs create new networks of security through their enrolment of key state and non-state nodes and aligning them to local issues that need attention. The IDs may sometimes act as coordinators of these networks and sometimes one node among many – again, depending on the context and issue to be addressed. Furthermore, in research conducted by one of the authors, it was found that in some IDs, the local Community Police

Forums (CPFs) – initially developed by the newly-formed democratic government to promote good relations and systems of oversight between SAPS and
the community – are used as the space in which this coordination and network-
building takes place.

IDs have developed as network coordinators through the circumstances in
which they operate (for instance their lack of formal policing powers or mandate
to resolve issues directly, or at all), thereby gaining power through their ability
to be adaptive; through constantly looking for (networking) opportunities to
resolve their client's issues; and through enrolment practices. As one private
security representative in an ID commented: 'We have to adapt, we have to be
proactive . . . we have to network.'[31]

The IDs have thus perpetuated a 'whole-of-society' response to security in
the ID spaces through drawing in essential nodes (in the CPFs or through joint
security meetings) to engage with diverse issues of spatial ordering (Shearing,
2008, p. 4). In other words, the IDs may use CPF spaces or sites of networking
to mediate or act as a conduit for the regulation of nodes – seeing to it that
each node carries out its functions. However, as mentioned, the site of
coordination may shift, with state nodes sometimes taking the lead.

It is clear that within the IDs there are multiple authorities of governance.
These authorities or auspices are interdependent on each other to resolve
security issues within the ID, but nevertheless can operate as independent
nodes. This challenges conventional understandings of neoliberalism where
there is one authority meant to coordinate multiple service providers. What
follows is a discussion of the implications of having multiple, shifting sites of
authority.

Implications of polycentric security governance

There are three major implications of polycentric security governance in terms
of the impact it has on effectiveness (whether or not effectiveness is improved);
the way in which regulation functions within polycentric formations (whether
or not it is enhanced or undermined); and the impacts of non-state power on
democratic governance and the equitable delivery of security.

Effectiveness of polycentric formations

Local crime statistics (notwithstanding its flaws), confirmation from virtually
all interviewed and general appearances of ID spaces, seem to suggest that IDs
are effective in improving the urban management of the spaces in which they
operate – at least more effective than sites without IDs (testimony to this is the
increasing popularity of IDs). The IDs undoubtedly fulfil a gap and contribute
in a unique way, as do the other nodes in the arrangement.

However, much of their activities are duplications of what is already provided
by a variety of other institutions. They provide additional cleansing to the

cleansing already provided by the City. They provide additional monitoring of law enforcement issues to that already provided by the SAPS and MPS. They provide additional parking control to that already provided by the City and so forth. In this polycentric arrangement, there are multiple authorities with duplicating functions or technologies of governance. That is, there exist multiple, shifting authorities exhibiting sometimes unique, sometimes over-lapping ways of thinking and doing security, resulting in a security landscape that is not dominated completely by one node.

The IDs may buy into state technologies usually epitomised by a punishment-orientated, backward-looking approach to crime (although this caricature is and has been changing). But their active monitoring and bobby-on-the-beat approach to security also brings into play the traditional ways in which private security conducts its business – through a risk management approach due to its desire and need to address a range of insecurity issues, not only crime issues (Johnston and Shearing, 2003).

If one node dominated the arrangement there would only be a focus on one technology of governance. Given the complexities of social disorder (especially public space issues of urban spaces management, by-law enforcement and petty crime and grime issues) and the challenges faced in policing South African cities in particular, a one-size-fits-all approach is inappropriate. And as it has been argued, security is best delivered when the diverse knowledges and capacities of a range of nodes are harnessed within a 'whole-of-society' approach – hence the effectiveness of the IDs (Johnston and Shearing, 2003). In other words, having multiple, overlapping and shifting authorities builds in redundancy which improves effectiveness:

> Instead of being a major detriment to system performance, redundancy builds in considerable capabilities. If there is only one governance unit for a very large geographic area, the failure of that unit to respond adequately to external threats may mean a very large disaster for the entire system. If there are multiple governance units, organized at different levels for the same geographic region, the failure of one or more of these units to respond to external threats may lead to small-scale disasters that may be compensated by the successful reaction of other units in the system.
>
> (Ostrom, 2001, p. 4)

Even though there may be weak players, and the research confirms that there are in fact weak nodes (such as the MPS or the SAPS), the polycentric nature of interaction means that the weakness of one is offset by the duplicating activities of another as the player(s) shifts from one node to the other.

Regulation as enhanced within polycentric formations

In terms of regulation,[32] polycentricity may be able to counter unequal and potentially abusive authority vested in a single source (Ostrom, 1999b, p. 55).

The multiplicity of sites of governance is arranged in such a way so that 'each may be a check on the other' (Ostrom, 1987, p. 37). This largely seems to be the case in the IDs. The IDs, as mentioned, assert authority in public spaces through enrolling others to meet their defined standards of safety and cleanliness, predominantly through information-gathering, donations, knowledge transfer, negotiation and inter-institutional conversations at all levels of the state and non-state.

They may also resort to more formalised systems of enrolment in their insistence that a service level agreement be signed with the City – this is as much a tool for IDs to enrol the City than anything else, as it is often used to ensure that the City performs the services it is meant to perform. The IDs in turn are regulated by the rate payers of the area and consider themselves accountable to them as well as morally accountable to the entire community in terms of their duty to perform the services assigned to them – reducing crime and grime. It is inevitable that they will themselves be the subject of oversight due to the fact that they 'do the ugly business end of dealing with anti-social behaviour'.[33] As a result, they have to remain financially open and transparent through regular meetings and frequent communication to all their stakeholders and all affected by their activities (including the broader public who spend time in the IDs, for work or for leisure).

There is also control over the IDs by the City, which can as mentioned, in theory, have them revoked at any stage. There is the understanding that, because they engage in the provision of security, the consequences of not doing this properly are even more pronounced than any other type of service delivery. It is more difficult to remain accountable when the quality of security service they provide is difficult to specify, unlike cleansing, for instance, which is quantifiably measurable (Freeman, 2006). They acknowledge the primary role that the state police plays and see themselves as accountable to them as well, especially in light of the fact that SAPS can at any time 'freeze [them] out' should they transgress the law.[34] However, the IDs and their ratepayers in turn can hold SAPS accountable, as indicated by the quote below:

> I mean business [or ratepayers] will soon notice if SAPS pulls out or doesn't do what they have claimed or promised to do, [ID] security personnel pick that up within five minutes, report it back to the business community and business community will say 'hang on, its not good enough'. It is a two-way accountability.[35]

The IDs also regulate the private security companies contracted to them – due to the nature of the contractual arrangement. Consider the following quote by an ID representative:

> We've had a couple [of complaints about the private security company the ID contracts with] ... so we feed the challenge back to the security company through their management and then leave it for a week or so,

keep track of it, and then find out what they've done about it and if it's a fairly challenging situation we will request immediate removal of that particular person, that's normally done within twenty four hours and then we get somebody else in. And it's that simple, so they're gone.[36]

This is not to say that this complex 'circular' accountability in place is necessarily watertight in practice, but it is to say that polycentricity seems to have created systems of informal regulation and gives effect to formal regulation (Braithwaite, 2002). That is, the IDs act out on the City's reneging of its duties, whereas individuals or non-ID communities may not have the capacity, inclination or motivation to do so.

Power disparities and inequitable security provision

IDs are hybrid bodies of governance; they are 'intertwined' with business and with government (Morçöl and Wolf, 2010). IDs have political power and voice: they 'can unduly influence the political system' and can be 'powerful enough to play important, and at times, controversial roles in urban politics' (Meek and Hubler, 2006, p. 48; Morçöl and Wolf, 2010). For instance, in Cape Town, a previous manager of the Cape Town Partnership was known as the 'unofficial mayor of Cape Town' (Miraftab, 2007, p. 613). So too in New York the president of the Grand Central Partnership was accused of 'creating his own fiefdom' by Mayor Rudy Giuliani (Morçöl and Wolf, 2010, p. 907).

IDs may also influence state policing on the ground and result in by-laws being (overly) enforced in ID areas, which impacts on the homeless (Garodnick, 2000). In this vein, IDs have been accused of undemocratic practices. In fact the very nature of how IDs operate is problematic: that they raise money from ratepayers in a *defined* space and that money is *ring-fenced* for spending *only* in ID areas. This means that only those who can afford IDs will be able to create them and will benefit the most from them. IDs thus create inequities in service delivery and challenge a fundamental anti-Apartheid tenet – 'one city, one tax base' or in an American context 'one person, one vote' – which seeks to address inequalities in service provision between formerly black and white communities (Garodnick, 2000; Didier *et al.*, 2012).

IDs obviously challenge this since additional taxes raised by comparatively wealthier suburbs (which usually correlate with formerly white areas) means that service provision is better in these spaces than in poorer areas that cannot afford ID rates. IDs have thus been accused of aggravating the problem of class-based fragmentation and socially polarised urban spaces in light of South Africa's history of racial/spatial segregation (Lemanski, 2007). In keeping with the transformation and image-building of public spaces, IDs have been accused of attempting to remove anything or anyone preventing that transformation or affecting the image of the ID – that is, the (forced or abusive) removal of 'undesirables' (Garodnick, 2000; Ward, 2006).

It is clear that, despite systems of democratic participation and input (as outlined by the SRA By-law above), it is difficult to ensure equal participation within communities. Some actors are more politically powerful than others and within mixed-use IDs for instance, the interests of big business may trump community needs. Inequalities may be created both within and outside of the IDs. Thus the ID as a security auspice may cause certain security threats, becoming prioritised through enrolling others and may therefore challenge the political authority of other (state) structures.

Conclusion

This chapter sought to describe policing within IDs as polycentric formations. The chapter began by defining what IDs are, the reasons for their adoption, and – using Cape Town as a case study – the normative framework that regulates their creation and operation. The chapter then described the policing practices undertaken within the IDs and found that the non-state enrols the state in order to fulfil its functions. The non-state also acts as a coordinator of new networks of security governance and promotes a whole-of-society approach to security. However, coordination may shift from node to node. It was found that shifting sites of authority improves the effectiveness of IDs and enhances regulation but that IDs, as polycentric formations, deepen power disparities and the inequitable delivery of security.

This chapter's focus on IDs begs the normative question about the democratic functioning of polycentric systems. The IDs may be effective, but effective for whom? They may be more regulated, but as Braithwaite (1999) reminds us, being accountable to others does not make one necessarily responsible for one's actions. That being the case, the question then becomes how to strengthen weak forms of regulation to ensure that the interests of an elite few do not trump security for the public good?

Scholars have thus engaged with polycentric systems to reflect on possible ways in which these systems could promote public goods in an equitable and democratic manner. In other words, how to govern in a polycentric way to promote the public interest and allow for democratic participation in new and novel ways so that the weak are politically empowered (Braithwaite, 2006). Gunningham (2008) for instance, has sought to identify features that need to be present for new forms of governance to function democratically – features such as participatory dialogue, local-level decision-making as well as inclusiveness and transparency. Others, such as Loader and Walker (2007), propose a means of tying new governance to these norms through a 'state-anchored' approach and argue that the state alone has sufficient capacity and resources to coordinate or anchor complex security governance arrangements. They argue that the state is the only node capable of bringing in a 'civilizing' function.

However, given the general blurring of nodes and functions – the hybrid nature of the IDs, the divergence of mentalities and technologies of governance and the political power demonstrated by the IDs and all within it – does it make sense to attempt to analytically separate 'state' from 'non-state'? In response to this question, many reject giving conceptual priority to the state to democratically anchor or regulate non-state nodes given the fact that the non-state may display political and sovereign power, as discussed. The challenge remains in finding a way in which security is enhanced and provided democratically and equitably while making use of a diversity of state and non-state knowledges, capacities and resources to achieve this.

Notes

1 Scholars conducting empirical work on the nature of security governance have increasingly found the terms 'private' and 'public' to be inadequate when describing the intermingled activities of the government, the business sector or that of communities (see for instance, Baker, 2004). Scholars have been left with the residual terms 'state' and 'non-state' to differentiate between various governance auspices and providers. However, these terms are also problematic in that they create a dichotomous reference to entities that are increasingly blurred in their mandates, activities and resources. Given the empirical reality of the blurring of the 'state' and 'non-state', these terms are used in this chapter as a heuristic device to refer to entities governing security in the IDs. State entities include the South African Police Service (SAPS), the Metropolitan Police Service (MPS) and the City of Cape Town. Non-state entities include ID management bodies, private security companies, property owners and ratepayers in the IDs.
2 Where someone benefits from the provision of services or goods but does not pay for it.
3 The empirical analysis in this paper is based on field research in Cape Town and to a lesser extent Johannesburg. Material gathered in 2002, 2006 and 2007 includes interviews with security analysts, police officers and security personnel, urban/ID managers, and other actors involved in policing and IDs in and around Cape Town.
4 Local Government Municipal Property Rates Act 2004. s.22(1)(a) and (b).
5 Local Government Municipal Property Rates Act 2004. s.2(a) and (b).
6 Local Government Municipal Property Rates Act 2004. s.2(a)(i) and (ii).
7 Local Government Municipal Property Rates Act 2004. s.3.
8 Local Government Municipal Property Rates Act 2004. s.3(ii).
9 Special Rating Areas Policy 2012/2013. s.5.1.
10 Special Rating Area By-law 2012. s.4(1).
11 Special Rating Area By-law 2012. s.4(3)(c)(ii) and 6(1).
12 Special Rating Area By-law 2012. s.5(1) and 5(3)(a).
13 Special Rating Area By-law 2012. s.5(2) and 5(7)(b).
14 Special Rating Area By-law 2012. s.5(2).
15 Special Rating Area By-law 2012. s.7(1)(a) and (b).
16 Special Rating Area By-law 2012. s.7(2) – (5).
17 Special Rating Area By-law 2012. s.8.
18 Special Rating Area By-law 2012. s.11(1) and (2).
19 Special Rating Area By-law 2012. s.11(3).
20 Special Rating Area By-law 2012. s.11(4).
21 Special Rating Area By-law 2012. s.11(7) and (8).

22 Special Rating Area By-law 2012. s.12(4).
23 Special Rating Area By-law 2012. s.12(5).
24 Special Rating Area By-law 2012. s.16(1)(a) and (b).
25 The Criminal Procedure Act 1977 equips private security personnel with the power to, for instance, arrest without a warrant, use force, if necessary, to affect this arrest, break open premises and so forth.
26 ID Executive Manager. 2006. Interviewed by Ricky Röntsch, Research Assistant, Centre of Criminology, University of Cape Town. Cape Town, 6 October.
27 This is seen as being a major obstacle to many of the private security companies and IDs involved in the research.
28 Private security company representative. 2006. Interviewed by Ricky Röntsch. Cape Town, 19 October.
29 See: Loader, I. and Walker, N., 2007. *Civilizing security*. Cambridge: Cambridge University Press.
30 One interviewee commented on the amount of information that originates from the cleaning staff in that particular ID.
31 Private security company representative. 2002. Interviewed by Julie Berg. Cape Town, 10 April.
32 By regulation we mean what happens 'when obligations are not being honoured' and which may thus involve holding others to account for their actions and attempting to modify their behaviour (Braithwaite, 2002, p. x; Black, 2003).
33 Cape Town City Councilor. 2007. Interviewed by Julie Berg. Cape Town, 9 May.
34 Cape Town Partnership. 2007. Interviewed by Julie Berg. Cape Town, 22 March.
35 Cape Town Partnership. 2007. Interviewed by Julie Berg. Cape Town, 22 March.
36 ID manager. 2006. Interviewed by Ricky Röntsch. Cape Town, 12 October.

References

Baker, B., 2004. Multi-choice policing in Africa: Is the continent following the South Africa pattern? *Society in Transition*, 35:2, 204–223.

Berg, J., 2004. Private policing in South Africa: The Cape Town City Improvement District – pluralisation in practice. *Society in Transition*, 35:2, 224–250.

Black, J., 2003. Enrolling actors in regulatory systems: Examples from UK Financial Services regulation. *Public Law*, Spring issue, 63–91.

Braithwaite, J., 1999. Accountability and governance under the New Regulatory State. *Australian Journal of Public Administration*, 58:1, 90–97.

Braithwaite, J., 2002. *Restorative Justice and Responsive Regulation*. New York: Oxford University Press.

Braithwaite, J., 2006. Responsive regulation and developing economies. *World Development*, 34:5, 884–898.

Braithwaite, J. and Drahos, P., 2000. *Global Business Regulation*. Cambridge: Cambridge University Press.

Briffault, R., 1999. A government for our time? Business Improvement Districts and urban governance. *Colombia Law Review*, 99, 365–477.

Caruso, G. and Weber, R., 2006. Getting the max for tax: An examination of BID performance measures. *International Journal of Public Administration*, 29, 187–219.

Clough, N. and Vanderbeck, R., 2006. Managing politics and consumption in Business Improvement Districts: The geographies of political activism on Burlington, Vermont's Church Street Marketplace. *Urban Studies*, 43:12, 2261–2284.

Didier, S., Peyroux, E. and Morange, M., 2012. The spreading of the City Improvement District model in Johannesburg and Cape Town: Urban regeneration and the neoliberal agenda in South Africa. *International Journal of Urban and Regional Research*, March issue, 1–21.

Freeman, J., 2006. Extending public accountability through privatization: From public law to publicization, in M. Dowdle (ed.), *Public Accountability: Designs, Dilemmas and Experiences*. Cambridge: Cambridge University Press, 83–111.

Garodnick, D., 2000. What's the BID deal? Can the Grand Central Business Improvement District serve a special limited purpose? *University of Pennsylvania Law Review*, 148:5, 1733–1770.

Gunningham, N., 2008. *The New Collaborative Environmental Governance*. Regulatory Institutions Network: Australian National University.

Johnston, L. and Shearing, C., 2003. *Governing Security: Explorations in Policing and Justice*. London: Routledge.

Lemanski, C., 2007. Global cities in the South: Deepening social and spatial polarisation in Cape Town. *Cities*, 24:6, 448–461.

Lippert, R., 2007. Urban revitalization, security, and knowledge transfer: The case of broken windows and kiddie bars. *Canadian Journal of Law and Society*, 22:2, 29–53.

Loader, I. and Walker, N., 2006. Necessary virtues: The legitimate place of the state in the production of security, in J. Wood and B. Dupont (eds), *Democracy, Society and the Governance of Security*. Cambridge: Cambridge University Press, 165–195.

Loader, I. and Walker, N., 2007. *Civilizing Security*. Cambridge: Cambridge University Press.

Meek, J. and Hubler, P., 2006. Business improvement districts in southern California: Implications for local governance, *International Journal of Public Administration*, 29, 31–52.

Miraftab, F., 2007. Governing post Apartheid spatiality: Implementing City Improvement Districts in Cape Town. *Antipode*, 39:4, 602–626.

Morçöl, G. and Patrick, P., 2006. Business Improvement Districts in Pennsylvania: Implications for democratic metropolitan governance. *International Journal of Public Administration*, 29, 137–171.

Morçöl, G. and Zimmerman, U., 2006a. Metropolitan governance and Business Improvement Districts. *International Journal of Public Administration*, 29, 5–29.

Morçöl, G. and Zimmermann, U., 2006b. Community Improvement Districts in metropolitan Atlanta. *International Journal of Public Administration*, 29, 77–105.

Morçöl, G. and Wolf, J., 2010. Understanding business improvement districts: A new governance framework. *Public Administration Review*, November/December issue, 906–913.

Ostrom, V., 1987. *The Political Theory of a Compound Republic: Designing the American Experiment*. Rev. ed. Lincoln: University of Nebraska Press.

Ostrom, V., 1991. *The Meaning of American Federalism: Constituting a Self-Governing Society*. San Francisco, CA: Institute for Contemporary Studies.

Ostrom, E., 1999a. Coping with tragedies of the commons. *Annual Review of Political Science*, 2, 493–535.

Ostrom, V., 1999b. Polycentricity (Part 1), in M. McGinnis (ed.), 1999. *Polycentricity and Local Public Economies: Readings from the Workshop in Political Theory and Policy Analysis*. Ann Arbor, MI: University of Michigan Press, 52–74.

Ostrom, E., 2001. *Vulnerability and Polycentric Governance Systems*. Newsletter of the International Human Dimensions Programme on Global Environmental Change, 3.

Ostrom, E., 2005. *Understanding Institutional Diversity*. Princeton, NJ: Princeton University Press.

Shearing, C., 2008. Making South Africans safe: Possibilities and prospects. *Acta Criminologica Conference Special Edition*, 1, 1–11.

Shearing, C. and Berg, J., 2006. South Africa, in T. Jones and T. Newburn (eds), *Plural Policing: A Comparative Perspective*. Oxon: Routledge, 190–221.

Vindevogel, F., 2005. Private security and urban crime mitigation: A bid for BIDs. *Criminal Justice*, 5:3, 233–255.

Ward, K., 2006. 'Policies in motion', urban management and state restructuring: The trans-local expansion of Business Improvement Districts. *International Journal of Urban and Regional Research*, 30, 54–75.

Wolf, J., 2006. Urban governance and Business Improvement Districts: The Washington, DC BIDs. *International Journal of Public Administration*, 29, 53–75.

Wood, J. and Shearing, C., 2007. *Imagining Security*. Cullompton: Willan.

Legislation and policy:

Cooperative Governance and Traditional Affairs, 2009. *State of Local Government in South Africa: Overview Report: National State of Local Government Assessments*. Pretoria: Cooperative Governance and Traditional Affairs.

Criminal Procedure Act 1977. Pretoria: Government Printers.

Local Government Municipal Property Rates Act 2004. Pretoria: Government Printers.

Special Ratings Area By-Law 2012. Cape Town: City of Cape Town.

Special Ratings Area Policy 2012/13. Cape Town: City of Cape Town.

Chapter 7

Security assemblages at the urban margins of Mexico City[1]

Markus-Michael Müller

Most political orders in the Global South are characterized by the fact that not one institution monopolizes the means of violence or a de facto sovereign position to do so. This has important consequences for a core element that stands at the heart of most forms of political order: The provision of security as well as the containment/regulation of internal violence and conflict.[2] In the absence of a monopolistic sovereign power, practices of violence, security provision as well as conflict resolution and order-making are dispersed among a variety of frequently competing but also collaborating actors, institutions and interests that cut across rigid state vs. non-state divides. Thus, a number of interests are played out simultaneously, entailing re-negotiations over the very definition of what "order" is.

Latin America fits well into this panorama of "complicated" political orders marked by "fragmented sovereignty" (Davis 2009). As recent research has shown, Latin American states never established a monopoly of violence that would have enabled them to impose projects of political order-making in an unmediated top-down fashion. Instead, the region's states have continuously negotiated informally with local power holders over their political, fiscal and coercive reach (Müller 2012a; Nugent 1999; Stepputat 2007; Waldmann 2006).

As Jenny Pearce has argued in this regard: "Rather than see this as a loss or absence of the monopoly of violence, I would argue that the state [in Latin America] has never aspired to exercise such a monopoly, welcoming these indirect alliances" (Pearce 2010: 298). Thus the *politics of sovereignty*, at least in their ultimate macro-level monopoly-claiming form, have been remarkably absent in the region. The result of this situation has recently been termed "violent pluralism," a notion designating the coexistence of states and organized violent non-state armed actors where "multiple forms of substate order . . . exist separately from, but in constant interaction with, the state-sanctioned rule of law" (Arias and Goldstein 2010: 20). Accordingly, any analysis of policing and the politics of order-making in Latin America must account for this violently plural political landscape and the related existence of multiple, competing and/or collaborating sovereign actors.

Moreover, due to the region's high degree of urbanization, this violent pluralism and the resulting politics of order-making have a predominantly urban face. They are mostly visible in marginalized city spaces where most of the region's urban denizens live (Angotti 2013; Arias 2006; Gay 2012; Koonings and Kruijt 2007; Perlman 2010).

In light of this scenario, and from the vantage point of Mexico City, the present chapter addresses the question of how those at the city's urban margins deal with the consequences of this violent pluralism in their everyday *practices of politics*. Through the analytical lens of assemblage theory, this chapter analyses this question by drawing on empirical research in the marginalized Mexico City neighborhood of Iztapalapa. It demonstrates how different practices of politics pursued by local actors assemble different component parts together in larger wholes that I will refer to as *urban security assemblages*. The latter, it will be shown, while providing different solutions to local problems of insecurity and violence, nonetheless contribute, albeit in different ways, to the reproduction of a highly uneven and informal political topography marked by the presence of local power brokers, clientelist relations and illegal actors.

Urban security assemblages

The chapter draws its analytical inspiration from *assemblage theory* (see DeLanda 2013). This theory is in general associated with the works of Gilles Deleuze (e.g. Deleuze 1968; Deleuze and Guattari 1986; Deleuze and Parnet 2007) and his notion of *agencements*, rather imprecisely translated into English as assemblages (Farías 2010: 14, see also Phillips 2006). It also draws inspiration from Actor–Network Theory inspired by Bruno Latour (2005). Assemblages can be defined as "contingent and shifting interrelations among 'segments'— institutions, powers, practices, desires—that constantly, simultaneously construct, entrench, and disaggregate their own constraints and oppressions" (Biehl and Locke 2010: 323). The assemblage perspective used in this chapter particularly draws on the (implicit and explicit) integration of basic insights of Deleuze and Latour by scholars working in the realm of Urban Studies (DeLanda 2013: 94–119; Farías and Bender 2010; Graham and Marvin 2001; MacFarlane 2011; see also Latour and Hermanet 1998),[3] Surveillance Studies (Ericson 2007; Haggerty and Ericson 2000; Lippert and O'Connor 2003) and International Relations (Abrahamsen and Williams 2009, 2011; Schouten 2010).

The security and surveillance-oriented studies that are influenced by assemblage theory and those within the field of International Relations view assemblages as contingent/emerging relational, decentered network-like configurations, composed of a variety of actors, institutions and rationalities. A security assemblage can be described as a "complex and multilayered arrangement" without "clear-cut hierarchical or vertical relationships, where power and authority runs in only one direction, or from one particular and clearly defined center" (Abrahamsen and Williams 2009: 8). It is:

> an open ended system of relations between diverse programmatic efforts that are "put together in novel and specific ways, and rationalized in relation to specific governmental objectives and goals." . . . Provided that its elements can be made to work together, it can be assembled from diverse elements . . . and can cut across private- and public-sectoral divisions.
>
> (Lippert and O'Connor 2003: 333)

In this regard, an assemblage perspective on security decenters dominant perspectives on security governance that think of security from the vantage point of the state and state institutions. Instead, an assemblage perspective does not privilege or prioritize any actor or institution but traces the relations and connections between different actors and how these interactions lead to the emergence of particular assemblages (see also Abrahamsen and Williams 2011: 95).

This emphasis on "making elements work together" and the direct dependence of an existing security assemblage configuration upon specific objectives and goals points towards two decisive elements of the assemblage. First, the flexibility and changing nature of the assemblage structure, and second, its relation to a specific, decisively context-dependent security problem or risk. Assemblages emerge out of the desire of and intentional efforts by local actors to merge component parts "into a larger whole," which "operates across both state and extra-state institutions" (Haggarty and Ericson 2000: 609). However, the concrete composition of this "larger whole," and the way its component parts are brought together and institutionalized is situational and context dependent (and impossible to fully predict). Far from being a "stable entity with fixed boundaries," an assemblage exists as a potentiality whose realization depends upon the way its component parts are brought together and "fixed" through "the intersection of various media that can be connected for diverse purposes" (Haggarty and Ericson 2000: 609–610)—all of which are ultimately related to the governance of security.

Due to this de-essentializing, relational and dynamic analytical perspective, assemblage theory is particularly useful for assessing the de-centered, fragmented and dynamic practices of politics and ordermaking in the Global South beyond clear-cut and dichotomizing perspectives such as state vs. non-state.

However, for the purpose of this chapter it is important to add a spatial dimension to this perspective. Recent studies on *urban assemblages* have pointed towards the fact that urban space itself, far from being static and given, is "multiple enacted and assembled at concrete local sites, where concrete actors shape time–space dynamics in various ways, producing thereby different geographies of associations" (Farías 2010: 6). This implies that far from being static and defined by essential properties:

> urban actors, forms or processes are defined less by a pre-given property and more by the assemblages they enter and reconstitute. The individual elements define the assemblage by their co-functioning, and can be stabilised (territorialised or reterritorialised) or destabilised (deterritorialised) through this mutual imbrication.
>
> (MacFarlane 2011: 208)

Seen through the lens of assemblage theory, urban space(s), politics and practices can thus not be predetermined due to the pre-existing properties of one of the elements of an assemblage. An assemblage perspective thus suggests a methodical move away from deductive reasoning based on predefined categories and instead proposes to explain processes through thick descriptions of place-specific relations of power, potential and agency (MacFarlane 2011: 205).

With the notion of *urban security assemblages*, I seek to integrate basic insights from the above studies into a heuristic lens for assessing security-related practices of politics and the corresponding forms of order-making in Iztapalapa. With urban security assemblages I designate different, context-dependent and dynamic networks. These networks are connecting different security actors, institutions and practices—public and private, formal and informal—and they are assembled through practices of politics emerging from a given urban space and in response to particular security threats/problems.

Practices of politics and security assemblages in Iztapalapa

Located in the south-east of Mexico City, Iztapalapa, one of the sixteen *delegaciones* (boroughs) of Mexico City, is home to about 1.8 million people, roughly 21 percent of Mexico City's population and one of its most marginalized boroughs. According to official data, about one third of Iztapalapa's residents are living in conditions of "high marginality" and another one third is living in conditions of "medium marginality."[4] Additionally, about 35 percent of the economically active population (including a large segment of under- and self-employed people) earn less than the official minimum wage that is currently set at 52.59 Mexican Pesos a day or 1,598.736 Pesos a month (roughly US$ 120). In this regard, a report from the borough administration concluded that most of the local workforce is living "in a situation of poverty, marked by a high degree of marginality that manifests itself in malnutrition, the dissolution of families, violence, illness, addictive problems and illiteracy" (Delegación Iztapalapa 2008: 3). To this picture of socio-economic marginality, we have to add a widespread lack or deficient quality of public infrastructure such as water supply, health services and public schools. It is telling in this regard that Mike Davis in his book *Planet of Slums* has listed Iztapalapa as one of the world's largest "Megaslums" (Davis 2006: 28).

Iztapalapa is also heavily affected by the "metropolization of crime" (Castillo 2008: 181) that has haunted the city since the mid 1990s. In fact, "Iztapalapa is infamous for being one of the most violent and criminally inclined *delegaciones* in Mexico City" (Boudreau *et al.* 2012: 76). In absolute numbers, Iztapalapa permanently ranks at the top of local crime statistics. Although these statistics are highly unreliable and marked by serious underreporting, due to the lack of confidence in the local administration of justice, they nonetheless indicate that crime and violence, ranging from petty theft, express kidnappings and organized criminal activity, such as the resale of stolen goods, and drug-trafficking, have become central ingredients of the local insecurity panorama, seriously affecting the everyday life of local residents, notably due to the coercive powers associated with drug-trafficking. In this regard, a report from the local Ministry for Social Development identified sixty-three areas, located in forty-three neighborhoods, as the principal generators and receptors of crime and insecurity in Mexico City. Nineteen of these areas, according to the report, are located in Iztapalapa, placing it at the top of this list (*La Jornada* 2006). As one observer recently stated, if there is one place that condenses the most pressing problems of poverty and criminality facing contemporary Mexico City, it is, in fact, Iztapalapa (*Frankfurter Rundschau* 2010).

This insecurity panorama exists despite a comparatively good police infrastructure, with some 3,700 officers of the Sectorial Police (*policía sectorial*) and some additional 1,170 agents of the so-called Auxiliary Police (*policía auxiliar*) operating in the borough (Boudreau *et al.* 2012: 84).[5] However, while these numbers indicate that there is a quite substantial state presence, local police forces, far from being a public and impartial actor effectively contributing to the safety of the local residents are more often than not real insecurity actors. For instance, they frequently collude with criminal actors, prey on local communities and are deeply embedded in factional party politics (see also Müller 2012a, 2012b).

Thus, Iztapalapa is a typical reflection of political orders in the Global South. It is marked by the absence of an all-powerful – or dominant – sovereign state capable of monopolizing the means of violence and providing efficient and impartial security for its subjects. This opens up the possibility of exploring the eventual emergence of urban security assemblages whose components are brought together through different practices of politics by local actors.

Assemblage 1: security beyond the state

One urban security assemblage that can be found in Iztapalapa emerges out of efforts by local residents to confront crime, violence or conflicts at the neighborhood level without the involvement of state agencies. This assemblage usually emerges out of family conflicts, problems stemming from petty crime or brawls involving residents from the same street or neighborhood. In all of these cases, patterns of conflict resolution around which this assemblage configuration emerges involves *politics of selfhood and social relations* in and through which local "moral authorities," local strongmen, but also family members, were called upon by local residents to intervene in order to solve the problem in question.

These local forms of *politics of selfhood and social relations* were made possible by the very high degree of social cohesion and the density of social relations among residents in many neighborhoods throughout Iztapalapa, reflected in frequently made statements such as: "Here, everyone knows each other." "Everyone greets everyone." "We have a particular sense of community" "You always keep an eye on your neighbor's house." Such expressions point towards the impact of what, following Thompson, we can identify as a "consensus of the community" (Thompson 1980: 69) or as a "moral consensus" (Thompson 1968: 87), characterized by specifically local notions of solidarity and morality that organize the social dynamics at the neighborhood level and that provide the basis for the previously mentioned forms of conflict resolution. The latter, however, are far from being some kind of disinterested self-help among equals. On the contrary, they are deeply embedded in local power structures and dominant perceptions about urban order and disorder. In this regard, one interview partner tellingly referred to a dominant form of "informal neighborhood morality," underpinned and enforced by political and coercive power of influential local actors.

> There is a set of norms within the neighborhoods, and this exists because otherwise there would be no daily coexistence [*convivencia*]. It has to do with certain unspoken codes. It is very typical that there are people in the *barrio* who have more power. Sometimes there are fights and if there are fights then everyone knows what the limits are. It is understood that I can't do this or that. Each person controls their blows. But of course, if certain lines are crossed, if it is not one on one, but several against one then it is very likely that someone powerful from the families will intervene.
>
> (Roberto, teacher, June 2007)

References such as "people who have more power" in general refer to the underlying informal political networks that structure urban life throughout Iztapalapa. Such notions usually refer to local political bosses, so-called *líderes*, many of whom emerged out of the struggles over the regularization of occupied land and the improvement of the public infrastructure since the 1970s and 1980s and who, due to their local standing as people who "get things done"— as well as their underlying capacity to mobilize potential voters—have become powerful informal political actors and brokers, mediating local state–society relations. Within the context of the expansion of political clientelism that accompanied the democratization of Mexico City politics since the mid 1990s and the emergence of the Party of the Democratic Revolution (PRD) as the leading political force in local politics, many of these leaders became integrated into the clientelist networks that underpin PRD-rule in the city (Hilgers 2008, 2009, 2011; Müller 2012c). But Iztapalapa is not just any borough, "it is the cradle of many different PRD-leaders" who mostly acquired their political capital through the tactical mobilization of clientelistic networks (Denissen 2009: 416). This inscribes clientelist practices deep into the micro-level workings of power at the neighborhood level. As one interviewee summed it up:

> Well, this is a PRD neighborhood, which is a left-wing party. So, many local politicians here are members of the local parliament. There are many people working for them as well, and because they are close to the PRD and because the government of the Federal District belongs to the PRD, there are obvious preferences. Here, they have always maintained these privileged relations, the tradition of having good connections to politicians or the police. . . . But the normal people of course don't have this kind of personal access. They must always establish a personal relationship with someone and thereby strengthen this person's political career.
>
> (Julio, merchant, October 2007)

As this passage indicates, access to clientelist networks and the people at the top of them is uneven and hierarchical. Not everyone has the political or social capital necessary for a direct and unmediated relationship with local political authorities. Therefore, the incorporation of ordinary people in these relations and the opportunities for them to gain access to the informal processes that distribute public security resources are in most cases mediated through political brokers. This practice represents a crucial feature of the practices of informal political negotiations or *gestiones* that are central to (clientelist) politics in Mexico City: in exchange for the delivery of "public" services or goods, local residents offer political support to people capable of providing these services. The brokers' political power is based on political capital derived from their capacity to mobilize people (and, eventually, votes). This capacity gives such brokers privileged access to state personnel and resources—including those related to public security—that can be appropriated to a certain degree for their private and political purposes and distributed across clientelist networks (Hilgers 2008).

The repercussions of the metropolization of crime in Iztapalapa increasingly converted the provision of security and conflict resolution into important elements within the broker's repertoire of clientelistic service delivery (Müller 2012b; 2012c; 2013; see also Denissen 2009: 240). In a somewhat paradoxical way, the formal state's incapacity to provide security for its subjects transforms the brokers' informal access to the state—and the political and coercive powers associated herewith—into an important resource enabling them to efficiently solve community conflicts without the formal involvement of local law enforcement agencies.

These are indeed practices of politics. They ultimately empower and reinforce the legitimacy of local political bosses as people who "get things done." In light of the limited capacity of state agencies to provide efficient responses to local violence and insecurity, residents of Iztapalapa "consider patron–client exchanges a strategic mechanism for achieving physical and economic security" (Hilgers 2009: 51). In doing so, they contribute to the reproduction of a decisively informal form of political order that, in turn, permanently enables the emergence of security assemblages operating "beyond the state," at least when state practices are exclusively understood in formal–legal terms.

While the resulting form of security provision is frequently highly efficient, it should not be overlooked that, as in all assemblages, possibilities and resources, such as enhanced security, are always accompanied by a set of constraints and limitations that the assemblage structure as a whole imposes upon its component parts, their interactions and practices (see DeLanda 2013: 34–35). As DeLanda observed:

> In the networks characterizing tightly knit communities, for example, a variety of resources become available to their members from physical protection and help to emotional support and advice. But the same density of connections can also constrain members. News about broken promises, unpaid bets and other not-honoured commitments travel fast in those networks: a property that allows them to act as enforcement mechanisms for local norms.
>
> (DeLanda 2013: 35)

In the case of the assemblage described in this section, such constraints frequently became a key factor in the efforts of local residents to search for security "beyond the state." In this regard, interviewees frequently mentioned that, what from the analytical perspective of this paper can be described as certain material and physical properties of the component parts of this assemblage literally force them to rely upon informal mechanisms of conflict resolution and impede them from turning to the police. Such properties include, for instance, the economic marginality of many residents that impedes moving to another *delegación;* the constraints put upon local spatial mobility due to the physical design of the urban infrastructure, including narrow and serpentine streets.

In addition to these more material aspects, constraints that force residents to search for security beyond the state also have a social dimension. For instance, physical proximity to neighbors and family members in social housing projects as well as in informally built homes frequently forces local residents to solve their security problems without external interference in order to avoid the perpetuation of a problem or the weakening of the density of social relations referred to above. In the words of Roberto, already introduced above:

> I go and accuse somebody from here, well the fight isn't going to just end there. If it were somebody from outside, from another *colonia* who has come to look for trouble, you go and you file a complaint. You go and accuse him, that's how the legal procedure works. But in the case of someone from the same *colonia*, you are going to have a constant fight, an interminable fight, because the dispute will no longer just be with him but with his mother, with his father, with his family. And it is something you are going to have to deal with day in and day out. As a result you prefer to just say, "It was the fight, this jerk was just drunk, he was on drugs." But you decide to just leave it at that, to that night's fight, because otherwise it becomes something bigger that goes beyond what happened.

Although urban security assemblages can make a positive contribution to the local (in)security situation, it must be recognized that they also function on the basis of symbolic and disciplinary power that puts constraints upon the security practices individuals can pursue within a given assemblage structure. In addition to their embeddedness in frequently highly exclusionary clientelist relations, such practices of politics and order-making thus also include the frequently unintentional imposition and reproduction of dominant norms, lifestyles and behavior that sustain the existing moral order inside the community. In this regard, they also reinforce restrictive forms of social control that are frequently based on the respect for family values, particular notions of honor or gender.

Assemblage II: security from state policing

While the first assemblage configuration operated beyond the state, another assemblage emerged from efforts to be protected from state security and law enforcement. These efforts, paradoxically, at least at first sight, frequently involved the active participation of state agencies and political actors. The main actors that assembled the different component parts of this assemblage structure —notably local police officers, their political patrons and public bureaucrats— together, were criminal actors. The latter strategically approached local police officers, political brokers and bureaucrats in order to assemble a network structure that provides them with protection from official law enforcement. In this regard this assemblage was (re-)produced by a specific type of local *politics of sovereignty* aimed at establishing what may be referred to as "criminal sovereignty" (Cribb 2009). The latter is a form of political authority that depends on illegal commerce for its own reproduction and that while subverting formal–legal practices associated with "official" sovereignty, establishes control over certain territory "which is then used for criminal purposes" (Cribb 2009: 8).

Local residents, including those participating in Iztapalapa's illegal economy provided frequent illustrations of how the political economy of illegal rent-seeking fused official state actors and illegal actors into mutually beneficial relationships in which security for and protection of illegal activities are traded for economic benefits. This consolidates an assemblage configuration centered on offering security *against* the state in order to reproduce criminal sovereignties at the neighborhood level. For instance, Juan, a local merchant from the market in Santa Cruz de Meyehualco, famous for the redistribution of and commerce in stolen goods explained:

> Everything that has been stolen in the city is sold in Santa Cruz de Meyehualco. At night, the trucks arrive and bring in the stolen goods. For example, you can see trailers from Liverpool or Palacio de Hierro. . . . You have to be there between 1 a.m. and 5 a.m. At 5 a.m., everything begins, including police protection. They collaborate. . . . When you arrive as a merchant and you don't accept the police protection, they are going to rob you, and when you accept their protection, you are really protected and safe inside the borders of Iztapalapa. Beyond the borders of the borough, they can take everything you have away. You are quote unquote safe, because the people from the market and the police protect you.
>
> (Juan, merchant, June 2007)

Patricia, another local merchant, who participated in the local commerce of stolen car parts, presented a closer view of how such forms of police protection occur and what costs they involve:

> — I was there everyday. From nine in the morning until dark, with another schedule until eight. It went well, but I was working.
> — *It was just doing business with car parts?*
> — Yes, everything from the scrapyard, but some people sold stolen parts and others not. But they paid their rent to the police so that they could work. Yes, the police came and raided them and sent them away, but not very often.
> — *It was the police?*
> — The police.
> — *When you say rent you mean they came by every certain period of time?*
> — Exactly.
> — *For example, how much did you give?*
> — No, I didn't give them anything. Well, there was one time when I worked there, and it was 50,000 pesos a month.
> — *Who paid it?*
> — Several people.
> — *Collectively?*

— No, individually. But we worked hard and earned more than 50,000.
— *What would the police do with so much money?*
— Well, it wasn't just them. It was their upper ranks as well. It was all divided. . . . It is what I have experienced. I am sure that it's true because out of 100, one police officer will listen to you.

(Patricia, merchant, November 2007).

However, while many of the consequences of such practices that contributed to the consolidation of spaces governed by the logics of criminal sovereignty were considered problematic by local residents, most worrisome for them was the emergence of spaces that were controlled by drug traffickers (see also Müller, 2012a: 186–188). As a consequence of the de facto control by traffickers over certain areas, local residents reported that they preferred to "ignore" or accept this phenomenon as a given fact—most of all because they fear violent retaliation: "No, it's not worth it [denouncing local drug traffickers]. They will kill you or someone of your family afterward. You see it, you hear it, but you remain quiet" (Miguel, taxi driver, September 2007). Another resident notes:

I tell you, there is a man here whom we all know, who doesn't have any legs. He was a diabetic and they cut off his legs. He is in a wheelchair. So he lives from selling drugs to minors. Right in front of the school! Just like that! Everybody knows that this man makes his living by selling drugs. . . . But he always has a godfather [*padrino*]. What do you do as a citizen? There are some folks here just around the corner, but they are the type that rob trailers like from Gigante. Everybody knows them and, well, they are untouchable.

(Lirio, sweetshop owner, September 2007)

However, we should be aware that it is not only the aggressiveness of drug users and the possibility of violent revenge from the local drug dealers that scare the inhabitants of Iztapalapa. It is also the presumed protection and toleration of local drug business by the police and local state functionaries. This relationship is frequently identified as the result as well as the basis of such *compadrazgos* (godparents) and the existence of "untouchables":

Here the people who sell drugs have protection. From the authorities. Because if they weren't being protected by the authorities they couldn't sell drugs. It's like if I were to come here and sell drugs, they would catch me in an instant. You understand? But there are people who have been doing this for years.
[They live] relaxed! Why? Why, because they have good contacts, good connections with functionaries who can help them out. Do you understand?

(Antonio, martial-arts trainer, September 2007)

On the street, such protection is enacted on and guaranteed through regular payments to police officers who collect the so-called *renta* that is distributed throughout the police apparatus. In addition to personal enrichment of the involved state actors, the *renta* also serves to compensate for financial shortcomings of the local police (Müller 2013). According to most interviewees the *renta* was the single most important element through which police–criminal connections were established. Therefore, the payment of the *renta*, as Carlos Alberto Zamudio Angles (2007) has demonstrated, is a precondition that local drug traffickers can keep their business running without interference from local police officers. But local police not only turn a blind eye on the activities of their "partners," they also try to maintain a certain appearance of order in the area they police. This orderly appearance is essential for assuring that local residents do not make a complaint to local authorities that could lead to the intervention of new, "external," police forces (Zamudio Angles 2007: 193–194).

Assemblage III: bringing in public security

The two urban security assemblages discussed above clearly demonstrate that when local state agencies and police forces get involved in local security governance they do so as decisively informal actors. The assemblage configuration that will be analysed in this section differs from the previously discussed cases as it is precisely the search for public actors by local residents that assembles the different component part into a larger whole. The underlying practices of politics have a material as well as symbolic dimension whose mobilization enables local actors to pursue a variety of different security strategies that, far from making security governance more public, permits them to pursue particularistic private and/or political goals.

As was already discussed with reference to the first assemblage, local norms, symbols and mechanisms of social control, stemming from dense and cohesive social relations at the neighborhood level, were perceived by many residents as providing efficient responses to particular security problems. However, interviewees also referred to conflicts and security problems that these responses that resulted from the first security assemblage were unable to deal with. In general, this meant situations involving serious acts of violence, such as physical assault, rape or homicide. Notwithstanding negative experiences with local policing, residents called for police intervention when such acts of violence were committed. This in general happened when the local "consensus of the community," which underpinned the first assemblage and its capacity of (re)enforcing established norms of behaviour and mechanisms of social control, was incapable of resolving conflict situations.

When local neighborhoods were facing such problems whose solution they considered beyond their capacity, they frequently turned to the police. In severe cases of violence, the formal image of the police as an impartial and public agency, apparently acting above and beyond the related conflict, is evoked in order to displace the potentially disruptive situation in a way that guarantees the integrity of neighborhood relations by creating the impression that the police did not intervene in favor of this or that person, but on behalf of the local "public" as such. This response, therefore has a clear political dimension, because bringing in the police as a *public* and impartial security provider also serves the purpose of maintaining the integrity of neighborhood relations and local order—including relations of power—through the intentional externalization of the respective security problem or conflict.

This strategy can be illustrated with reference to an "autonomous" *colonia* (neighborhood), which was taken over by the radical-left Independent Popular Front Francisco Villa UNOPI (FPFVI) and which is the home of some 4,000 residents. Through clientelist relationships with the local administration (Hilgers 2008), the *colonia* provides free housing and infrastructure for its members and has established an informal security governance structure. For example, there is a permanent presence of guards at the two main entrances of the *colonia* who check and question everyone wanting to enter. Each member of the FPFVI is obliged to do a guard service once a month. In this respect, the people are organized in twenty-eight brigades, and each brigade is responsible for one day of guard service. The daily shifts, always covered by at least five members of the respective brigade, are divided into three turns. The first turn is from 6 a.m. to 2 p.m., the second shift from 2 p.m. to 10 p.m., and the night shift is from 10 p.m. to 6 a.m. Besides the guard system, there is also an alarm whistle that can be used by all members in order to inform and mobilize them in the case of an emergency—including any questions of insecurity.

The FPFVI's political interest in managing their own security affairs notwithstanding, there are situations in which outside security actors are approached in order to preserve internal cohesion and order. The following account from an interview with a member of the FPFVI provides some impression of how justice is administered in the *colonia* and identifies where this kind of administration of justice 'beyond the state' encounters its limits. Asked if there are instances in which the FPFVI is obliged to contact the authorities, Rosario responded:

> Yes there are. When, for example, someone from the outside comes in and robs, he tries to steal a water tank or break into a house, so they get in, but the people stop them. So what do we do? One day they caught somebody and they took away his clothes and hung a sign on him that said "I am a thief," and they took him on a walk all over the neighborhood so that people could see that he was a thief. In some cases some of the guys will give him a few slaps in the face and throw him out, because the problem isn't very big. At one point there was another type of internal

problem. For example, one of the compañeros raped a four-year-old girl, here inside. So the mother denounced him. The people were outraged by this. They beat him up, but we decided to hand him over to the police because in the end we can have our own rules. We can have a different vision [of justice], but there are some cases where we can't go beyond what exists, so the law that exists is the only one. The other option was to leave him at the hands of the people, and this would have generated a quite different situation. So what happened was that the police were called. . . . We've called them, we said that we have this guy, that we will wait for them at the door; we handed the person over and they took him away. So there are questions like this. I don't know – for example, some youths are fighting in the doorway, they pull out guns and shoot at each other. In that case we don't expose ourselves either. What we do is keep the door closed and we call [the police] and say: "This and this is happening. Come over here and solve it."

(Rosario, FPVI member, September 2007)

Informal security assemblages at the neighborhood level in Iztapalapa become dependent on state resources in order to solve security problems or conflicts that are perceived as having a highly disruptive potential and/or whose resolution is beyond the capacities of micro-level security governance arrangements and therefore threatens to create disorder. In such cases, formal police involvement through the externalization of the security problem contributes to the maintenance of the integrity and cohesion of social relations in the affected community and the reproduction of order at the neighborhood level.

In addition to such situations, local residents also draw the police as a public institution for pursuing highly particularistic goals. For instance, it is common to informally appropriate and instrumentalize the police's coercive powers for individual or collective protection purposes, as well as for the coercive intimidation or the "punishment" of "troublemakers" (see Müller 2012b: 339–340 for details). In fact, many local residents described a variety of cases where they—individually or as organized collectives of neighbors or merchants—donate money, food or drinks to local police agents in order to "establish good relations" or "friendships" with them. Creating such "good relations" by offering informal incentives in money or kind is expected to establish some form of obligation for the involved police officers to offer more protection, to pay more attention and to demonstrate more responsiveness to their "donors'" security needs in the case of an emergency.

Another example is the practice of "contracting" policemen, who when off duty offer protection services as local *vigilantes*, frequently to entire neighborhoods. Although such practices are illegal, as police officers are not allowed to engage in private security provision, they are widespread. In such arrangements, neighbors either collect a certain amount of money, or the vigilantes go from door to door in order to ask for their payment. In return for payment, the vigilantes walk or drive around the area, often blowing a whistle, to indicate that the area is "under surveillance."

What converts these actors into attractive security providers is their assumed affiliation with the police as an official state institution, which is expected to guarantee an immediate response from the local authorities in the case of an emergency. Additionally, the common knowledge that the vigilantes could belong to the police is expected to provide a substantial deterrent potential, thereby indicating to potential criminals that it is "dangerous" to prey on this neighborhood. Such practices, as I show in greater detail elsewhere (Müller 2013) are commonly based on the initiatives of local political bosses who are interested in enhancing their political capital by demonstrating that they can provide security for "their" constituencies. They also benefit personally from the protection and coercions services provided by the vigilantes. Such practices are deeply embedded in the reproduction of a decisively informal political order that structures everyday forms of security governance, which has resulted in three urban security assemblages in Iztapalapa.

Conclusion

Through the analytical lens of assemblage theory, this chapter has analyzed different strategies and practices of politics in and through which the residents of the marginalized Mexico City neighborhood of Iztapalapa engage in everyday practices of micro-level security governance and conflict resolution. All three assemblages that have been addressed in this chapter, undeniably contributed to the governance of specific (in)securities and risks. However, they also reproduced local power relations and informal political structures that dominate local urban politics.

As a consequence, local political bosses, patrons heading clientelist networks, and illegal actors are the main beneficiaries of the different assemblage configurations and the local political order that underlies them. This clearly indicates the ultimately political nature of security provision, conflict resolution and order-making at the margins of contemporary Mexico City.

Are these conceptual reflections and empirical findings relevant for the analysis of security governance beyond the case of Mexico City? I think they are. Nonetheless, some qualifications are necessary. First of all, the findings of this paper reflect the underlying dynamics of a decisively urban context. Although other urban settings throughout the so-called Global South, as many contributions to this book demonstrate, are marked by similar processes, and in an increasingly urbanized world, violence, insecurity and conflict are becoming more and more urbanized; each city has its own particular historical legacies, producing different institutional arrangements and constellations of actors involved in the governance of security. Therefore, I do not claim that Iztapalapa is and will be everywhere. This holds true in particular for more "rural" and peripheral settings.

Urban security dynamics may become increasingly relevant and even predominant in both quantitative and qualitative terms. Security problems and governance in rural settings, where state presence has historically been less dense than in urban areas, may look quite different, giving rise to assemblage structures unlike those observed in Iztapalapa. However, and notwithstanding these qualifications, I would like to close this paper with the tentative suggestion that the concept of security assemblage, precisely through its relational focus on practices and processes through which local actors connect different "component parts" (security practices and actors) into a "larger whole," offers a promising analytical lens for the development of a more comprehensive research agenda on practices of politics and the related (in)security dynamics in "most of the world" (Chatterjee 2004).

Acknowledgements

Research for this article was conducted between 2006 and 2009 within the context of the Research Centre (SFB) 700 "Governance in Areas of Limited Statehood," funded by the German Research Foundation and located at the Freie Universität Berlin. I am thankful for the invaluable research assistance provided in Mexico City, including conducting interviews with local residents, by Carlos Alberto Zamudio Angles and Nils Brock.

Notes

1 This chapter has drawn upon material from within Markus-Michael Müller, "Addressing an Ambivalent Relationship: Policing and the Urban Poor in Mexico City," *Journal of Latin American Studies* Volume 44(2), pp. 319–45, 2012 © Cambridge University Press and from *Public Security in the Negotiated State: Policing in Latin America and Beyond*, 2012 © Palgrave Macmillan, reproduced with permission from the publishers.
2 But see Clastres (1974).
3 For a critical discussion of "assemblage urbanism," see Brenner *et al.* (2011).
4 The degree of marginality takes into account questions of education, income, patrimony of the household and quality of the dwelling. These are divided up into six indicators: residents age fifteen and over without junior high school degree; employed residents with a monthly work-related income up to two minimum wages; residences without telephone; residences without ground lamination; residences without indoor tap water; and average number of people sharing a bedroom. See www.siege.df.gob.mx/copladet/index.html.
5 On the formal organization of Mexico City policing, see Müller (2012a: 66–75).

References

Abrahamsen, R. and Williams, M. C., 2009. "Security Beyond the State: Global Security Assemblages in International Politics." *International Political Sociology*, 1:3, 1–17.
Abrahamsen, R. and Williams, M. C., 2011. *Security Beyond the State: Private Security in International Politics.* New York: Cambridge University Press.

Angotti, T., 2013. "Introduction: Urban Latin America: Violence, Enclaves and Struggles for Land." *Latin American Perspectives*, 40:2, 5–20.

Arias, E. D., 2006. *Drugs and Democracy: Trafficking, Social Networks, and Public Security*. Chapel Hill, NC: University of North Carolina Press.

Arias, E. D. and Goldstein D. E., 2010. "Violent Pluralism: Understanding the New Democracies of Latin America." In E. D. Arias and D. E. Goldstein (Eds.), *Violent Democracies in Latin America*. Durham: Duke University Press, 1–33.

Biehl, J. and Locke, P., 2010. "Deleuze and the Anthropology of Becoming." *Current Anthropology*, 51:3, 317–351.

Boudreau, J.-A., Davis, D. E., Boucher, N., Chatel, O., Élizabeth, C., Janni, L., Philoctète, A., and Salazar Salame, H., 2012. *Constructing Youth Citizenship in Montreal and Mexico City: The Examples of Youth–Police Relations in Saint-Michel and Iztapalapa*. Montréal: Institut national de la recherche scientifique Centre – Urbanisation Culture Société. Online available at: www.im.metropolis.net/medias/ RapportSynthese-YouthENG.pdf (accessed March 23, 2013).

Brenner, N., Madden, D. J. and Wachsmuth, D., 2011. "Assemblage Urbanism and the Challenges of Critical Urban Theory." *City*, 15:2, 225–240.

Castillo, J., 2008. "After the Explosion." In R. Burdett and D. Sudjic (Eds.), *The Endless City*. London: Phaidon, 174–185.

Chatterjee, P., 2004. *Politics of the Governed: Reflections on Popular Politics in Most of the World*. New York: Columbia University Press.

Clastres, P., 1974. *La Société contre l'État: Recherches d'anthropologie politique*. Paris: Éditions de Minuit.

Cribb, R., 2009. "Introduction: Parapolitics, Shadow Governance and Criminal Sovereignty." In E. Wilson (Ed.), *Government of the Shadows: Parapolitics and Criminal Sovereignty*. London: Pluto, 1–9.

Davis, D. E., 2009. "Non-State Armed Actors, New Imagined Communities, and Shifting Patterns of Sovereignty and Insecurity in the Modern World." *Contemporary Security Policy*, 30:2, 221–245.

Davis, M., 2006. *Planet of Slums*. London: Verso.

DeLanda, M., 2013. *A New Philosophy of Society: Assemblage Theory and Social Complexity*. New York: Bloomsbury.

Delegación Iztapalapa (Dirección General de Desarrollo Social), 2008. *Reglas de Operación 2008*. Mexico City: Delegación Iztapalapa.

Deleuze, G., 1968. Différence et répétition. Paris: Presses Universitaires de France.

Deleuze, G. and Guattari, F., 1986. *A Thousand Plateaus: Capitalism and Schizophrenia*. Minneapolis, MN: University of Minnesota Press.

Deleuze, G. and Parnet, C., 2007. *Dialogues II*. New York: Columbia University Press.

Denissen, I., 2009. "New Forms of Political Inclusion: Competitive Clientelism." In Dutch Ministry of Foreign Affairs (Ed.), *Quality and Effectiveness: A Rich Menu for the Poor: Food for Thought on Effective Aid Policies*. The Hague: Ministry of Foreign Affairs. Online available at: www.minbuza.nl/en/Key_Topics/Quality_and_ Effectiveness/A_Rich_Menu_for_the_Poor (accessed September 14, 2013).

Ericson, R. V., 2007. *Crime in an Insecure World*. Oxford: Polity Press.

Farías, I., 2010. "Introduction: Decentering the Object of Urban Studies." In I. Farías and T. Bender (Eds.), *Urban Assemblages: How Actor–Network Theory Changes Urban Studies*. London: Routledge, 1–24.

Farías, I. and Bender, T. (Eds.), 2010. *Urban Assemblages: How Actor–Network Theory Changes Urban Studies.* London: Routledge.

Frankfurter Rundschau. 2010. Drogen und andere Dummheiten. In *Mexiko ist Schulbildung die stärkste Waffe gegen Gewalt und Armut*, September 15, 2010.

Gay, R., 2012. "Clientelism, Democracy, and Violence in Rio de Janeiro." In T. Hilgers (Ed.), *Clientelism in Everyday Latin American Politics.* Basingstoke: Palgrave Macmillan, 81–98.

Graham, S. and Marvin, S., 2001. *Splintering Urbanism: Networked Infrastructures, Technological Mobilities, and the Urban Condition.* London: Routledge.

Haggerty, K. D. and Ericson R. V., 2000. "The Surveillant Assemblage." *British Journal of Sociology*, 51:4, 605–622.

Hilgers, T., 2008. "Causes and Consequences of Political Clientelism: Mexico's PRD in Comparative Perspective." *Latin American Politics and Society*, 50:4, 123–153.

Hilgers, T., 2009. "Who is Using Whom? Clientelism from the Client's Perspective." *Journal of Iberian and Latin American Research*, 15:1, 51–76.

Hilgers, T., 2011. "La relation complexe entre clientélisme et démocratie (cadre de référence fondé sur le cas du PRD dans la ville de Mexico)." *Politique et Sociétés*, 30:2, 123–146.

Koonings, K. and Kruijt, D. (Eds.), 2007. *Fractured Cities: Social Exclusion, Urban Violence and Contested Spaces in Latin America.* London: Zed Books.

La Jornada. 2006. Ubican zonas generadoras de delincuencia, January 19, 2006.

Latour, B., 2005. *Reassembling the Social: An Introduction to Actor–Network Theory.* New York: Oxford University Press.

Latour, B. and Hermanet, E., 1998. *Paris: ville invisible.* Virtual Book. Online available at: www.bruno-latour.fr/virtual/EN/index.html, accessed August 22, 2013.

Lippert, R. and O'Connor, D., 2003. "Security Assemblages: Airport Security, Flexible Work and Liberal Governance." *Alternatives*, 28:33, 331–358.

MacFarlane, C., 2011. "Assemblage and Critical Urbanism." *City*, 15:2, 204–224.

Müller, M.-M., 2012a. *Public Security in the Negotiated State: Policing in Latin America and Beyond.* Basingstoke: Palgrave Macmillan.

Müller, M.-M., 2012b. "Addressing an Ambivalent Relationship: Policing and the Urban Poor in Mexico City." *Journal of Latin American Studies*, 44:2, 319–345.

Müller, M.-M., 2012c. "Transformaciones del clientelismo: Democratización, (in)-seguridad y politicas urbanas en el Distrito Federal." *Foro Internacional*, 52:4, 836–863.

Müller, M.-M., 2013. "'Public' Security and Patron–Client Exchanges in Latin America." *Government and Opposition*, 58:4, 548–569.

Nugent, D., 1999. "State and Shadow State in Northern Peru circa 1900: Illegal Political Networks and the Problem of State Boundaries." In J. McC. Heyman (Ed.), *States and Illegal Practices.* Oxford: Berg, 63–98.

Pearce, J., 2010. "Perverse State Formation and Securitized Democracy in Latin America." *Democratization*, 17:2, 286–306.

Perlman, J., 2010. *Favlea: Four Decades of Living on the Edge in Rio de Janeiro.* Oxford: Oxford University Press.

Phillips, J., 2006. "Agencement/Assemblage." *Theory, Culture and Society*, 23:2–3, 108–109.

Schouten, P., 2010. "Security as Controversy: Privatizing Security Inside Global Security Assemblages." Paper presented at the International Studies Association Annual Conference, New Orleans, February 17–20, 2010.

Stepputat, F., 2007. "Insecurity, State and Impunity in Latin America." In L. Andersen, B. Møller, and F. Stepputat (Eds.), *Fragile States and Insecure People: Violence, Security and Statehood in the Twenty-First Century*. Basingstoke: Palgrave Macmillan, 201–226.

Thompson, E. P., 1968. *The Making of the English Working Class*. Harmondsworth: Penguin.

Thompson, E. P., 1980. *Plebejische Kultur und moralische Ökonomie. Aufsätze zur Sozialgeschichte des 18. und 19. Jahrhunderts*. Frankfurt am Main: Ullstein.

Waldmann, P., 2006. *El Estado anómico. Derecho, seguridad pública y vida cotidiana en América Latina*. Madrid: Vervuert.

Zamudio Angles, C. A., 2007. Las redes del narcomenudeo. Cómo se reproducen el consumo y el comercio de drogas ilícitas entre jóvenes de barrios marginados. Unpublished Masters Thesis, Escuela Nacional de Antropología e Historia, Mexico City.

Chapter 8

Closure of bars, cantinas and brothels

Practices of civil in/security, state formation and citizenship in urban Bolivia[1]

Helene Risør

On 17 October, 2007, bottles of alcohol, furniture and other goods were burning in the streets of La Ceja, the overcrowded city centre of El Alto, Bolivia. The fire was the culmination of a demonstration, or *marcha*, organized by students of the FES (Federation of Secondary Students of El Alto). *Cholita* hawkers and their customers, workers, young professionals and Alteños in general watched the youngsters rally for computers and chemistry laboratories for their school as well as for the closure of illegal bars, cantinas and brothels. 'What do we want?' chanted the students, and the rhetorical question was answered with a roar: 'Close the bars and cantinas!' The *marcha* turned into a riot as the youngsters threw stones at the windows of the bars, invaded the premises and brought the furniture and alcohol outside, where it was torched in broad daylight. By the time the police had managed to disperse the crowd at least four bars had been destroyed, and afterwards nobody was held legally responsible for the destruction. Rather, the youngsters have since been honoured for their actions.

In this chapter I present an ethnographic analysis of the *clausura*. The analysis illustrates how experiences and protests regarding civil in/security are entangled with understandings and practices of statehood and citizenship. Particularly, I discuss how illegal practices such as the *clausura* may result in the mutual strengthening of civil society groups and the state. Engaging with James Holston's (2008) notion of insurgent citizenship I illustrate how the claims of marginalized populations to substantial rather than simply formal citizenship take the form of illegal actions. Pushing this argument, I indicate that popular actions situated in the interstices of formal and informal civil participation and legal and illegal actions, do not necessarily stand in an antagonistic relationship with the state and state authorities. In El Alto, for instance, the state is not an absolute and absent 'other' contrasting the figure of the marginalized poor and mainly indigenous population. Rather, the municipality and the police (as state representatives) often depend upon the citizens' (illegal) order-making activities. Thus, while the state's capacity to ensure civil security and order is a key aspect of its 'stateness', this enactment depends on the collaboration of citizens. Eventually this relationship grows tenser and people's search for safety and security adopts the form of defiance of state sovereignty, for instance as illegal burnings of the inventory of bars and brothels, or more spectacularly, as mob lynching of presumed criminals. We should nevertheless be careful not to unequivocally consider actions of this kind as the defiance of state sovereignty, because they may also be understood as a desperate attempt to call for the state's attention (cf. Goldstein 2004, 2012) or as ways of giving shape to the state and adopting a state language (cf. Risør 2010). Following from this, in the present chapter I analyse the *clausura* with regards to state formation in contemporary Bolivia and how it also represents 'citizen-formation', which allows for the coming into being of novel political actors and subjectivities, in this case of youth.

In the chapter I first introduce the urban context of El Alto, focusing on how citizenship is enacted through community based collectives and trade unions. These collectives constitute the institutional formation through which poor urban inhabitants engage with the state and vice versa. In the second section I analyse how this particular state–citizen relationship is played out with respect to civil in/security as this is the arena of state sovereignty par excellence. In the following three sections I return to an ethnographic analysis of the events and actors of the *clausura*. Analysing it with regards to practices of state and citizen formation I argue that although the *clausura* did not substantively improve the living conditions and civil security situation of the Alteños it should not simply be dismissed as a violent form of clientelism or as an inutile battle over access to scarce municipal resources. It also stands out as an instance through which otherwise marginal populations engage in negotiations with the state and engage in its transformation.

El Alto: state–citizens relationships in the new Bolivia

To most people, El Alto is the poor urban area surrounding the international airport of Bolivia's capital La Paz. It is a marginal area that one must necessarily drive through to reach more attractive locations. Nevertheless, this city houses approximately one million people, and it is thus Bolivia's second largest city. The city is known for its high degree of socio-political organization, impelled by everyday necessities of ensuring basic services and the need for political and civic recognition. People organize themselves in *junta de vecinos* (neighbour-hood associations), school committees and trade unions in order to obtain everything from tap water, electricity and a sewerage system to pavement of streets, schools and civil security. Therefore, being a citizen in El Alto is a collective matter and demands of state authorities are carried out collectively rather than on an individual or household basis (Arbona 2006; Lazar 2008; Risør 2012).

While state authorities are not absent in El Alto and other marginal urban areas of Bolivia they seldom appear in the form that people wish for. More often than not the state is made present through the state-like activities of organized neighbourhoods among which we find self-help security squads (Goldstein 2004; Risør 2010; Risør 2013). As such, it is the local social organizations that constitute the principal authority in the everyday of El Alto's inhabitants. These social organizations are in part an inheritance from the trade unionism of ex-miners and the collective nature of governance in *ayllus* of the rural indigenous Aymara communities. Yet, despite their collective nature these social organizations can also be considered a neoliberal form of citizenship. Peasants and poor urban dwellers have come to occupy the space of governance and protection left by the withdrawal of the state since neoliberal reforms were initiated in 1985, even if they have also used this platform to question the ideological framework on which these reforms were made and demand more state presence (Arbona 2006, 2008; McNeish 2006; Postero 2007; Goldstein 2012).

Understanding current transformations of Bolivia – often epitomized by the 2005 presidential election of Evo Morales as the country's first indigenous president – requires attention to the new expressions of citizenship that led to his election. These expressions are turning into a hegemonic form of socio-political participation and enactment of citizenship in Bolivia. The *clausura* as a kind of political action only makes sense when analysed in relation to similar forms of popular protests, growing unrest and political participation that have marked Bolivia since 2000. This unrest peaked during the so-called Gas War of 2003 when the then president Sanchez de Lozada deployed the army to dissolve massive protests against the government's plan to export gas to the US through Chilean ports. Seventy people were killed in and around El Alto before the president was forced to resign and flee to the USA where he remains until this day (Mamani Conde 2006; Hylton and Thompson 2007).

The event put El Alto on the political map as the city where social movements managed to change a country's political agenda: after the Gas War most of the traditional post 1952 national revolution parties were dissolved or went through a fundamental restructuring process. Consequently, the social organizations gained further strength. As a movement that coordinates trade unions, indigenous organizations and neighbourhood associations such as the MAS (Movemiento al Socialismo or Movement towards Socialism) grew stronger and in December 2005 its leader Evo Morales was elected president of Bolivia. With his presidency, social movements now form part of the government, and representatives from both the FEJUVE (Federación de Juntas Vecinales, or Federation of Neighbourhood Associations of El Alto) and the COR (Central Obrera Regional Workers' Central, which organizes the many trade unions) have become ministers. Yet, social demands from citizens are still made through social organizations, either through collective pleas, *marchas* or eventually by means of protests such as the *clausura*.

During my fieldwork in 2007–2008, the social organizations of El Alto were simultaneously involved in governmental positions and state activities and in challenging state authority. In sum, the socio-political reality of El Alto is messy, making it difficult to define in practical terms who and where the state and the citizenry are located. In practical terms, the line between the state and civil socio-political organizations of the urban poor is therefore unclear. While the suffering and abstentions of the poor are very real, the state adopts a much more shadowy character, and therefore insurgent citizenship is not always directed towards a clearly identified state, which seems to be the underlying logic of Holston's (2008) terminology, a point that I return to below.

Civil in/security and police–citizen relations

Concerns and practices regarding civil in/security constitute a privileged space for the analysis of fluid state–citizen configurations. In particular, quarrels over crime and public order bring to light citizens' expectations towards the state as provider of protection, and they also indicate, sometimes in very concrete and violent ways, who among the community members are considered worthy of protection and who are not. Elsewhere, I have described how Alteño neighbours organize in a more or less structured manner to prevent crime in their areas of residence. This is done through safety-seeking practices that involve 'reading' the urban landscape and recognizing the strategy of criminals in the flow of the city before they identify a household as their next object. People mimic police work and private security companies as they write warning signs in the name of 'the law' and seek to trick potential criminals into believing that private security companies protect their street. For instance, they put up sign-boards of fictitious security companies that supposedly patrol the neighbour-hood. In this way, people adopt different and ambiguous subject positions, alternatively appearing as the 'neighbours', the 'law', and private security firms. It is in this regard essential that these shifting subject positions at once work to conceal the concrete subjects that may engage in illegal activities such as community punishments and mob lynching and to make visible the neighbours as crime victims and citizens with a right to state protection (see also Risør 2010, 2013).

While the police are not absent in El Alto they do not provide security consistently or in a structured manner, because of their limited presence and corrupt practices. Most of the time it is the neighbours who perform their own version of proper police work in the form of self-help security groups, even if these practices are of a shadowy nature because they are illegal according to state law. The most violently spectacular expression of these practices is that of mob lynching of presumed criminals. Yet, even these evident transgressions of the state monopoly of violence are not solely state defying practices. They mimic the state language by incorporating interrogation, including torture, of the presumed criminal and frequent reference to the 'law'.

Despite widespread criticism and complaints about the police, the neigh-bourhoods also demand more police presence, and in turn the police seek to establish constructive police–community relations. Also, the municipality in its 2007 report on civil security states that safety and security are shared responsibilities between community members and authorities. However, this relationship is not straightforward and accusations of police corruption (see also Mansilla 2003; Quintana 2005) and extra-legal and excessive violence by the local population are always lurking under the surface. The following description of a police–municipality–community meeting in the city's third district that I participated in is a good illustration of this. The meeting took place one Saturday afternoon and after the neighbours' regular meeting two police officers and two of the municipality's civil guards appeared on motorbikes. They distributed flyers and then began to illustrate different ways in which community members could be tricked or assaulted by criminals. The police officer and the municipality guard performed a short play on *el cuento del tío* ['the uncle's tale' or trick thievery], and they warned women against wearing expensive jewellery at marketplaces and people in general against carrying large amounts of money in the street. The focus of the presentation was on prevention, and the officers stressed that crime prevention was a shared responsibility and that community members should self-organize, put bars in front of their windows and look out for each other. The police officer also recommended that they use whistles as a form of alarm that would scare criminals away and call upon the attention of their neighbours so that thieves could be apprehended.

The issue of collective apprehension of criminals by community members was a delicate matter. First, because, 'it could be dangerous' to deal with criminals as the police officer explained. Second, because apprehensions were matters for the police to deal with, and, 'lynching is illegal' and a morally sanctioned deed, the officer emphasized. The officer noted that if community members carried out lynching activities they would put themselves on the level of criminal murders and risk legal prosecution. The issue of lynching caused unrest among the community members who were reluctant to accept a label that criminalized their practices. Until this point in the presentation, people had listened to the officer and studied the flyers, but now they began questioning the utility of the officers' advice: If they should not apprehend the thieves then who would? Why did the police never answer their calls? Why were there no patrols? Why would they not put the criminals away in prison for long periods of time? The officer replied that the police lacked equipment and manpower, that the law favoured the criminals, and that justice could not be done because the law was unjust. The officer pointed out that the law was issued as if 'Bolivia was the United States' where the police allegedly have endless forensic and technical equipment at their disposal to enhance the investigation, generate evidence and apprehend the criminals. 'But this isn't the United States, it is Bolivia and this is why the criminals are laughing at all of us', the officer added. In this way, he managed to convince community members that both the police and the citizens were caught in a web of unjust laws, lack of resources and the elite's aspirations to adopt Western norms. The community members' calmed down a bit. Guilt was externalized towards the judicial system and the modification of the penal code facilitated in 1997 by the then Minister of Justice, René Blatmann, and a certain consensus was reached among participants at the meeting. Nevertheless, the overall picture was that of a lose–lose situation. We were all partaking in a common frustration, and the issue of collective punishment and lynching remained as a latent and unresolved matter. The officer stood up, and in a final attempt to reach some degree of consensus with the crowd he announced: 'You may beat them up, but you cannot kill them, because if you kill them then Human Rights will come.'

On this background of common frustration, and in spite of its obvious illegal elements, the *clausura* stands out as successful mutual community–police enhancement. As has been illustrated in the above analysis, the point is that to ensure order and some version of the law, the police effectively draw upon the dirty work of the community. As the *clausura* had addressed a widespread concern with excessive alcohol consumption and the proliferation of criminal assaults in the city centre, the commanding officer of the municipality's Civil Security Department praised the action. This was the case, even when he recognized the fact that the burning of private property obviously was illegal.

In public discourse the commanding officer honoured the students for their deeds. He associated the *clausura* with the police's preventive work and in this way strengthened the police's position on the background of the community's extra-legal activities (even if he denied that the police were involved in or condoned any illegal activity). The Alteño police, as with police forces in general (cf. Hansen 2006), rely upon community cooperation, which is conceptualized as the entity that knows what is 'really' going on in the city (Jensen 2004, 2009). However, the police are not just a parasite, as it were, benefitting from community actions. As a state institution they also grant legitimacy to the citizens' activities, in this case the *clausura*. In this particular case it is a win–win situation in which police, community members and students form police–citizen relations successfully. Hence, in a skilful navigation of an unstable terrain of mutual distrust and accusations, state structures can actually be strengthened through the community's actions and the community can be validated by the endorsement of state authorities.

Participating in the *clausura*

The *clausura* in October 2007 was the continuation of a demonstration (*marcha*) against the bars that the students held in 2006. It bore reference to former closures that adults and students had carried out in their zones of residence: a week earlier the *Juntas Escolares* (School Committees) of the southern zones of El Alto had looted bars at a traffic nodal point in Rio Seco near the Public University of El Alto (UPEA). The day before the students' demonstration, the *Junta de Vecinos* of the central zone of Villa Dolores had brought 'closure' to bars in the city centre. As such the *clausura* was not a unique event. Yet, it gained the status of being just that because of the way the students managed to turn the protest into a political negotiation that was organized by the FES.

The planning of the demonstration was not a simple task: students had to be convened and FES normally does so through the official regional office of educational affairs, indirectly placing student protests under the control of state institutions. The students also coordinate with the COR, which the FES is affiliated with, in this way associating the students' demands with a long history of working class struggle in Bolivia. Thus, while FES is a recent relevant actor in Alteñan politics, its *modus operandi* draws on a long tradition of labour activism and political protest within Bolivia and El Alto. Characteristic of the fluid nature of state–citizen relations, a detailed account of the organization of the protests illustrates the participation of the municipality in the students' demand for the closure of bars. A municipal official says:

> We have worked to make the youngsters aware about gangs, domestic violence, alcohol consumption and drug consumption. Sad as it is, for some time now we have seen an increase in alcohol consumption in the city of El Alto, right. For that reason on August 31, 2007, we carried out a mobilization of students that was called 'The First Walk of the Alteño Youth for Civil Security'. It was a big mobilization and approximately 10,000 youngsters participated, and the demand of the students was the immediate closure of bars and cantinas in El Alto.

The official situates the youngsters' concern with the bars as a consequence of the municipality's work of 'making the students aware' [*sensibilizar*], and he underscores that the municipality organized the first mobilization.

The FES *dirigentes* recognize their mutual cooperation with state authorities. The point is that FES, as a trade union affiliated to the COR, operates as a recognized social organization that monitors the principals and teachers of the schools. They form part of a system of mutual recognition between state authorities and social organizations, which bestows a certain authority on trade unions. It is for this reason that FES calls for *marchas* and parades through the system of SEDUCA (Servicio Departamental de Educación), the state department of education. The *marchas* of a trade union are made obligatory by means of the stamp of a state organization. In this sense, FES depends on a state institution to carry out its activities in the best possible manner, which means showing a great number of participants in the streets. Yet, it is also because of its capacity to organize large numbers that FES can get tangible results from its negotiations with the state authorities. Therefore, the FES *dirigentes* can also negotiate directly with the principals of the schools. One student leader, 'Claudio', says:

We put conditions on the schools also. For instance, we have obtained laboratories for physics and chemistry so we go to the educational institutions and we say to them, 'those who want laboratories will have to participate in the *marcha* that FES has called for – if they don't participate, they will lose their laboratories'. So, looking out for their interests, because there are good principals out there, they send their students [to the *marcha*] and they will get their laboratories.

In this sense, FES is a de facto political power in El Alto, although its strength rests on its ambiguous relationship with state authorities, on whom it depends as well as challenges. Occasionally, FES also holds *marchas* without the support of the SEDUCA. The *clausura* of 2007 was one such instance. Since this *marcha* ended up with the torching of private property, the municipal authorities claim no connection:

> The Directorate of Civil Security and the Unit of Prevention had no knowledge of these activities. The organized secondary students and the Padres de Familia [school committees] of El Alto planned it. [. . .] In fact you could say that they took justice in their own hands. So we believe that this act weakened [the authority of] the municipality, because basically they stated that the municipality was not on top of the situation. After the burnings of the brothels in the city of El Alto on October 12, the municipal order 132 was immediately effected, or I mean the decree [*ordenanza*] that prohibits these bars in the vicinity of educational centres.

The official simultaneously defines the *clausura* as an illegal act with no reference to the municipality and yet recognizes that it led to the new law being enacted. Yet, not all local authorities share this position: renowned city council member Roberto de la Cruz, seemed less concerned with maintaining a division between legality and illegality when I interviewed him in July 2008. He framed the *clausura* as a legitimate act against bars and bar owners who 'illicitly make money with alcohol in the city of El Alto'. As a city council member and leader of the political party Movimento de Octubre (M-17), he willingly associated himself with the burnings carried out by the neighbors. However, he claimed no connection with the actions of the FES (who did not associate themselves with him either) and he underscored that he did not participate in person, although his 'followers' did.[2] According to Cruz, certain bar owners had been untouchable before the *clausuras* due to corruption among the municipal officials who should control the bars' licences. He describes El Alto before the *clausura* as 'a city of nobody [in charge]', meaning that the law was constantly being broken and that (state) sovereignty was an absent feature. In this sense, he defines the *clausura* as an extraordinary measure in an extraordinary situation. The council member knows that the burnings are illegal, but he emphasizes that they have made the bars 'calm down', and states: 'To me, it is not legal, but it is legitimate when we think of the demands of the *Padres de Familia*, who do not want the youth to continue drugging themselves, damaging their mental health.'

The *clausura* did not only have winners but also losers. From the perspective of the *dirigentes* of the legal bar owners in the ASPEBREK (Asociación de peñas, bares, restaurantes y karaokes) the *clausuras* simply work to underscore the status of El Alto as 'nobody's city', or as he phrased it, 'a city without law'. Lily Cortez, the *dirigente* of the sex workers who in the aftermath of the *clausura* in 2007 initiated a hunger strike as a means of protest because they were impeded from carrying out their legal activities, made similar statements to me. Conversely, the municipal official does not think that the *clausura* has radically changed anything in El Alto. To him the illegal burnings, however understandable and legitimate, simply confirm El Alto as 'a city of nobody'.

The protest

The degree of violence and the magnitude of the *clausura* came as a surprise to the youngsters who participated. Though the *marcha* was carefully planned, the violence is explained as an unpredicted result of the masses' rage and rebelliousness. It appears as if the violent actions simply took place. The torchings were not planned. Rather, they are described as a consequence of the heat of the moment, and the *dirigentes* emphasized that a leader 'must obey the will of the masses'. Normally, this understanding of leadership is practised by means of assemblies where matters are discussed (often for many hours) until an agreement is reached, either through consensus or by vote. *Dirigentes* are thus considered as literally enacting the will of the people, rather than directing them in accordance with their beliefs. Of course a *dirigente* tries to convince the masses of their own point of view, and oratory skills are important for a leader, but at the end of the day he or she is considered the embodiment of the will of the people. In this sense, the *dirigentes* are not so much considered to be individualized figures through which the demands of the masses become expressed. The central political subject is the collective, be it students, Padres de Familia, neighbours or Alteños.

Thus, the student leaders describe the initial throwing of stones at the bars as a demand from the base members that they had to obey. This argument resembles the narratives circulating about the Gas War in which the leaders were said to be 'overflowed' by the ordinary members. During the *clausura* it was almost as if they were an instrument of mass rage. According to one student:

> We lifted a really big stone and there it was, the first bar, which was protected with burglar bars, really well secured, and we threw the big stone and went in. After much effort we entered and grabbed some drunkards. Then we started to bring outside all the materials of the disco – its chairs, its speakers and all that, but we had nothing flammable [so we used] the very alcohol they serve as drinks.

What is striking about these narratives is that the violence is described as something that naturally emerges from the crowd of youngsters, who are overtaken by their rage against everyday insecurity, alcoholism and violence.

Other students emphasize how the torchings were supported by the *cholita* hawkers, who gave them matches and pure alcohol so that the burnings could go on from bar to bar. Thus, the narratives situate the youngsters as an instrument of the will of the Alteño people, and individual agency is atomized in the body of the collective. According to Claudio: 'The most important thing that I will never forget is that the *señoras* that sell potatoes in La Ceja began to give us matches and alcohol when we started the burnings.' In his narrative, the *señoras*, the street vendors of El Alto, represent the popular subject. The fact that they handed over alcohol and matches to the youngsters turns the protesters into the enactors of the demands of the people. However, Claudio's narration of 'the most important thing' continues, and he says: 'and the whole world, all of El Alto, has noticed that the students have taken the streets [and seen] what we have done, and since then FES has been known for its ability to mobilize.'

Just like the community members' warning signs against potential criminals referred to earlier in this chapter, the students' narratives are indicative of how the Alteño as an active socio-political agent is difficult to categorize clearly. Whether we look at warning signs signed by the 'neighbors' or the students' narratives of the *clausura*, subject position switches between first and third person positions. Sometimes they act as the mass and the people, sometimes in the name of the 'youth' and sometimes they constitute the FES. That is why it can simultaneously be the 'most important thing' that it was the *cholitas* that handed over the matches *and* that FES has gained political respect and credibility due to its 'ability to mobilize'. The art of managing these fluid subject positions is a matter of political skill that was shown during the negotiations in the aftermath of the event itself.

Hence, the political power Claudio refers to does not appear automatically. Neither do the bars become stabilized and fixed as sites of insecurity simply because a few of them were set alight. It is due to the youngsters' political skill that it is the bar owners and the sex workers, not them, who end up being criminalized. This is managed by means of the hunger strike and political negotiations with the mayor. As a matter of fact, the students tell how during the *clausura* the police initially treated them as gangsters and vandals, as a consequence of which the youngsters felt most offended. However, they were not arrested, and they soon managed to attribute a political rationality and utility to the violence. This took place as the students initiated a hunger strike.

Hunger strike as negotiation

The students did not end their activities with the burnings. Once the crowd had dispersed, eight of them initiated a hunger strike. Hunger strike is a recognized political language in Bolivia (Fabricat and Postero 2013) and it may be understood as the initiation of a political negotiation that performatively situates the civil security issue as a matter of life and death.

One of the participating girls told me:

> Then we went into eight days of hunger strike. The two first days nobody took notice of us, but on the third day people from the municipality began to come by, telling us that we should give up the strike and that they would give in. On the fifth day they worried a bit and the media and everything came by. On the seventh day we made an agreement and on the eighth day we signed the agreement [with the mayor] but by then I had had to give up and they [the municipality] took me to the hospital.

As the days passed, the students' demands went from specific petitions regarding the schools and security to a political demand for the mayor's resignation, because he failed to control the bars and hence the civil security situation. As such, the *clausura* took the form of a small-scale version of former protests in which demonstrations, roadblocks and hunger strikes are common elements.[3] As the form of the protest went from demonstration to torching to hunger strike, the students' demands went from free breakfast to closure of bars to the resignation of the mayor. This latter demand was dropped once the mayor showed up and explained to the youngsters the difficulties he had with corrupt employees.

An agreement was finally signed in which the mayor promised implementation of the new municipal law prohibiting the existence of bars within 500 metres of public schools, hospitals and churches. It was further agreed that FES could participate in the public inspections of bars, cantinas and brothels. Today the students occasionally accompany the municipality's officials and the police on their random nightly raids on bars and brothels. As such, FES has turned into a relevant political actor and the students participate in activities of the COR and periodically organize public activities and *marchas* in coordination with the municipality. They mobilize people, as Claudio puts it.

Conclusion

In the present chapter I have indicated how concerns with civil insecurity constitute a privileged arena where state-citizen relations, however tensed they may be, are re-negotiated in such a way that state and community organizations are mutually strengthened. While the police as state representative may appear as weakened, insufficient or incapable of fulfilling the citizens' expectations of civil security, the community's (illegal) actions in search of safety and security do not necessarily undermine state authority and sovereignty. They can also work to enforce the state's credibility or at least compel the necessity for more and better police presence. The *clausura* stands out as an example of this state-citizen complex. As such, state formation can also occur in contexts of apparent state defiance and, when state authorities endorse the citizen's actions, civil society organizations are simultaneously ratified.

The analysis of the *clausura* indicates the importance of civil insecurity in the city of El Alto, and how this issue has been articulated in such a way that FES is now a relevant political actor. It also indicates how the realm between formal and informal politics is intertwined in El Alto, as in many other sites. The youngsters have worn the faces of angry protestors, local authorities that inspect bars and brothels (or inspect the municipality's inspectors) and trade union leaders, while they attempt to navigate an unstable terrain in search of better life opportunities. As such, the analysis of the *clausura* indicates how politics and the becoming of political actors take form in a political terrain where state and non-state, law and the breaking of it, constantly change their shape and adopt each other's form. It is this indeterminacy of the political terrain that opened up the possibility of the students' engagement in it in the first place, and it is their skill to adopt subject positions according to prevalent circumstances that allow them to be taken seriously. Civil security is an important arena for these processes because it is an issue that severely affects people in their everyday life. It is also a political arena that, taken at its extreme, and following Schmitt (2007 [1929]), defines who is friend and who is enemy. The outcome of the *clausura* was the moral positioning of the students, not as gangsters and drunkards (which is a common image of the Alteño youth), but instead as responsible citizens and local leaders. The losers were the bar owners and the sex workers who ended up as morally dubious figures with no place in the future of the Bolivian nation.

In October 2008 I participated in the national FES congress, which was held in El Alto at the premises of the COR. Delegations from student federations from all over Bolivia were there to discuss educational matters and youth politics. Among the local authorities present was Colonel Peréz, head of the municipality's Civil Security Department who, in uniform, honoured the youngsters for their capacity to take justice into their own hands to create a safer El Alto. At the time it did not seem bizarre that the head of civil security and a representative of the Bolivian police was honouring people for taking the law into their own hands. As a matter of fact, it would only seem bizarre from a formalist perspective that assumes a clear-cut division between state and non-state actors, law and law-breaking. At that particular moment, the youngsters appeared to be the law, or better put, one law among others. As the law-enforcing entity, the colonel depended on the youngsters and the community members generally, and as a state officer he graced the youngsters with a stately twinkle; but he also simply recognized de facto co-governance between local government and the social organizations of El Alto. In this sense, we may understand the *clausura* as a form of insurgent citizenship. Yet, it is insurgency with a twist because the aim or the result of the protest was not simply a substantiation or expansion of the Aleños' civil rights. The *clausura* was also, and more importantly, an opening for the students not just to be seen by the state, but also to enact sovereignty and 'stateness' themselves.

These forms of socio-political organization and activities remind us that politics and state formation do not solely take place from the centres towards the periphery but also very much in the state margins, here understood as: 'sites of practice on which law and other state practices are colonized by other forms of regulation that emanate from the pressing needs of populations to secure political and economic survival' (Das and Poole 2004: 8). Following this perspective, the insurgency of my Alteño interlocutors is visible in their attempts at trying, not only to improve their living conditions and civil rights, that is, to become more visible to the state, but also to make state–citizen relations visible and stable. In other words, they try to exorcise what Daniel Goldstein (2012) recently defined as the Bolivian 'phantom state'. They strive to give corporality to the state in the marginal areas; even if they themselves must embody this stateness and eventually reproduce the very spectral character of the state that they try to circumscribe (cf. Risør 2010). In this way, the Alteños impel us to consider political actions (such as the *clausura*) and figures (such as the state and the citizenry) not in abstract and static terms but as a perform-ative practice (cf. Hansen and Stepputat 2001, 2005); that is, as figurations (cf. Krøijer 2010) in movement that people seek to socially navigate (cf. Vigh 2006) in order to position themselves in a favourable position and eventually to stabilize and manage them by means of violence (Risør 2013).

It remains an open question whether the *clausura* has effectively addressed and improved the civil security situation of El Alto. Most probably the municipal officer quoted above is right insofar that status quo more or less persists. The bars still form part of the cityscape of La Ceja, and it is probable that new protests, and new political negotiations, will take place. Yet, the fact that the *clausura* did not resolve the severe problems of civil insecurity in El Alto should not lead us to simply dismiss actions of the *clausura* as plain riots or as the struggle over scarce municipal resources. That is, to consider actions of this kind as incessant rebellions rather than decisive revolutions, as Henrik Vigh (2009) has suggested in a recent article regarding violent youth in West Africa. Drawing on Gluckman (1963), Vigh argues that successive rebellions cannot be seen as precessions of a revolution since rebellions and revolutions are different in their aims and effects. From this perspective, a 'revolution designates a change in the political system in question – that is, a change in the distribution of resources and organization of power within the system', while 'rebellions are fought for a change in the personae holding political positions' (Vigh 2009: 148). When seen in this way, the *clausura* and its outcomes can rightly be considered as an inutile rebellion that does not offer any profound structural transformation of the living conditions and security of the Alteño population. However, the *clausura* also indicates that actions of that kind stand out as instances through which otherwise marginal populations engage in negotiations with the state and manage to stand out as citizens with rights and to define and expand the scope of who can be considered worthy of protection and as valid political actors. In this sense, the *clausura* did not only allow a group of students to gain access to recourses and political positions; it also expanded the understanding of which groups are entitled to constitute the state.

The extended analysis of the *clausura* is an example of how state–citizen relations are not stable, but rather a set of practices that are constantly being reshaped and transformed – in El Alto and beyond. Finally, the ethnography of the *clausura* also underscores that the study of civil in/security and social dis/order is a privileged arena for the study of these processes. Indeed, this volatility of state–citizen relations points to the core of our understanding of the state as the holder of the monopoly of legitimate violence and our understanding of proper citizenship. It is with these considerations in mind that the *clausura* case allows us to consider that sometimes what appears as defiance of state authority and sovereignty might as well be considered as state enhancing and state transforming activities.

Notes

1   The present chapter would not have been possible without the support and collaboration from friends, interlocutors and institutions in El Alto and beyond. I am particularly grateful to the leaders and base members of the Federación de Estudiantes Secundarios de El Alto (FES) who during my fieldwork in El Alto in 2007–2008 allowed me a glimpse into their lives, struggles and concerns. I hope they find that the descriptions and reflections presented in the present chapter resonate with their own experiences, even if the analysis, and hence also the responsibility for eventual errors and misinterpretations, are solely mine.
2   In the aftermath of the *clausura* Roberto de la Cruz was accused of corruption, and of demanding money from bar owners in exchange for not setting their possessions on fire. These accusations made news headlines, and so when I met with him, he was particularly interested in denying them and explaining them as the result of the bitterness of the bar owners who used to be 'untouchable', as he puts it.
3   According to my Alteño interlocutors, hunger strike is seen as the first step of the radicalization of a conflict. Writing posters with one's blood, extracted in public with a needle, is also a performative form of protest. More extreme measures are crucifixion (first with ropes and then with nails) and auto-confinement, in which the entrances to the room of confinement are blocked off with bricks until only a small window is left to communicate with the outside world and receive water and coca leaves.

References

Arbona, J. M., 2006. Neo-liberal ruptures: Local political entities and neighbourhood networks in El Alto, Bolivia, *Geoforum*, 38, 127–137.
Arbona, J. M., 2008. Sangre de minero, semilla de guerillero. Histories and Memories in the Organisation and Struggles of the Santiago II Neighbourhood of El Alto, Bolivia, *Bulletin of Latin American Research*, 27:1, 24–42.

Das, V. and Poole, D., 2004. State and its margins: Comparative ethnographies, in V. Das and D. Poole (eds), *Anthropology in the Margins of the State*. Oxford: James Currey, 3–34.

Fabricat, N. and Postero, D., 2013. Contested bodies, contested states: Performance, Emotions, and new forms of regional governance in Santa Cruz, Bolivia, *Journal of Latin American and Caribbean Anthropology*, 18:2, 187–211.

Gluckman, M., 1963. *Order and Rebellion in Tribal Africa*. New York: The Free Press of Glencoe.

Goldstein, D., 2004. *The Spectacular City: Violence and Performance in Urban Bolivia*. Durham and London: Duke University Press.

Goldstein, D., 2012. *Outlawed: Between Security and Rights in a Bolivian City*, Durham and London: Duke University Press.

Hansen, T. B., 2006. Performers of sovereignty: On the privatization of security in urban South Africa, *Critique of Anthropology*, 26:3, 279–295.

Hansen, T. B. and Stepputat, F., 2001. Introduction: States of Imagination, in T. B. Hansen and F. Stepputat (eds), *States of Imagination: Ethnographic Explorations of the Postcolonial State*. Durham and London: Duke University Press, 1–40.

Hansen, T. B. and Stepputat, F., 2005. Introduction, in T. B. Hansen and F. Stepputat (eds), *Sovereign Bodies: Citizens, Migrants and States in the Postcolonial World*. Princeton, NJ and Oxford: Princeton University Press, 1–36.

Holston, J., 2008. *Insurgent Citizenship: Disjunctions of Democracy and Modernity in Brazil*. Princeton, NJ and Oxford: Princeton University Press.

Hylton, F. and Thompson, S., 2007. *Revolutionary Horizons: Past and Present in Bolivian Politics*. London: Verso.

Jensen, S., 2004. Claiming community: Local politics on the Cape Flats, South Africa, *Critique of Anthropology*, 24:2, 179–207.

Jensen, S., 2009. Gendered connections: Politics, brokers and urban transformation in Cape Town, *Critique of Anthropology*, 29:1, 47–64.

Krøijer, S., 2010. Figurations of the future: On the form and temporality of protests among left radical activists in Europe, *Social Analysis*, 54:3, 139–152.

Lazar, S., 2008. *El Alto, Rebel City: Self and Citizenship in Andean Bolivia*. Durham: Duke University Press.

McNeish, J.-A., 2006. Stones on the road: The politics of participation and the generation of crisis in Bolivia, *Bulletin of Latin American Research*, 25:2, 220–240.

Mamani Conde, J., 2006. *Octubre: Memorias de dignidad y massacre*. El Alto, Bolivia: Centro de Estudios y Apoyo al Desarrollo Local (CEADL) and Agencia de Prensa Alteña.

Mansilla, H. C. F., 2003. *La Policia Boliviana: Entre códigos informales y los intentos de modernización*, La Paz: Plural Ediciones.

Postero, N., 2007. *Now We Are Citizens: Indigenous Politics in Postmulticultural Bolivia*. Stanford CA: Stanford University Press.

Quintana, J. R., 2005. *Policia y Democracia en Bolivia: una política institucional pendiente*. La Paz: PIEB.

Risør, H., 2010. Twenty hanging dolls and a lynching: Defacing dangerousness and enacting citizenship in El Alto, Bolivia, *Public Culture*, 22:3, 465–485.

Risør, H., 2012. The *vecino* as Citizen: Neighbourhood organizations in El Alto and the transformation of Bolivian citizenship, in D. Rodgers, J. Beall and R. Kanbur (eds), *Latin American Urban Development into the 21st Century: Towards a Renewed Perspective on the City*, Basingstoke: Palgrave Macmillan, 103–122.

Risør, H., 2013. Captured with their hands in the dough: Insecurity, safety-seeking and securitization, in M. A. Pedersen and M. Holbraad (eds), *Times of Security: Ethnographies of Fear, Protest and the Future*. London: Routledge studies in Anthropology, 57–79.

Schmitt, C., 2007 [1929]. *The Concept of the Political* (expanded Version). Chicago, IL and London: University of Chicago Press.

Vigh, H., 2006. *Navigating Terrains of War: Youth and Soldiering in Guinea-Bissau*. New York and Oxford: Berghan Books.

Vigh, H., 2009. Conflictual motion and political inertia: On rebellions and revolutions in Bissau and beyond. *African Studies Review*, 52:2, 143–164.

Chapter 9

Security governance in Hout Bay

A study of three local communities' capacity to engage in policing

Øyvind Samnøy Tefre

The South African experience with policing is a fragmented history of multiple actors working both within and outside the law. At times it is performed by the state police or aided by it, at other times policing actors work independently of the state. Initially the Post-Apartheid South African government had a strong emphasis on community policing, exemplified by the establishment of Community Police Forums (CPF). However, by the late 1990s public outcry over high levels of crime supported more centralised state policing and 'get tough on crime' initiatives (Gordon 2006). Feelings of insecurity in South Africa nonetheless remain high and private and community-based policing orders have continued to expand. This has supported unequal access to publicly provided security and exacerbated the differences between rich and poor communities in their ability to provide security for themselves (Baker 2002). While middle and upper class citizens are able to confront their growing insecurity through their purchasing power, the lower-income citizens are left with an increasingly under-resourced and overworked public police, giving room for widespread vigilantism (Minnaar 2002) and other forms of local level self-help groups. As sections of society insulate themselves inside security bubbles, there is also the danger that dialogue across political class and racial lines withers. Social exclusion and urban fragmentation prevent a common national identity, echoing the Apartheid days of racial segregation (Baker 2002).

This chapter examines how crime and insecurity are confronted by three communities in Hout Bay, Cape Town, that are characterised by widely different socio-economic conditions and racial compositions (White, African and Coloured).[1] In particular, it explores each community's ability to generate collective capacity to provide enhanced policing in their own neighbourhoods. I argue that two factors are important to the effectiveness of everyday policing. First, the ability of a group to form a shared identity that is capable of generating and sustaining collective capacity for action. Second, the ability of a group to network with other security actors and gain access to external resources and technologies that can aid it in the pursuit of its policing agenda.

I combine a nodal governance approach with Mouffe's (2005) concept of the political in relation to group formation. This provides for an enhanced focus on how political conflict is always present when groups attempt to enforce order. The finding is that agonistic handling of political conflict, both between members within a node and in networking with other nodes, combined with an identity that is constructed on the basis of a shared ethos, is crucial for establishing an effective policing node, and for communities to affect their shared security challenges.

Thus, networking, identity formation and the social relations surrounding the various nodes are crucial variables in explaining a group's ability to effectively mobilise the technologies and resources that are necessary to make order. The relationship between the three communities under scrutiny in the chapter is characterised by distrust. Increasing differences in access to security is likely to exacerbate tensions. The study shows that order-making will lead to further social fragmentation unless the people of Hout Bay are able to build common projects, based on shared goals and relations that will enhance the security of all.

Nodal governance, networks and collective capacity

This study employs a nodal governance approach (Burris *et al.* 2005; Wood 2006) to map the active policing auspices and providers of Hout Bay and the networks they form that make up local order-making. However, the nodal perspective does not explain the relative strength of nodes. Nor is it capable of explaining how effective nodes come about, and what separates them from less effective nodes. The comparison of different communities in Hout Bay illustrates that the governing capacity of nodes depends on two important variables: first, their collective identity formation, and second, their capacity to enrol other nodes by access to different types of networks.

Along with Mouffe (2005), I see political identities as relational constructs; 'we' is understood in relation to the significant other, 'they'. Effective cooperation requires political identities to be based on 'agonism' rather than 'antagonism'. If the distinction becomes antagonistic there is no room for cooperation because 'they' are the enemy. Conversely, 'agonism' means accepting the legitimacy of conflicting viewpoints, leaving room for disagreements, while keeping the door open for cooperation in areas where interests overlap. Agonistic identity formation is central to effective group action.

Collective capacity for action requires group members to share a belief in their conjoint capability to achieve intended effects. It is not the strength of social ties themselves, but the way ties are activated to achieve desired outcomes that matters (Sampson *et al.* 1999). Converting social ties to collective capacity for action is most effective when all members are committed to a shared group 'ethos'; a set of constitutive goals, values or standards that give the group motivating reasons for action. Shared commitment to group ethos is crucial because it binds members together in the realisation that the desired outcomes can only be achieved as a group. Aggregate private reasons cannot substitute this shared ethos (Tuomela 2007).

Effective group action requires members to be collectively committed to the shared ethos, but at the same time agonism requires space for disagreement, in order to keep disruptive conflicts at bay (Briggs 2008), allowing members space to address the shared ethos in different ways, so long as the ethos itself is respected. It is the commitment to what can be achieved that is important, not strong ties between individual members. This is also important to agonistic conflict resolution. Because the group is bound by its ethos, private and emotionally charged identity politics may be sidestepped (Kempa 2008) when they do not directly affect the ethos itself, allowing cooperation to continue despite disagreements.

The point that the strength of social ties is secondary to the commitment to an ethos is important to networks as well; sharing an ethos means that a group can consist of weaker ties but still rely on each other to perform. 'Weak' ties are beneficial, because they are more likely to constitute 'bridges' that can enable the flow of resources, ideas, and information between separate networks (Granovetter 1973; 1983), thus giving the group the benefit of greater reach to enrol and align with other groups. Policing nodes with access to many bridging ties will be more effective at enrolling and aligning other policing nodes through networks.

In the following I utilize the nodal governance approach to map out the key nodes that actively attempt to influence policing in Hout Bay. I show that an emphasis on how policing nodes are capable of converting social ties to collective commitments to a shared group ethos and handling political differences agonistically, can lead nodes to become significantly more effective at enhancing security provision. Networking with other policing nodes is also necessary for effective order-making, and I argue that the identity construction is important to the ability of nodes to interact and cooperate effectively.

Presenting Hout Bay

Hout Bay is situated a few miles south of Cape Town and is home to three distinct communities. The Valley occupies the largest area and is home to mainly White middle-to-upper-income residents. There are some gated communities in the Valley, but the majority live in single houses surrounded by high fences. The Hangberg community is located by the harbour and is home to the majority of the Coloured population. The area is dominated by hostels and flats, but there is also an informal settlement dominated by freestanding houses and bungalows. Traditionally a fishing village, the loss of fishing quotas has made unemployment a major issue in later years. The third community is the mainly Black African township Imizamo Yethu, also known as 'Mandela Park'. Established in 1991, it was designed to accommodate the African population of Hout Bay which numbered roughly 2,500 people who had previously resided in five separate squatter camps in the area. Imizamo Yethu has grown rapidly and is today estimated to number about 16,000 people (Adams *et al.* 2006).

Prior to 1950 people of all races lived mixed together in the Valley of Hout Bay, but following the Group Areas Act of 1950 it was designated an area for Whites. The Coloured population was forcefully moved to the harbour, and the Blacks were removed almost entirely. The White community increasingly regarded the growth of squatter camps as an eyesore, and from 1975 measures were taken to evict unwanted elements from the Valley, and limit African and Coloured influx. During the next ten years racial tensions peaked as detection and pass raids, demolition of shacks, forced removals, and imprisonment became the order of the day (Froestad 2005). Today the relationship between the different communities of Hout Bay remains strained and fragmented. Their interaction is restricted to the economic domain. Though there are few signs of open hostility between the communities, people stick to their own. Cooperation between them is rare.

The Valley – pragmatic partnerships and community ethos

In only a year, from April 2005 till April 2006, the residents of the Valley managed to reduce property crime by 70 per cent, mainly due to the Hout Bay Neighbourhood Watch (HBNW) (SAPS Deputy Station Commissioner, 29 March 2006). While previous efforts to combat the rising problem of property crime since the late 1990s had failed, the HBNW made a change for three reasons: first, the establishment of a clear agenda and a collective commitment to a shared group ethos; second, the ability to handle internal conflicts by fostering agonistic social relations; and last, extensive networking with the police and private security companies.

Networks with private and public providers

HBNW was established in April 2005 by members of the Hout Bay Community Police Forum (HBCPF) who had tired of the yearlong conflict with Hout Bay SAPS (South African Police Service). Most blamed the expansion of Imizamo Yethu for the rise in crime. The launch of HBNW was attended by over 500 people and many signed up to participate in patrols. A year later HBNW was the largest civic organisation in Hout Bay with more than 1,500 members.

HBNW operates on a range of different levels. They raise awareness about and bring community members together in crime prevention. With about 100 members doing active night patrols this is perhaps the most important HBNW activity. An extensive radio communications network has been established with about 120 radios in circulation, which have been distributed to the police and private security companies. The idea is that HBNW provides manpower for and acts as the eyes and ears of the police, without directly performing arrests. However, some HBNW sectors have in fact done arrests. While most HBNW activities are within the law, there are actions with a questionable legal character. One of the sectors, for instance, put up an electric fence on council land and placed a guard at the entrance. Although strictly illegal, the government has done nothing to prevent it. Residents claim that if the government is not in a position to ensure their safety they have to do it themselves. There is also the questionable legality of citizens' arrests and the way HBNW members confront people in the streets who are seen to not belong to the area. Concerns related to these practices are the racial profiling involved, which is a highly sensitive political issue in South Africa. Moreover, the police worry that citizens' arrests could eventually result in someone getting killed as people with little or no training do police work. The police are aware of these activities but have so far turned a blind eye to them when performed by HBNW members. In general, the relationship to the police is close. The police also have a member on the executive committee of HBNW.

A similarly close relationship exists with the two private security companies in Hout Bay. ADT is the largest and dominates with their armed response service. The other is Deep Blue Securities, a newly established local company that provides guarding and response services. The HBNW control centre, WatchCon, is provided by Deep Blue free of charge. The fact that SAPS and ADT have also been provided with HBNW radios also ties them to Deep Blue. Deep Blue has a small client base. For this reason it spends a lot of time backing up HBNW and also uses this to actively recruit new subscribers. ADT provides a much more standardised service, and has been reluctant in using their personnel to back up HBNW activity. They argue that engaging in activity in areas where they are not contracted will place their employees at unnecessary risk and could mean lawsuits for the company. As Deep Blue has increasingly been seen as the strong community supporter, ADT has started sponsoring HBNW with R15,000 (approx. $2,500) a month to avoid being seen as detached from the community. HBNW ties to the private security industry are strengthened by the fact that one of its executive committee members is part owner of Deep Blue.

The partnership between HBNW, the SAPS and the primary private security providers has proven very effective in reducing property crime in the Valley. According to an ADT executive:

> It's a three way partnership, the police can't do it alone they don't have the resources, we can't do it alone we don't have the powers . . . the residents are key to that. If you look at Hout Bay over the last ten years, the residents have to a large extent left security issues to the police and service providers.
>
> (ADT General Manager Western Cape, 11 April 2006)

One reason for the success of HBNW is that its members have managed to constitute HBNW as a structure where the different security nodes can come together and coordinate their efforts.

HBNW members have enrolled the resources of the police and private security companies to suit their own needs. Utilising Deep Blue's wish to be seen as a community company and setting this up against ADT which wishes to be seen as contributing on an equal footing with its competitor has generated enormous resources for HBNW. Further, the relationship with the SAPS is not as straight forward as would seem to be the case. Many members are dissatisfied with alone being the eyes and ears of the police. They rather see the police as a resource to further the needs of HBNW. The relationship between HBNW and SAPS is one where it is never quite clear who is doing the enrolling, and who is being enrolled. There is a constant struggle between them as to which party is to govern. On the one hand, the night patrolling by HBNW has given the police more time to deal with serious crimes in neighbouring communities. On the other hand, HBNW members place strong demands on the police to respond immediately to their calls, often to deal with trivial matters such as a 'suspect' person walking in the neighbourhood. Further, many HBNW members viewed the average SAPS officer with low esteem and saw them as inexperienced and incompetent, lacking sufficient knowledge of the local area to police it. Members actively sought to direct the police in how to respond to calls from HBNW. Despite complaints, the SAPS tolerated this behaviour because they depended on the HBNW to provide effective policing. On the whole both parties benefitted from the relationship: the SAPS can show their superiors improved statistics and extra manpower: the HBNW gains legitimacy through their cooperation with SAPS, e.g. by borrowing extensively from the symbolic power that accrues from being associated with the police.

Political conflict and agonistic solutions

To understand how HBNW became the vessel through which the people of the Valley came to organise security it is important to understand the breakdown of the Hout Bay Community Police Forum (HBCPF). The HBCPF was made up of civic organisations in all three communities. It was intended to operate as a statutory body overseeing the overall safety and security in Hout Bay and liaise with the SAPS. However, HBCPF became the centre of strong political contestation between the police and the HBCPF chairperson, as well as between member organisations choosing sides in the struggles.

The strained relationship between the police and the HBCPF started when the chairperson took up allegations of corruption within the Hout Bay SAPS leadership with the SAPS Area Commissioner. Although the leadership was cleared of all charges, the seed had been planted for a complete breakdown in the relationship between the Hout Bay SAPS and the HBCPF. The Hout Bay SAPS were ordered to distance themselves from the HBCPF while the SAPS sought to have the HBCPF disbanded to constitute a new CPF. However, the Cape Town High Court ruled that the SAPS did not have the authority to do so, and ordered the police to resume cooperation with the HBCPF. But it was too late:

> there is a total lack of trust, almost hate between them [the station commissioner and the HBCPF chairperson]. It cannot function without changes . . . there is a need for either a new station commander or a new chairperson of the CPF, there is no other way of solving it.
> (SAPS Deputy Station Commissioner, 29 March 2006)

During the conflict member organisations split within the HBCPF as they took sides in the conflict. Many members stopped attending the HBCPF meetings.

The chairperson of HBCPF later announced a class action law suit against the government for failure to provide security to the people of Hout Bay by letting the influx and growth of Imizamo Yethu go unchecked. This further alienated many organisations from the HBCPF, particularly within Imizamo Yethu and Hangberg. They saw the HBCPF as a political vessel for the DA (Democratic Alliance). The actual goal, many thought, was to attack the ANC before the upcoming municipal elections. The vice chair of HBCA explained:

> politics here play a major role . . . especially in the [Valley]. You know exactly who is DA or whatever party, we all know [the HBCPF chairperson] is DA. When we get together there's always a political side coming out, especially at meetings this political thing sticks its head out. It always sticks its head out because they, I don't want to say rich people, but they don't care what happens in the Harbour.
> (HBCA deputy chair, 30 April 2006)

This view was supported by the chairperson of the HBNW who saw the HBCPF as being:

> hijacked by political organizations . . . I'd go so far as to say that they've weighed the CPF with community organisations that had very little to do with community policing. So just to put it very plainly is; White organisations have got control of the CPF . . . I've made myself very unpopular for saying that, but it's the truth.
> (HBNW Co-chair, 14 March 2006)

The actions taken by the HBCPF chairperson and her supporters had strong political implications. It antagonised large parts of the member organisations, in all three communities, as well as the police, making it impossible for the HBCPF to operate effectively in its policing role.

The HBNW was launched shortly after the HBCPF announced its intention to sue the government. While the HBNW is formally constituted under the HBCPF it has distanced itself from its mother organisation, opting for a very pragmatic orientation to dealing specifically with what citizens can do to prevent property crime. It is this commitment to what 'we' can do to prevent property crime that holds its members together. This is the basis for its collective ethos. The Valley is not a closely integrated community, but the feeling that they were all being victimised by criminal elements, mainly stemming from Imizamo Yethu, was effectively used to tie people together to a common goal. Whereas the HBCPF took a very aggressive stance towards relocation of the township, the HBNW explicitly distanced itself from any such action and instead chose to focus on an ethos of self-reliance: if the government is not going to provide sufficient policing, we must do it ourselves. The HBNW also committed members to an understanding that 'we' stand and fall together. Crucially, HBNW consists of members with different views about the lawsuit or any other political issue, such as police corruption, that may concern residents of the Valley, but they do not let this interfere with their goal of increasing public awareness and action against crime. This makes HBNW able to function well despite disagreement among its members.

Where antagonism and conflict ruined the HBCPF's chance of functioning as a collective vessel for enhanced policing, HBNW rose to take its place. By focusing on a shared ethos and establishing pragmatic networks with other policing nodes in Hout Bay, HBNW has become the primary drive for enhanced security and policing for the residents of the Valley. HBNW has established weaker ties among its members, committing them to collective action to reduce property crime in the Valley. It has been able to do so by sidestepping the political conflicts that were previously preventing action through the HBCPF.

Imizamo Yethu – a community divided

Imizamo Yethu is a mixed Black community that consists of a majority of about 50 per cent Xhosas. Other groups include Zulus, Angolans, Nigerians, Ovambos, Malawians and Congolese. The ethnic diversity of the township has resulted in some tension, and the relationship between the different groups remains cautious. Unemployment and alcohol abuse are widespread and breed problems of assault, rape and domestic abuse. The ethnic diversity is also reflected in organisational life. Division, lack of trust, allegations of corruption and nepotism are frequently mentioned when speaking to the residents.

A lot of the criticism is directed at the main civic association, SANCO (South African National Civic Organization) and at the local ANC (African National Congress), which many see as serving their own interests and aiding those close to them. The leaders of SANCO and ANC are, however, regarded by most as the top community leaders in the township. The vast majority of resources that enter the township go through them. Another community civic is the Sinethemba. It claims to represent the 'original beneficiaries', i.e. those present at the establishment of the township. Their numbers are few, but they have two seats on the HBCPF executive (both of whom are DA members) and have allied themselves closely with the Ratepayers in the Valley. They are supported by the HBCPF chairperson as well as the DA Ward Councillor. Sinethemba's main thrust in the area of policing has been to support the HBCPF in both the allegations of police corruption and in initiatives to prevent further expansion of Imizamo Yethu through law suits aided by the HBCPF and the Ratepayers. Like the Ratepayers and many in the Valley they believe that the only way to prevent crime and other social ills from escalating is for the majority of the township's population, those they refer to as 'the illegals', to be relocated. This has alienated them from the wider community of the township and they are regarded by many as little more than 'puppets for the Whites'; several instances of violence against them have been reported, with blame pointed at SANCO as the instigators. A lot of the malcontent in Imizamo Yethu is grounded in a housing project that was to allocate plots and houses to the people who were present when the township was established in 1991. Accusations of corruption and nepotism were quickly directed at SANCO who were in charge of allocating the plots.

The level of conflict and lack of trust between different groups in Imizamo Yethu is detrimental to establishing any cooperation and development in the township. The lack of trust in the community leadership combined with conflicts over housing issues and influx control have spilled over to other issues facing the community. This makes it difficult for organisations to work together on any issue, though the problems facing them may be shared.

Weak policing and politically contested networks

Complaints that the police do not prioritise Imizamo Yethu are common. The police admit that they have great difficulties with doing patrols in the township because of the bad infrastructure. They have also been attacked and stoned when attempting to shut down shebeens. A central problem is that the township currently has few viable alternatives to the police. This has resulted in instances of mob justice and vigilantism. In early 2003 a group of about twenty businessmen got together and attempted to impose a curfew on the township in order to secure their businesses. This resulted in random shootings in the streets. A number of young people were beaten up by the businessmen. While organised vigilantism seems to be short lived, there are still occasional beatings by civilians of persons caught doing burglaries. In September 2003 a neighbourhood watch was established. Twenty-seven volunteers were trained for a week by the SAPS to perform night patrols. Over the holidays in December the Department of Community Safety (DOCS) recruited the volunteers to keep the beaches of Hout Bay safe for tourists, and members received financial compensation. After this project ended the neighbourhood watch dissolved, presumably because there was no longer any financial compensation.

For a while there were several Block Committees in Imizamo Yethu that functioned as community courts. Though most have been abandoned some are still operating. These committees provide an important source of social control and dispute resolution. This includes direct intervention in cases of domestic violence or fights in shebeens. The committees do not distinguish between civil and criminal matters, but rather deal with all problems. Because of this they seem to have enjoyed a great deal of local legitimacy. The focus on making peace between parties rather than distributing guilt is the key to how they operate: 'The main thing is to make peace, not to create friction. Psychologically you must know that although these people have been fighting, they love each other because they know each other' (Block Committee leader, 23 May 2006).

The relationship between the police and the Block Committees was seen as mutually beneficial. Conflict resolution by the committees saves the police a lot of time and effort. It also means that the already strained judicial system becomes less overburdened. Committee members were also used by the police as victim support in cases of rape and child abuse. Members of the Block Committees noted that the police were quick to respond to their calls. They use the police as a last resort if they are unable to solve a matter themselves, or if the violation is too serious for them to handle.

The majority of the committees have been abandoned because of disagreements with the community leadership in SANCO. Though the Committees operate relatively autonomously they belong to the larger SANCO structure. Many members felt that the SANCO leadership reaped the benefits of their hard work without contributing anything:

> [The Block Committees] stopped when they started building houses . . . I think when SANCO also wanted to be involved in the Block Committees . . . We were working so hard but they were not doing so much, but they wanted to be the ones who got praised, so then people got fed up with it and so they left . . . When it came to the elections of the SANCO . . . people wanted to elect someone on those groups because they could see how we were working. But the SANCO committee . . . they don't give the people their own choice.
> (former Block Committee leader, 30 May 2006)

The loss of Block Committees has left large parts of Imizamo Yethu with the police as the only option. Yet the Hout Bay SAPS are understaffed and lack sufficient resources.

Group fragmentation and conflict

The groups operating in Imizamo Yethu are all characterised by following their own agenda, and a lot of it seems to be motivated by personal interests. There is no common 'we' in Imizamo Yethu. Instead there are many smaller groups with strong internal ties. This is influenced by the level of poverty, which has given rise to a system of patronage where people are dependent on those few sources of resources that exist.

A central reason for why SANCO has maintained its central position in the township is because it is seen by the government agencies, the ANC, as well as NGOs and social entrepreneurs as representing the community. SANCO has an almost exclusive possession of the bridging ties that go out of the township to private entrepreneurs and the government. This leaves SANCO in a position to decide who is to be involved with and benefit from the projects they are able to provide.

SANCO members act as patrons for a network of people who depend on them for what little resources they can provide, but the fact remains that there are not enough resources to go around for everyone. The exclusive possession of bridging ties to resources outside of the township by SANCO is reinforcing fragmentation and increasing dependency. The pattern of dependency is likely to be crucial to why people in the township are clustered into smaller groups with relatively few connections to each other. Inside these groups they can form strong ties to each other, which make it more likely that other group members will come to their aid if need arises.

What is striking about Imizamo Yethu is the degree to which politics and conflict have a paralysing effect on collective capacity to perform tasks that are not directly related to the dispute. The housing issue does not need to affect the work on security, but it clearly does. The experience with the housing issue and the lack of influence on SANCO elections seems to have been the final straw for the Block Committees. The loss of the Block Committees represents a severe blow to the hopes of establishing a wider collective capacity to confront the challenges to security in Imizamo Yethu. The lack of trust in the community leadership makes it unlikely that SANCO will be able to re-establish the Block Committees. It is difficult to see how a community wide initiative to provide additional security should come about, given the level of fragmentation that currently characterises the township.

Hangberg – weakness in strong ties

Hangberg is home to approximately 5,500 people with the vast majority of them being Coloured. Most of the people living here come from families that have resided in Hout Bay for generations. This also means that most people are in some way related to one another. Hangberg is a strongly integrated community with less explicit conflicts, but despite this they have not been able to act collectively to address their shared problems. Instead, conflict resolution is done privately between the families concerned.

Hangberg has a massive drug problem and there is concern that this will destroy an entire generation of youth. Because of the large unemployment in

Hangberg, poaching of crayfish has become very common. The drug trade and poaching operations overlap, and are part of serious organised crime. The people behind the poaching are seen to be paying their poachers in drugs, rather than money. The drug abuse leads to lots of other problems such as theft, robberies and break-ins, as well as serious problems of child abuse. Hangberg has also faced an escalation in burglaries for some time, but a lot of these crimes go unreported.

Personalised policing and civic networks

The organised character of criminal activity in Hangberg makes it very difficult for the police to get help from the community. Intimidation prevents people from coming forward with information about crime. It is not just the drug dealers they fear. There is also a widespread belief that at least some of the police officers are involved with the drugs and the poaching.

Also, the slow response time by police in relation to more ordinary crimes, such as burglaries, theft, abuse and violence, contributes to even more crimes going unreported. Moreover, the fact that so many people are related to one another makes people reluctant to report crimes. This leads to personalised, ad hoc forms of conflict resolution:

> People steal from others who are family members, distant down the line, and then people find who it was and they will go to the family and say 'look here, I heard that your son stole from me at this and this time, do you know about it?' and they would approach him and get the item back if possible. And if that person has already sold it, they will maybe ask the family to pay them, and just leave the case. That is one option. The other option is that when the family member discuss, they will actually hit that family member [the perpetrator], and after they've hit that family member they will say 'ok, the case is now finished'. Because they're both brought in trouble you see. One could go down for stealing and the other could be brought charges against for assault.
>
> (Lay Minister St Simon Anglican Church, 22 May 2006)

Private conflict resolution and fear of causing family feuds prevent issues from being collectively recognised and dealt with as a shared problem that affects all. Problems are thus fragmented into single instances. Attempts at organising community actions related to policing and security matters have for this reason met many obstacles. For instance the Hout Bay Civic Association (HBCA) held talks with HBNW about starting a neighbourhood watch sector in Hangberg. The talks were promising, but failed to generate interest in the Hangberg community: 'If you talk to people they say yes. But when you come to the actual meeting nobody turns up' (HBCA Vice-chair, 30 April 2006).

Like SANCO, HBCA has close ties with ANC. Its chairperson is vice-chair of Hout Bay ANC. Despite their mutual engagement in ANC there is little cooperation between the civics in the two communities: 'We don't want to get involved in their politics. They've got their own politics in that place. We've heard about [the allegations of SANCO corruption] because that's a big issue there, and you hear people talking about corrupt leaders' (HBCA Vice-chair, 30 April 2006). HBCA also broke ties with HBCPF following the announcement of the lawsuit against the government. Conversely, the chair of the HBCPF said there was little they could do to aid Hangberg because their challenges were related to organised crime that has to be handled by the police. Unlike SANCO, the HBCA is not represented on the local Ward Committee. This perpetuated the ignorance of government to the plights of their community, according to HBCA. The DA Ward Councillor saw it differently:

> There is no legitimate civic association out there. There's a grouping who call themselves Hout Bay Civic Association, which is a bit of a joke . . . they represent just about no one in the Harbour community . . . it's really just an ANC office.
>
> (DA Ward Councillor, 28 March 2006)

The lack of outreach to organisations outside of Hangberg as well as the failure to get internal community commitment has led the civic to concentrate most of its efforts on aiding small initiatives and helping other organisations through networking, such as the local churches.

The twenty churches in Hangberg occupy an important position in the community and hold the potential for contributing to resolving security matters. The relationship between the residents and the churches is close, and many residents attend several churches because of intermarriages. In some cases the churches have been involved in dispute resolution as mediators. However, the extent of this form of mediation is difficult to establish because of its very informal nature. While the personal involvement of church leaders in the lives of their congregation is likely to have been around for a long time, this does not seem to have done much to prevent the spread of crime. Matters are still handled in a very private manner by the families affected, even when church leaders are brought into the picture.

Another significant civic is the Eye on the Children. It is set up to handle child abuse in the community and comprises nineteen volunteers trained by Child Welfare. They act as community social workers and have a legal mandate to remove children from their homes. The fact that they can enter people's homes and take their children says a great deal about their standing in the community. Several of the members are people who have been involved with community work through the churches for a long time, making them respected members of the community. The fear that families will be split up, which leads to a lot of crime not being reported, seems to be lessened by the approach taken by Eye on the Children. They are able to communicate with the families as concerned helpers, not as outsiders, and become less of a threat. By using their local knowledge they are in a position to do what professional outsiders cannot: break the silence and bring help to those who previously suffered from fear of being severed from their families. Because they work to preserve the families where possible, they gain respect from the community. This also makes it easier for them to find evidence in cases where the police and social workers need to be involved. By building networks with Child Welfare, Social Services and the SAPS, Eye on the Children are, as one of the very few organisations in Hangberg, able to bridge the gap between the community and outside agencies.

Family relations and challenges to collective action

Hangberg is faced with a double, mutually reinforcing, problem when it comes to creating collective capacity. First, there is not a lot of external aid coming into Hangberg. Second, there is a lack of engagement by community members in actively resolving their problems. It seems that the common identity is based on a notion of 'who we are' rather than an idea of 'what we do'. This could be essential to understanding why the strong collective identity does not easily lend itself to group action. As argued by Sampson *et al.* (1999), strong social ties may have negative outcomes, such as fatalism, apathy, and a shared sense of hopelessness. This viewpoint was shared by several of my Hangberg informants: 'The people don't try, the churches try . . . the people have no initiative, no drive, no willpower, no strength . . . They've given up!' (Volunteer, St Simon Anglican church, 9 May 2006). Although the different organisations individually may have a defined goal, they do not share a common ethos that they can engage with collectively.

The strong ties between members of the Hangberg community reinforce the necessity for self-reliance. Because of the fear that families may become enemies, it is of vital importance to resolve disputes in ways that keep the peace. This leads to private, ad hoc solutions between families that prevent a wider community sanction against the perpetrators. It may also be part of what prevents the community from coming together to confront their problems collectively.

The heavy reliance on strong family ties is not accompanied by weak ties capable of acting as bridges to external actors and agencies. This has left Hangberg in isolation, which very likely has reinforced the reliance on strong internal ties, increasing the necessity of self-reliance, and further diminishing the ability to reach outside the community for aid and resources. The organised character of crime in Hangberg is accompanied by intimidation and fear of being targeted if one comes forward with information. The deep fear that the police cannot be trusted is also contributing to the lack of collective action. Combined, all of these factors may be seen as reinforcing each other and perpetuating the difficulties of establishing group action. Despite the existence of organisations that attempt to build and encourage communal action, the initiatives invariably fail to gather any wide response in the community. In striking contrast to the other communities of Hout Bay, there is an almost total lack of political engagement in Hangberg. No one is challenging the authority of existing civic structures or coming up with alternatives. Rather, most of their efforts are simply ignored as people go about their daily lives.

Conclusion

This chapter has examined how identities and networks affect the collective capacity of three different communities to influence security provision in Hout Bay, Cape Town. As shown, there are great differences between the communities in both how collective identities are constructed and in the ability to form networks with significant players outside the community. My findings support that collective action benefits greatly from a combination of basing identities on an issue specific common ethos in combination with agonistic conflict resolution.

The Valley has successfully established a vessel for collective capacity for action, through the HBNW, by generating collective commitment to a common ethos and by focusing on agonistic social relations for handling conflict. Imizamo Yethu groups are isolated by antagonism and dependency on local political patrons. The antagonism prevents any form of cooperation between groups that share the same problems, because their wider political differences lead them to regard each other as enemies. What HBNW have realised is that they need to put aside their wider differences in order to work on a shared problem, while at the same time accepting that they still hold very different political views on important questions, and not let this interfere with the task at hand, namely their shared ethos of preventing property crime in the Valley. Hangberg lacks a focus on specific issues. While there is a strong shared identity, the conversion of this identity into collective commitment to generate capacity is missing, and this has a direct impact on ineffective local policing. What the empirical studies illustrate is that the combination of agonistic social relations and the conversion of identity into collective commitment are vital for achieving collective capacity for joint action.

Another important factor is each community's relative access to weak ties capable of forming bridges and strong internal ties. The combination of utilising weak and strong ties in the Valley has led HBNW to take the leading role in coordinating security provision between the participating nodes. This has also greatly increased the collective capacity to provide security. The fostering of weak ties that involve a large part of the community, as well as connecting HBNW to other governing nodes, has been crucial. Both Hangberg and Imizamo Yethu lack the benefit of weak bridging ties. While Imizamo Yethu has some bridging ties, these are controlled by local patrons who use them to serve specific power interests. Hangberg is characterised by an almost complete lack of bridging ties capable of bringing resources and innovation to the community. While strong ties may help to generate and sustain commitment, the empirical case studies show that weak bridging ties are crucial for the effective networking that is needed to generate collective capacity for the provision of security.

The relationship between networking and identity construction may be synergetic. In the Valley the issue specific identity and agonistic relations lend themselves easily to networking because they have a clear ethos that can be aligned with the interests of the SAPS and with those of the private security companies. This is mutually reinforcing, because the strong level of networking also helps clarify what the contribution of HBNW should be. This in turn supports a common ethos. In Imizamo Yethu the antagonistic social relations and fragmented ethnic identities make networking very hard. There is no common ground on which civic organisations can interact that could benefit the entire township population. Instead, the few bridging ties are controlled by narrow political power interests. The lack of networks that reach a wider part of the population is in turn reinforcing social antagonism and fights over controlling the few available networks. It also increases a situation of dependency on those who currently control the networks. The strong internal ties in Hangberg and lack of commitment to a common ethos make networking difficult to achieve. Lack of outreach also contributes to apathy in the community because its members see nothing worth aspiring towards. It becomes a vicious circle. The lack of bridging ties to bring in innovation and aspiration reinforces an identity based on the feeling of being cast aside and of being a pariah. This breeds apathy, which prevents the kind of commitment to collective action that could otherwise support the capacity to improve conditions in the community.

While the Valley has clearly been most successful at establishing a policing node capable of effective order-making, there have been promising tendencies in the impoverished communities as well. Especially the Block Committees in Imizamo Yethu show the potential for effective identity building around a common ethos. Their capacity for networking with the police also had a good record. In Hangberg the civil structures, including the churches, show that there are those who are willing to make a collective effort, but they lack networking capacities of bridging ties to external support.

The antagonism and mistrust that prevail between the three communities means that there is currently no basis for joint action across the communities that could enhance the provision of security to all in Hout Bay. Even though the HBNW has managed to construct a local collective capacity that benefits the Valley, this is unlikely to be a strategy that will reconcile and bring the communities closer together. Rather, the increasing differences in the provision of security may further the distance between them. This prospect is likely to have a negative impact on everybody in Hout Bay. The years since the fall of Apartheid have shown that security is difficult to sustain when it is concentrated on a minority. This makes it unlikely that HBNW will be able to sustain its effect on security provision in the long run, unless the neighbouring communities are included in some way.

Note

1   The study is based on a field work of four months in 2006. Data consist of interviews, documents and observation.

References

Adams, B., Esau, F., Horner, D. and Marindo, R., 2006. *Migration to two neighbourhoods in the suburb of Hout Bay, Cape Town, 2005: Survey report and baseline information.* Cape Town: SALDRU. Available at: www.capetown.gov.za/en/stats/CityReports/Documents/Migration_in_Hout_Bay_.pdf (Accessed 4 December 2013).

Baker, B., 2002. Living with non-state policing in South Africa: The issues and dilemmas. *Journal of Modern African Studies*, 40:1, 29–53.

Briggs, X., 2008. *Democracy as Problem Solving: Civic Capacity in Communities Across the Globe.* Cambridge, MA: MIT Press.

Burris, S., Drahos, P. and Shearing, C., 2005. Nodal governance. *Australian Journal of Legal Philosophy*, 30, 30–58.

Froestad, J., 2005. Environmental health problems in Hout Bay: The challenge of generalising trust in South Africa. *Journal of Southern African Studies*, 31:2, 333–356.

Gordon, D. R., 2006. *Transformation and Trouble: Crime, Justice, and Participation in Democratic South Africa.* Ann Arbor, MI: The University of Michigan Press.

Granovetter, M., 1973. The strength of weak ties. *The American Journal of Sociology*, 78:6, 1360–1380.

Granovetter, M., 1983. The strength of weak ties: A network theory revisited. *Sociological Theory*, 1, 201–233.

Kempa, M., 2008. Les processus policières au contexte de mondialisation: la politique économique de la sécurité humaine. *Revue Criminologie*, 41:1, 153–175.

Minnaar, A., 2002. The 'new' vigilantism in post-April 1994 South Africa: Searching for explanations, in D. Feenan (ed.), *Informal Criminal Justice (Advances in Criminology)*. Burlington: Ashgate, 117–134.

Mouffe, C., 2005. *On the Political.* London: Routledge.

Sampson, R. J., Morenoff, J. D. and Earls, F., 1999. Beyond social capital: Spatial dynamics of collective efficacy for children. *American Sociological Review*, 64:5, 633–660.

Tuomela, R., 2007. *The Philosophy of Sociality: The Shared Point of View.* New York: Oxford University Press.

Wood, J., 2006. Research and innovation in the field of security: A nodal governance view, in J. Wood and B. Dupont (eds), *Democracy, Society and the Governance of Security*. Cambridge: Cambridge University Press, 217–240.

Chapter 10

Young but not alone

Youth organizations and the local politics of security provision

Louis-Alexandre Berg

Introduction

Young men and women play central roles in conflict-affected settings. Youth tend to be disproportionately affected as victims of violence, but they are also prime contributors to security and insecurity. As members of militias, rebel groups and urban gangs, youth are directly responsible for violence. Youth may also serve as providers of security, as members of community watch, youth movements or advocates. Especially where state institutions are unable to guarantee security, organized youth often serve either as core providers of security or perpetrators of insecurity. Which of these roles they take on elucidates the core dynamics of political order and security provision at the local level.

This chapter explores the local politics of security provision through an examination of organized youth in countries affected by violent conflict. Youth organizations serve as legitimate and trusted sources of protection for communities affected by insecurity, but they are also subject to manipulation by powerful authorities and prone to engage in violence themselves. Like other local actors, whether they act as protectors or as perpetrators depends largely on the context in which they operate. I examine two features of local context that shape their role: the density of social ties within their communities, and the extent of linkages between their communities and the state. In divided communities with limited access to services and external resources, youth organizations tend to fuel insecurity as they exploit their positions to the detriment of their communities. In the presence of denser community ties and multiple channels to external resources, youth organizations play a more beneficial role. Variations in these conditions can alter the role of youth organizations even within the same community.

I explore these dynamics through comparisons of youth organizations in two countries. I first compare neighbourhood youth groups in two urban neighbourhoods of Port-au-Prince, Haiti, which followed distinct paths with divergent effects after both fuelling insecurity in the context of a broader political conflict. I then examine the evolution of the Bike Riders Unions of Sierra Leone, which facilitated economic opportunities for former combatants after the civil war, but whose impact on security shifted from fuelling conflict to contributing to urban safety. I explore how variations in the local social context and state–society relations affected the role of these organizations as providers of security. These comparisons illustrate the varying roles played by youth in shaping local order, and point to the need to examine social and political context to understand the role of local actors in order-making.

Brokers and bridges: the role of youth organizations in local security

While the impact of youth on security has been widely recognized, their roles as providers of security have received less attention.[1] Youth are often viewed as subjects of the social and political forces that fuel conflict. Large youth populations are correlated with increased risk of armed conflict (Mesquida and Wiener, 1999; Collier and Hoeffler, 2004; Urdal, 2006), as they fill the ranks of rebel groups, militias and gangs. Youth are also recognized as victims of violence as a result of forcible recruitment into militias and gangs, social stigmatization, and the traumatic effects of conflict (Hilker and Fraser, 2009). Yet, youth also serve as agents who shape these forces and affect security. Organized into neighbourhood groups, clubs or associations, youth self-police their members to prevent involvement in violence, organize 'community watch' and other informal policing schemes, serve as interlocutors with state security forces, or mobilize citizens for democratic participation. Youth also play leading roles in criminal gangs or militias, engage in crime and extortion, and serve as agents of political repression. From impoverished urban neighbourhoods of Jamaica, Nigeria and Haiti to post-civil war Sierra Leone, Liberia and Timor-Leste, youth organizations play a central role in people's experience of security.

Youth play especially salient roles where the state is unable to guarantee security in parts of its territory. Scholars increasingly recognize that 'where state agencies are incapable of delivering (or unwilling to deliver) security and other basic services', people turn to 'other social entities and support' (Boege et al. 2008, p. 9). While such 'hybrid political orders' are most evident in fragile and conflict-affected states, they occur in a wide range of settings. Leaders of post-colonial states that are unable to penetrate society have 'traded a hands-off policy that allowed the strongman to build enclaves of social control for the social stability such strongmen could guarantee' (Migdal, 1988, p. 247). In weak states, leaders have relied almost entirely on local figures while allowing the state bureaucracy to whither (Reno, 1998). Even in more developed contexts, state provision of security is exercised through intermediaries or absent in some parts of the territory. Like their national counterparts, local leaders in these areas must amass sufficient political loyalty and revenue to maintain their authority (Tilly, 1990). In rural areas local 'strongmen' mobilize votes and extract taxes in exchange for the provision of public services. In urban settings, street gangs and vigilante groups fight to control 'turf' in which they can extort local businesses or assault the public. At this local level – in the neighbourhoods and villages in which most violence occurs – youth play a crucial role in these processes. As they are embedded in social networks, they can serve as effective instruments of mobilization and coercion and contribute to either protecting or exploiting their communities.

The role of youth organizations at the local level depends on the characteristics of the neighbourhoods in which they operate and the nature of the communities within them. Since the importance of youth stems from their deep connection to local social networks, the structure of these networks shapes their role within them. Even after they join militias and gangs, young men and women are known as the children of community members, and social ties foster communication and trust. Armed groups that are embedded in local social networks tend to play a more beneficial role in their communities (Reno, 2008). Where their relationships cut across sub-groups within a neighbourhood, youth organizations can reinforce these ties by facilitating information flows and mobilizing to address issues of common concern (Granovetter, 2005). They can quickly identify perpetrators of violence and report them to authorities or mobilize to prevent further bloodshed. By playing the role of 'bridges', organized youth can help to resolve disputes before they escalate (Varshney, 2002). Research on urban neighbourhoods in the United States has found that denser ties within communities account for lower violence, partly as a result of shared expectations and social pressure among youth (Sampson, 2012).

In areas in which divisions along ethnic, language or other lines inhibit social ties, information-sharing and collective action are more difficult. Youth organizations reflect these divisions as they mobilize to protect their own sub-neighbourhood or group against others, leading to 'turf battles' between rival gangs and rapid escalations in local conflicts over water, property and other issues. Violence among the martial arts groups in Timor Leste, for example, emerged from resource conflicts between neighbouring groups in Dili's urban slums (Scambury, 2009). Divisions also generate opportunities for politicians to build their authority by selectively distributing services in exchange for political loyalty (Alesina *et al.*, 1999; Banerjee and Somanathan, 2007). Youth organizations that identify with an ethnic or religious group play the ideal 'foot soldiers' in mobilizing members of their group, often through violence.

The potential for youth to protect or exploit also depends on the availability for the residents of a given neighbourhood or village of channels to the state and to other sources of services, authority and protection. In his study of colonial Sierra Leone and Mauritius, Lange (2003) found that limited ties between the state and society allowed local actors to exploit their leadership roles, while multiple ties enabled them to expand services. Where access to critical services is scarce, entrepreneurial leaders can act as 'brokers', exploiting positions as the sole providers, especially for internally cohesive communities (Burt, 2005). By 'imposing themselves between segments of the population and critical resources' they can extract rents from both the state bureaucracy and recipient communities. (Migdal, 1988, p. 257). Politicians and state actors in this position use local youth to provide basic security, and to mobilize supporters and repress opponents. Youth organizations can themselves exploit such a position. By claiming to speak for a neighbourhood or group under their control, youth groups secure weapons and funding from politicians, and use those resources to bolster their authority. In urban neighbourhoods, street gangs run extortion rackets that seek payment in exchange for protection, often with the tacit cooperation of police and local authorities. The Bakassi Boys of Nigeria, for example, improved security for businesses and communities, but also engaged in extreme violence and rent-seeking (Smith, 2004).

Residents of neighbourhoods with access to multiple channels through which to access, services and protection are less likely to face such exploitation. Individuals depend less on any one actor for services and can reject the authority of those who make their lives worse. To ensure their legitimacy, youth leaders are forced to play constructive roles in serving their communities, or risk remaining marginal. Youth organizations also have more opportunities to play productive roles by drawing upon various institutions and actors to access services. They serve as 'bridges' not only within their neighbourhoods, but between their communities and essential services (Lange, 2003, p. 377).

The density of ties within local areas and the extent of linkages between communities and the state combine to shape opportunities and constraints for youth organizations. Societies affected by conflict, as well as urban areas, tend to be divided, traditional social norms and authority structures have frequently broken down, and limited access to essential services leaves citizens vulnerable to manipulation. In such contexts, youth organizations tend to act as 'brokers', manipulated by more powerful patrons and exploiting their position to extract rents through violence. The presence of dense social networks and a variety of channels to access resources generate opportunities and incentives for youth organizations to contribute more positively to public safety. Although other factors – ranging from cultural norms, prevailing values and psychological risk factors to socio-economic conditions – affect the propensity for violence among youth (Winton, 2004), these two features of the social context shape the opportunities for organized youth to serve as providers of security or perpetrators of violence in a given neighbourhood.

Youth organizations in Haiti and Sierra Leone

In Haiti and Sierra Leone, youth organizations have played a central role in violence. They have channelled widespread frustration and facilitated youth involvement in armed conflict and civil unrest. Yet they have also played con-structive roles in enhancing security. I compare youth organizations in different neighbourhoods and different time periods, to show how varying conditions affect the role of youth organizations in enhancing or undermining security.[2]

The first comparison focuses on two urban neighbourhoods in Haiti's capital, Port-au-Prince. Local youth organizations played different roles as a result of variations in their communities' cohesion and access to state and international actors. I then examine the Bike Riders Unions in the secondary cities of Sierra Leone, focusing on their evolution over time. Dense, cross-cutting ties and an increasing number of channels to access information, resources and support from local and international actors enabled these unions to play gradually more effective roles in providing security.

The politics of youth violence in Haiti

Youth organizations began to flourish in Haiti after the transition from authoritarian rule. Local organizations known as *organisations populaires* emerged to promote solidarity and channel popular participation. These organizations were rooted partly in neighbourhood associations called *organisations de bases*, or *baz* in Creole, mostly comprised of youth.[3] Especially after the fall of the Duvalier regime in 1987 and during the coup regime that removed President Bertrand Aristide in 1991, these groups helped to protect members of their communities and resist violent repression (Americas Watch, 1993).

In addition to serving their communities, the *baz* served as instruments of mobilization for Haiti's politicians. After his return to the presidency in 1994, Aristide cultivated ties with youth groups that had actively opposed the coup regime. Rather than building a formal party structure, however, he relied heavily on informal ties to local leaders (Fatton, 2006, p. 123). As his *Lavalas* party fragmented after his first term and around the contested 2000 elections, Aristide relied increasingly on armed *baz* within Port-au-Prince's poor urban neighbourhoods to mobilize supporters and repress opponents. In response, his political opponents cultivated their own ties to local youth groups to mobilize opposition. Politicians thus maintained the long-standing practice of relying on 'local religious, administrative, and even criminal leaders' to maintain order (Muggah, 2005, p. 2). They afforded these leaders a monopoly on local political and economic control in exchange for their support in mobilizing the electorate and protecting their interests.

In the marginalized, urban neighbourhoods of Port-au-Prince, youth organizations played central roles in this pattern of local order. Local *baz* competed for control over neighbourhoods in order to claim the authority that would allow them to seek weapons and funds from political patrons, and to monopolize local economic opportunities such as ports, state-owned enterprises, extortion and petty crime (Muggah, 2005). These conflicts sometimes escalated when local rivals sought the assistance of political patrons, or politicians mobilized their local supporters to intimidate opponents. The most sustained violence of this nature occurred in the aftermath of Aristide's forced departure from power in 2004. In the context of national level political tension, politicians increased their support to armed youth in urban neighbourhoods, and competition among these groups escalated. The resulting wave of kidnapping, rape and other violent crimes most severely affected the poorest urban neighbourhoods of Port-au-Prince. Estimates of violent deaths range from 1,600 to 8,000 in 2004–2005 (Kolbe and Hutson, 2006). In the most affected neighbourhoods, the homicide rate reached as high as 450 per 100,000 residents (Médecins Sans Frontières, 2008).

Within this context, patterns of violence varied, including among the most marginalized neighbourhoods. In two of the worst-affected neighbourhoods of Port-au-Prince – Cité Soleil and Bel Air – variations in the social context contributed to divergent responses by youth organizations and different outcomes for their communities.

Division and exclusion in Cité Soleil

Cité Soleil represents the extreme of social division and state weakness in Haiti. Originally built to house 30,000 workers for a nearby export processing zone, the neighbourhood expanded to a population of over 300,000. The inhabitants live in dire conditions, with unemployment as high as 80 per cent, and limited access to basic services.[4] Having mostly migrated from rural areas in search of jobs, residents complain that 'there is no presence of the state', and 'remain suspicious of the state'.[5] As violence escalated following Aristide's departure in 2004, access to services further declined as government actors fled the neighbourhood. Police stations and courthouses in the area were destroyed, while water, electricity and other services were available only through theft. International humanitarian organizations pulled out their personnel, and even the United Nations Stabilization Force (MINUSTAH) rarely set foot in the area.[6]

The neighbourhood was also characterized by internal division and sparse social ties among its residents. Most residents remained more closely tied to their rural communities of origin than to their new neighbours, and many stayed in Cité Soleil only until they had the means to move on. The neighbourhood was divided into thirty-four sub-neighbourhoods, or *blocs*, each with its own leadership and few social ties across them. Residents of neighbouring *blocs* competed over access to resources and basic services, with the biggest rivalries between Upper and Lower Cité Soleil. As a local activist described, 'each area has its chief, there are divisions among each *bloc* . . . but the frontline for the gang wars is between Lower Cité Soleil and Upper Cité Soleil – Lower Cité Soleil is seen as more violent and poorer.'[7]

Within the context of limited access to services and internal divisions, armed *baz* with ties to politicians emerged as the dominant security actors. Business owners sought assistance from the *baz* to protect their factories and warehouses, while rival politicians used them to mobilize supporters. International organizations relied on *baz* to distribute humanitarian aid. The *baz* leaders used access to weapons and finances to entrench their authority in each of Cité

Soleil's *blocs*, while displacing other community leaders, such as pastors and teachers, who opposed their violent form of control.[8] Since controlling territory was crucial to controlling these resources, the *baz* spent much of their energy engaged in turf battles with rival groups. Residents recalled the 'tension when [rival political parties] came to Cité Soleil and provided support to members of local groups to become well-armed, which led to conflicts between neighbourhoods'.[9] *Baz* leaders also intervened in conflicts over access to water, sanitation or electricity to establish themselves as protectors of their sub-neighbourhoods. Although the armed *baz* did in some cases protect their communities against rivals, conditions mostly favoured exploitation of neighbourhood residents by youth leaders and their patrons. Especially at the height of political conflict between 2004 and 2007, youth leaders used their weapons to kidnap, rape and extort local businesses.

When Haitian government and international actors stepped up efforts to improve security in Cité Soleil after 2007, local conditions continued to favour an exploitative role for local youth leaders, thereby undermining the impact of these efforts. After the election of President René Préval in 2006, political tensions declined and political parties decreased their financial support to *baz* leaders. In the face of mounting international pressure, Préval approved a set of joint operations in 2007 by MINUSTAH and the Haitian National Police (HNP) aimed at capturing or exiling the leaders of armed groups (Dziedzic and Perito, 2008). International donors began an intensive effort to generate a 'peace dividend' in Cité Soleil through programmes that created short-term jobs, built infrastructure and expanded services.

Although the area became more accessible, divisions in the community continued to fuel tensions and reinforced the authority of abusive local leaders. The 2007 security operations weakened the armed *baz* by arresting the top leaders, but their members remained active within Cité Soleil.[10] Although access to services and jobs improved, competition among neighbourhoods remained fierce and frequent confrontations erupted 'over turf and resources, like access to water and sanitation, and as [the *baz*] compete to get their people the jobs'.[11] In response to this competition, 'the gap between population and international community was filled with gang leaders, but they didn't play a constructive role for the community'.[12] Armed youth leaders continued to serve as brokers, forcing aid organizations to rely on them to identify beneficiaries of the aid while channelling most resources to their supporters.[13] Residents found that 'despite all of the international aid . . . the situation hasn't changed. Each organization works with one group and the rest of the community doesn't benefit'.[14]

The authority of the state was also mediated through the leadership of local *baz*. Local government officials who returned to the area colluded with the *baz* who had helped secure their elections. Meanwhile, many residents remained distrustful of local officials, who, they believed, continued to 'monopolize jobs and take most resources for themselves and their supporters'.[15] Other state actors also colluded with local *baz*, or remained too ineffective to overcome the legacy of mistrust of the state. A new police sub-station constructed in 2009 was plagued by insufficient personnel and resources, and residents complained of crimes committed right outside the station with no response.[16] Armed youth groups remained the only authoritative security presence in the area. One resident summed up the situation:

> We are not protected by the state . . . When you go to the police station to talk to police [concerning security], they tell you to go and talk to the municipal authorities . . . When we tell the mayor that we have a security problem, he responds by saying that only God can provide security.
>
> (INURED, 2010)

With little alternative source of protection, residents were forced to rely on the protection of the armed groups who perpetrated violence. In the words of another resident, 'Before it was the *macoutes*[17] and former soldiers who had the guns, now, it's the people who live in your own neighbourhood who commit the violence' (Small Arms Survey, 2006). Between 2004 and 2007, up to a third of the residents of Cité Soleil fled the area (Willman and Marcelin, 2010). Although security improved in Port-au-Prince after 2007, in 2008 36 per cent of survey respondents in Cité Soleil reported being the victims of violent crime, an increase over the previous year, while 71 per cent named youth gangs as perpetrators (Ibid., p. 523). In the words of one resident, 'It's different than it used to be. Shots are no longer being fired. But the divisions are still there' (Ibid., p. 528). The situation improved slightly in 2009, but following the 2010 earthquake crime in the area once again spiked after prisoners escaped from the National Penitentiary.[18] As assistance was diverted to other dire needs, the conditions in Cité Soleil remained unchanged.

Community mobilization in Bel Air

While the nearby neighbourhood of Bel Air also experienced insecurity during the same period, the situation improved after 2005. This was in part a result of changes in the behaviour of local youth groups in response to local conditions. Although Bel Air appeared similar to Cité Soleil, it differed in important respects. Like Cité Soleil, the area was divided among several sub-neighbourhoods, youth *baz* leaders supported by patrons extracted revenue through violence, and competition over turf and access to patronage fuelled violent competition. Marginalized from state services and distrustful of the state, residents relied on armed *baz* for protection. Yet Bel Air had been a middle class neighbourhood with more stable residency than Cité Soleil. Although the socio-economic character of the neighbourhood had changed as a result of rural–urban migration, its residents still took pride in the neighbourhood's historical reputation as a political centre of the city and in its tradition of art, music and culture.[19] The area was also more accessible than Cité Soleil due to its more developed infrastructure and closer proximity to downtown Port-au-Prince. Unlike Cité Soleil, where economic life revolved primarily around the nearby manufacturing zone, Bel Air had been home to a wide variety of businesses with ties outside the neighbourhood.

The relative accessibility of Bel Air facilitated efforts by international and national actors to improve conditions in the neighbourhood before they began in Cité Soleil. As early as 2005, the HNP and MINUSTAH established a presence in the neighbourhood. A disarmament and demobilization programme sponsored by the UN focused on Bel Air as one of its first target areas in its efforts to persuade youth to give up their arms in exchange for cash and training opportunities.[20] Non-governmental organizations (NGOs) began to operate in the area. A Brazilian NGO called Viva Rio aimed to reduce crime, drawing upon its experience in the Brazilian *favelas*. It established a centre in the neighbourhood and began to cultivate relationships with local youth leaders.[21] These efforts resulted in a higher level of interaction between neighbourhood residents and authorities, for example, through participation of MINUSTAH, HNP and community leaders in monthly meetings and in sports tournaments, concerts and other community events.

Increased access to services, combined with stronger ties within the neighbourhood, facilitated a shift in the role of the youth leaders in Bel Air. Well-positioned youth leaders, many of them associated with armed *baz*, used their access to these resources to build their stature relative to other leaders and groups. An activist involved in the process recalled that 'when the National Commission on Disarmament, Demobilization and Reintegration (CNDDR) offered jobs and money, gang leaders facilitated entry into the community, some joined NGOs but stayed as leaders who could reach people'.[22] Rather than disbanding armed groups, the CNDDR co-opted their leaders into the commission to incentivize their participation.[23] Similarly, Viva Rio engaged directly with youth leaders – some of whom were affiliated with armed groups. A local Viva Rio official recounted that 'in 2006–2007, we said if you could facilitate services and peace, you would be community leaders'.[24] The same leaders who had been active in violence could now claim credit for the benefits of Viva Rio and other NGOs, and they developed a stake in their presence. From the perspective of *baz* leaders, this approach created 'incentives to keep things peaceful and to start to collaborate with the police, with NGOs, and others'.[25]

This new approach took root as a result of the relatively dense ties among youth leaders and residents in the neighbourhood. Viva Rio and other NGOs sought to reinforce these ties by sponsoring activities such as soccer tournaments, musical competitions and carnivals that brought together members of rival communities. These efforts encouraged community leaders to reach across sub-neighbourhood boundaries. For instance, to prevent violence instigated by musical groups known as Rara bands that would 'go into another *bloc*, start a fight and violence', they created a 'mixed' Rara band involving representatives from the various *blocs*.[26] These efforts culminated in a 'peace accord' among *baz* leaders in Bel Air, in which they promised to stop fighting in exchange for resources provided to their communities, such as festivals, sports tournaments, and scholarships to children. The accords legitimated their authority while reducing violence.

Intra-neighbourhood ties also generated pressure on these leaders to honour their commitments. In the words of a Bel Air youth leader:

> Before the peace accords, the word 'community leader' did not exist. Leaders were only used by outside actors to put pressure on the community. Now leaders are expected to provide for their communities, if they do not, people reject them as leaders.[27]

Their new roles also fostered more productive cooperation with authorities in trying to prevent violence. As another leader described, 'now, we see the police at soccer tournaments and regular meetings. As soon as I have information about a criminal in the area, I pass it on to [a senior member of the police]'.[28]

These interventions contributed to a marked but precarious reduction in violence in the area. One survey (Fernandes and Nasciemiento, 2007) found that the percentage of respondents who reported being the victim of violent crime dropped from 45 per cent in 2005 to 14 per cent in 2006. Yet many of the same leaders who participated in violence remained empowered and their organizations remained intact, leading to occasional spikes in violence. Youth leaders also remained dependent on the support of externally funded NGOs such as Viva Rio to maintain their peaceful posture. While local conditions enabled a change in the role of youth leaders, this shift remained tentative in the face of broader economic and political pressures.

The Sierra Leone Bike Riders Unions

Youth played a central role in the civil war in Sierra Leone and in its subsequent reconstruction. Having been excluded from social, political and economic opportunities, young men swelled the ranks of the major combatant groups, including the Revolutionary United Front (RUF) rebels, the pro-government Civil Defence Force (CDF) militias and the Sierra Leone Army, as a result of voluntary and forced recruitment (Abdullah, 1998; Gberie, 2005). Following the war, disruptions in traditional social structures resulting from the flight of 'big men' and government officials from much of the country created the space for youth organizations to play an expanded role in local orders (Peters, 2007). While in some cases organized youth contributed to violence as they took the law into their own hands or staged violent protests, in other cases they contributed to public safety.

The Bike Riders Unions (BRUs) evolved from rough beginnings as a source of conflict and violence, to eventually contribute to security for its members and for the residents of Sierra Leone's cities. The first BRU was established in 2000 in Bo, the country's second largest city and the centre of the CDF militia movement (Richards *et al.*, 2004; Fithen and Richards, 2005). The association was set up by former combatants to help their peers find jobs. Given the destruction of most four-wheel taxis, damage to the roads and the need to link isolated areas to the urban centre, providing motorcycle transportation to local traders became a successful niche. The union quickly grew in size, reaching 600 riders by 2003. Similar unions emerged in the country's other cities, including Kenema, Makeni, Koidu and Freetown. In each city, a Bike Riders Union affiliated with the national Bike Riders Association (BRA) emerged to coordinate the activities of riders, provide financial and social support, and help them in case of accidents, conflicts with the police or other troubles.[29] The unions benefited from a high level of internal solidarity, as well as dense ties to other groups in their urban environments. Although they initially found themselves in conflict with authorities, expansion in the number of channels to services provided by the state and other actors enabled them to contribute more effectively to public safety.

The Bike Riders Union formation and initial conflicts

A high level of internal cohesion among the bike riders and other groups within Sierra Leone's urban centres provided a foundation for their contribution to security. Although the founders initially drew from their own combatant networks, they quickly reached across ethnic and wartime divisions to integrate ex-combatants from all of the major groups. Ex-combatant youth were united by their feeling that they had been manipulated by various 'big men' and should work together – across combatant lines – against future exploitation (Fithen and Richards, 2005). One study (Fithen and Richards, 2005, p. 134) highlighted 'the sense of common purpose among young men fighting each other only a few years earlier, and their recognition they had been manipulated to fight'. This broad base served as the foundation for ties to other groups, such as market women and traders who relied on them for transportation. These ties developed in the context of declining ethnic tensions in urban centres that had become inter-ethnic 'melting pots' as a result of migrants attracted by the economic opportunities (Peters, 2007, p. 18). The BRUs' dense networks enabled them to provide services to their members, and to work with other groups for common benefit.

Yet the bike riders initially struggled to secure essential services, and fell prey to the influence of powerful patrons who exploited sparse ties to authority and resources. During the war, urban residents had relied on local commanders for protection and services. After the war, riders generally secured their motorbikes by renting them from these local patrons, or by purchasing them on credit from businessmen in exchange for a portion of their wages. Yet they lacked training, knowledge of the rules of the road, or permits. Limited training contributed to frequent accidents, and they remained vulnerable to thefts and assaults. Few options were available to overcome these challenges. Although the Sierra Leone Police (SLP) was one of the first institutions to deploy outside of Freetown starting in 2002 (Albrecht and Jackson, 2009, p. 33), it remained plagued by insufficient personnel – with less than 40 per cent needed to cover the country – as well as limited equipment, mobility and capacity (Middlebrook and Miller, 2006, p. 12). As police officers deployed, they began to harass the motorbike riders and subject them to fines. The chairman of the BRU in Bo explained that 'when we decided to start the commercial bike riders, people were suspicious, since many of us were ex-combatants, and initially we had problems with the police – they used to arrest us for not having licenses, we weren't familiar with the rules of the road'. [30] Those who rented bikes from local patrons with connections to the police could secure some protection from these threats. Yet these patronage relationships generally left them with little share of the profits, and vulnerable to exploitation and assault.

The BRUs succeeded in freeing riders from dependence on these exploitative relationships. By pooling their earnings, the unions would help members purchase their own motorbikes, and pay for medical care and family expenses. By improving the behaviour of their members, the unions' leaders sought to enhance their relationships with the market women and other traders who relied on the riders to carry their goods (Richards *et al.*, 2004). According to the executive of the Makeni Bike Riders Union:

> Our members were quite wild before, when they were still carrying guns, they could intimidate everybody, but now they have to stick to the rules. . . . if for instance someone rides too fast, we confiscate the bike for a few days. [31]

Yet they also found themselves in conflicts with other members of the public, and subject to accidents, thefts and harassment by the police. The riders remained stigmatized as ex-combatants, and their inability to secure permits or training did not help. As their earnings increased, without the protection of their former patrons thefts and assaults also increased. Attempts to report these incidents to the police rarely received a response. Instead, police officers viewed the bike riders as a source of revenue, and routinely harassed them, according to a rider, 'charging high rates for licences that we couldn't afford, then arresting us and charging us to court – this led to confrontations with the police'. [32]

Tension with the police escalated, resulting in a series of violent confrontations in February 2003. Mass protests by the riders in Kenema and Bo led to the arrest of thirty-two riders and the levying of high fines by the police (Richards *et al.*, 2004). The incident sparked a general strike by the motorbike riders, who were joined by market women in solidarity. Given the important role both groups played in local commerce, the strike disrupted daily life in these cities. The escalation only ended following a direct intervention by the Inspector General of police, legal assistance to bring the case to court, and engagement by internationally funded NGOs. As a result of these responses, however, new opportunities emerged for the BRUs.

The Bike Riders Unions as security providers

The conflict with the police led to an expansion of channels to access services and resources and enabled the BRA to play a more effective role in providing security. Within the police, support by the UK, including a British officer seconded to serve as the Inspector General, led to major expansion and reform including hiring and training new personnel, provision of new equipment and infrastructure, and significant changes in management (Albrecht and Jackson, 2009). The police established Local Policing Partnership Boards (LPPB) that aimed to involve community leaders to coordinate security policy and improve responsiveness. A security sector architecture was set up to improve coordination and oversight of the security sector, including through the establishment of District Security Committees (DISEC) to monitor security in the provinces and coordinate responses.

The BRUs also received the support of international actors to help them access these new channels. A UK-funded programme by the international NGOs Conciliation Resources and Search for Common Ground 'held workshops that included the bikers, police and civil society, where they taught [the riders] how to use the road, rules and ethics'.[33] These discussions led to the designation by the police of liaison officers who cultivated direct relationships with the BRUs, and the BRUs designated representatives to deal with the police. The NGOs also facilitated an agreement with the Sierra Leone Roads and Transportation Authority (SLRTA), under which it would issue licences to the BRUs in exchange for the payment of fees for each licensed rider. This agreement enabled more riders to secure licences, thereby eliminating a source of tension with the police who had been levying fines for driving without licences.[34] Representatives of the BRUs were also invited to appear at monthly meetings of the DISECs to raise concerns.

These new channels enabled the BRUs to more effectively promote security for their members and communities. The riders had new incentives to follow traffic laws in order to secure and maintain their permits and to cultivate relationships with the police. As one bike rider explained:

> the police started to see that the riders knew how to use the road, and they started encouraging them. Later when the Local Police Partnership Boards were set up, we realised the police could also be helpful – they helped bring us close and establish understanding with the police.[35]

The riders now had multiple channels through which to report crimes, and the police began to assist in recovering stolen motorbikes. The police also relied on the BRUs to respond to crime and accidents. 'Disciplinary officers' in the BRUs were charged with enforcing the law among the riders, and the SLP provided training for them. A BRU executive in Bo explained:

> we work together with the police . . . whenever there is an accident, the police officer calls the [union] so we can come and work it out if possible . . . if the accident involves a private rider, we try to compromise. If we can't, we go to the police, who investigate and bring charges . . . if we see a crime, we inform the police.[36]

Other state institutions also came to see them as an asset. For example the manager of the national Anti-Corruption Commission referred to the BRA as 'very strategic in the fight against corruption'.[37]

Although the motorbike riders continued to serve as both victims and perpetrators of crime and accidents, strong networks among themselves and their communities and expanding channels to the state and international actors enabled the BRUs to evolve into more constructive security players in Sierra Leone's cities. With the police 'handicapped by logistical problems', the BRUs have helped resolve some issues on their own and prevented others from escalating.[38] In 2007, for example, after a bike rider in Bo was assaulted and killed by thieves, other riders 'went on a rampage' since they felt the police had not responded to their call for help.[39] The matter was brought before the DISEC, which helped to broker an agreement between the police and the BRU to work together to investigate crimes and prevent violence. The BRUs have also mostly succeeded in avoiding politicization.[40] Incidents of violence continue both against and by bike riders, and union executives remain frustrated by the inability of the police to prosecute criminals. Nonetheless, the BRUs have contributed to public safety in a challenging environment.

Conclusion

Youth organizations play a central part in the security of their communities. In societies where the state is too weak to provide security, organized youth groups can protect their neighbours, or they can extract revenue through violence. Their effects on security depend on their role in local political orders, as legitimate sources of authority with the capacity to mobilize people, develop links to politicians and exert coercive power. The role of youth as security providers must therefore be understood within the local politics of how leaders achieve and maintain authority in contested environments.

The youth organizations examined here illustrate how variations in the density of ties within a community and the extent of linkages to external authority and resources affect their roles by generating opportunities and constraints on the exercise of authority. In Haiti, divided urban neighbourhoods with limited access to basic services enabled neighbourhood-based youth groups to serve as 'brokers' between politicians and communities, while engaging in violent competition and crime. In neighbourhoods with denser ties and less internal division among sub-communities, the opening of new channels to international and state actors enabled these groups to take on a more protective role, and local public pressure created incentives to do so. In Sierra Leone, the Bike Riders Unions built upon dense ties in post-conflict, urban environments to create successful organizations. As new channels opened to access services and protection from various branches of the state and the international community, they played increasingly effective roles in providing security to their members and the residents of their cities. In both cases, broader socio-economic challenges ranging from poverty to weak state capacity proved detrimental to security. Yet within these contexts, local conditions shaped opportunities for local youth groups to serve as perpetrators or protectors in specific neighbourhoods and cities.

Understanding hybrid political orders requires an expansive view of the actors involved, and a deep understanding of the context in which they operate. While youth are most often viewed as subjects of broad political forces, they play crucial roles as agents in providing security or fuelling violence. They can be understood as political actors who operate in response to the pressures and constraints in their environments. The role of youth, like that of other local leaders, depends upon the local contexts in which they are embedded, and that shape these pressures. While broader socio-economic dynamics matters, the local environments they face affect their impact on the safety and security of their communities.

Notes

1 According to the World Health Organization and United Nations, youth is defined as men and women, 15 to 24 years old, although ages of individuals who self-identify or are identified as youth vary.
2 The narratives are based on interviews and focus groups with youth leaders, community members, state and donor officials conducted between December 2009 and October 2010, as well as published surveys and studies.
3 The term *baz* refers to a diversity of local groups. While I focus on armed *baz*, not all are armed, and their roles and activities vary.
4 In a 2008 survey, 86 per cent of residents said they were unemployed, while 81.4 per cent claimed they did not have enough money to feed everyone in their household (Willman and Marcelin, 2010, p. 519).
5 Interview, Cité Soleil civil society activist, Port-au-Prince, 6 July 2010.
6 One exception was Médecins Sans Frontières which maintained a clinic to treat victims of violence from Cité Soleil.
7 Interview, Cité Soleil civil society activist, Port-au-Prince, 6 July 2010.

8 Interview, Haitian civil society activist, Port-au-Prince, 15 October 2010.
9 Focus group, Residents of Cité Soleil, Port-au-Prince, 8 July 2010.
10 Interview, UN Official, Port-au-Prince, 9 July 2010.
11 Interview, Haitian civil society activist, Port-au-Prince, 6 July 2010.
12 Interview, Haitian civil society activist, Port-au-Prince, 15 October 2010.
13 Interviews, international NGO officials, Port-au-Prince, 6 and 10 July 2010.
14 Focus group, Residents of Cité Soleil, Port-au-Prince, 8 July 2010.
15 Focus group, Residents of Cité Soleil, Port-au-Prince, 8 July 2010.
16 Focus group, Residents of Cité Soleil, Port-au-Prince, 8 July 2010.
17 The *macoutes*, also called *tonton macoutes*, was the popular name given to an armed militia used by the Duvalier regime to control political dissidents in Haiti.
18 See Logos Technologies, 2010. Haiti Stabilization Initiative (HSI) Monitoring and Evaluation Final Report. p. 25. Available at www.logostech.net/documents/HSI_Phase_3_final_report_for_distribution_Logos_19Aug10.pdf (Accessed 26 December 2013).
19 Interview, youth leader in Bel Air, Port-au-Prince, 14 October 2010.
20 The programme managed by the National Commission on Disarmament, Demobilization and Reintegration (CNDDR) was later changed to the Community Violence Reduction (CVR) program.
21 See www.vivario.org.br and www.comunidadsegura.org for an overview of their activities.
22 Interview, Haitian civil society activist, Port-au-Prince, 15 October 2010.
23 Some of these decisions were highly controversial since they were perceived as legitimating armed actors. See Bercovitch 2007.
24 Interview, Viva Rio official, 14 October 2010.
25 Interview, youth leader from Bel Air, Port-au-Prince, 9 July 2010.
26 Interview, youth leader from Bel Air, Port-au-Prince, 9 July 2010.
27 Interview, youth leader from Bel Air, Port-au-Prince, 7 October 2010.
28 Interview, youth leader from Bel Air, Port-au-Prince, 9 July 2010.
29 Interviews, members of Bike Riders Unions, Bo and Makeni, December 2009–January 2010. See also Richards *et al.* 2004.
30 Interview, Chairman of Bike Rider's Union, Bo, 6 January 2010.
31 Interview, Bike Riders Union executive, Makeni by Hoek and de Jong 2004, cited in Peters, 2007, p. 20.
32 Interview, Bike Riders Union executive, Bo, 6 January 2010.
33 Interview, Bike Riders Union executive, Bo, 6 January 2010.
34 Interview, Bike Riders Union executive, Makeni, 21 December 2009.
35 Interview, Bike Riders Union executive, Bo, 6 January 2010.
36 Interview, Bike Riders Union executive, Bo, 6 January 2010.
37 Kamara, M. J., 2012. ABC meets with Bike Riders Association. *Awoko*. Available at http://awoko.org/2012/01/20/abc-meets-with-bike-riders-association (Accessed 10 September 2013).
38 Interview, Bike Riders Union executive, Bo, 6 January 2010.
39 Interview, SLP Officer, Bo, 5 January 2010. This incident was discussed in interviews conducted by the author with members of the BRU, the DISEC and the police in Bo in January 2010.
40 An effort by a political party to assert control of the BRU in Bo following the 2007 elections was defused when union members sought help from the DISEC and NGOs. An agreement to hold internal elections avoided a split in the union. Interview, civil society activist, Bo, 5 January 2010.

References

Abdullah, I., 1998. Bush path to destruction: The origin and character of the Revolutionary United Front Sierra Leone. *Journal of Modern African Studies*, 36:2, 203–235.

Albrecht, P. and Jackson, P., 2009. *Security System Transformation in Sierra Leone, 1997–2007*. Global Facilitation Network for Security Sector Reform (GFN-SSR).

Alesina, A., Baqir, R. and Easterly, W., 1999. Public goods and ethnic divisions. *The Quarterly Journal of Economics*, 114:4, 1243–1284.

Americas Watch, 1993. *Silencing a People: The Destruction of Civil Society in Haiti*. New York: Human Rights Watch.

Banerjee, A. and Somanathan, R., 2007. The political economy of public goods: Some evidence from India, *Journal of Development Economics*, 82, 287–314.

Bercovitch, D., 2007. Less guns, more peace in Haiti: Interview with Alix Fils-Aime. Published on *Comunidade Segura*, available at: www.comunidadesegura.org.br (accessed 10 September 2011).

Boege, V., Brown, A., Clements, K. and Nolan, A., 2008. On hybrid political orders and emerging states: State formation in the context of 'fragility', *Berghof Handbook Dialogue No. 8*. Berlin: Berghof Research Centre for Constructive Conflict Management.

Burt, R. S., 2005. *Brokerage and Closure: An Introduction to Social Capital*. Oxford: Oxford University Press.

Collier, P. and Anke Hoeffler, A., 2004. Greed and grievance in civil war. *Oxford Economic Paper*, 56:4, 563–595.

Dziedzic, M. and Perito, R., 2008. Haiti: Confronting the gangs of Port-au-Prince. *United States Institute of Peace Special Report* 208.

Fatton, R., 2006. Haiti: The saturnalia of emancipation and the vicissitudes of predatory rule, *Third World Quarterly*, 27:1, 115–133.

Fernandes, R. C. and de Sousa Nasciemiento. M., 2007. *La Violence à Bel Air, Port-au-Prince, Haiti: Étude sur la Victimisation*. Port-au-Prince: Université de Quisqueya and Viva Rio.

Fithen, C. and Richards, P., 2005. Making war, crafting peace: Militia solidarities and demobilization in Sierra Leone, in P. Richards (ed.), *No Peace, No War: An Anthropology of Contemporary Armed Conflicts*. Oxford: Currey, 117–136.

Gberie, L., 2005. *A Dirty War in West Africa: The RUF and the Destruction of Sierra Leone*. Bloomington, IN: Indiana University Press.

Granovetter, M., 2005. The impact of social structure on economic outcomes. *Journal of Economic Perspectives*, 19:1, 33–50.

Hilker, L. M. and Fraser, E., 2009. *Youth Exclusion, Violence, Conflict and Fragile States*. Report prepared for DFID's Equity and Rights Team. London: DFID.

INURED. 2010. *Voices from the Shanties: A Post-Earthquake Assessment of Cité Soleil*. Port-au-Prince: Institut Interuniversitaire de Recherche et de Développement.

Kolbe, A. R. and Hutson, R. A., 2006. Human rights abuse and other criminal violations in Port-au-Prince, Haiti: A random survey of households. *The Lancet*, 368:9538, 864–873.

Lange, M., 2003. Structural holes and structural synergies: A comparative-historical analysis of state–society relations and development in Colonial Sierra Leone and Mauritius. *International Journal of Comparative Sociology*, 44:4, 372–407.

Médecins Sans Frontières, 2008. *Violence, Mortality and Access to Health Care in Cité Soleil: Results of an Epidemiological Survey.* Port-au-Prince: Médecins Sans Frontières.

Mesquida, C. G. and Wiener, N. I., 1999. Male age composition and severity of conflicts, *Politics and the Life Sciences,* 18:2, 181–189.

Middlebrook, P. J. and Miller, S. M., 2006. *Sierra Leone Security Sector Expenditure Review.* London: UK Department for International Development.

Migdal, J. S., 1988. *Strong Societies and Weak States.* Princeton, NJ: Princeton University Press.

Muggah, R., 2005. *Securing Haiti's Transition: Reviewing Human Insecurity and the Prospects for Disarmament, Demobilization, and Reintegration.* Geneva: Small Arms Survey.

Peters, K., 2007. From weapons to wheels: Young Sierra Leonean ex-combatants become motorbike taxi-riders. *Journal of Peace Conflict and Development,* 10, 1–23.

Reno, W., 1998. *Warlord Politics and African States.* Boulder, CO: Lynne Rienner.

Reno, W., 2008. Bottom-Up Statebuilding? in C. T. Call with V. Wyeth (eds), *Building States to Build Peace.* Boulder, CO: Lynne Rienner.

Richards, P., Bah, K. and Vincent, J., 2004. *Social Capital and Survival: Prospects for Community-Driven Development in Post-conflict Sierra Leone.* Washington, DC: The World Bank.

Sampson, R. J., 2012. *Great American City: Chicago and the Enduring Neighborhood Effect.* Chicago, IL: University of Chicago Press.

Scambury, J., 2009. Urban conflict in East Timor. *East Asia Forum,* available at: www.eastasiaforum.org/2009/09/18/urban-conflict-in-east (accessed10 September 2011).

Small Arms Survey, 2006. *The Call for Tough Arms Control – Voices from Haiti.* Geneva: Small Arms Survey.

Smith, D. J., 2004. The Bakassi Boys: Vigilantism, violence, and political imagination in Nigeria, *Cultural Anthropology,* 19:3, 429–455.

Tilly, C., 1990. *Coercion, Capital and European States, A.D. 990–1990.* Cambridge: Blackwell.

Urdal, H., 2006. A clash of generations? Youth bulges and political violence, *International Studies Quarterly,* 50:3, 607–629.

Varshney, A., 2002. *Ethnic Conflict and Civic Life: Hindus and Muslims in India.* New Haven, CT: Yale University Press.

Willman, A. and Marcelin, L. H., 2010. If they could make us disappear they would! Youth and violence in Cité Soleil, Haiti. *Journal of Community Psychology,* 48:4, 515–531.

Winton, A., 2004. Urban violence: A guide to the literature, *Environment and Urbanization,* 16, 165–184.

Chapter 11

Secret societies and order-making in Freetown

Nathaniel King and Peter Albrecht

Introduction

The security landscape in Sierra Leone's capital, Freetown, is characterised by a plurality of policing actors and practices. They combine mutually reinforcing and conflicting forms of physical and esoteric–spiritual authority to provide security and make order. This chapter explores a set of actors that plays a central role in urban order-making, represented by a particular variety of urban secret societies, the Odelays. Specifically, we analyse the role of the Firestone Secret Society (in the following referred to as Firestone). Like other Odelays it is situated on the socio-economic and geographical margins of Freetown. Its security functions encompass apprehending criminals, investigating and solving crimes in collaboration with the Sierra Leone Police (SLP), at times through Firestone's expansive social networks.

Odelays are of a relatively recent origin. They emerged after the Second World War in pace with urbanisation, and grew out of Freetown's older Yoruba-based societies, such as Agugu, Hunters, Gelede and Akanjia (King 2012). Odelays are socially integrative bodies that are rooted in the spatial territoriality of specific neighbourhoods (Abdullah 2002: 23), and built up around medicinal-esoteric practices (King 2012). Membership is historically dominated by the young and excluded urban poor and is coveted because it generates social, economic and political authority. By extension, it affords members the capacity to bargain with the political elite and take on the role of security providers.

The main argument of the chapter is that people on the urban margins interact with centres of power through institutions such as Firestone, which provide the means to engage with the central government from a position of authority. This does not detract from the relative marginality of Firestone, but through its gatekeeper function, the society generates strategic value from its marginality. Membership becomes a route to building up relations with state representatives from a position of power and a means to expose the limits of the latter's reach.

Odelays are practical manifestations of the fact that no institution monopolizes the authority to produce order and a sense of security or is in a de facto position to do so.[1] The mechanics of local order-making practices through Odelays is best understood if Sierra Leone is analysed as a multi-centred governance system in which a variety of institutional formations take on a security function. Order is a continuously negotiated and relational category of distributed authority that is constituted by the enactment of an integral system of mutually reinforcing, beneficial and sometimes antagonistic relationships and partnerships (Albrecht 2013: 19).

The multiplicity that Firestone represents is captured in much of the empirically grounded literature that explores the fragmented, local and often personalised nature of authority in contexts where order-making is not necessarily the prerogative of a set of centrally governed institutions associated with the state (e.g. Das and Poole 2004; Hansen and Stepputat 2001, 2005, 2006; Lund 2002, 2006, 2008). On the one hand, this perspective enables us to understand 'the operation of authorities in a disaggregated manner and to de-emphasize the state as the ultimate seat of power' (Sharma and Gupta 2006: 9). On the other hand, it supports the importance of 'examining the dispersed institutional and social networks through which rule is coordinated and consolidated, and the role that non-state institutions, communities and individuals play in the mundane processes of governance' (ibid.). Odelays can be seen as locally rather than central-bureaucratically constituted networks of governance that the SLP and other state representatives may access through negotiations and by invitation.

The chapter begins with a brief historical overview of how different types of secret societies emerged in Sierra Leone and the varying functions they have across the rural–urban divide. Specifically, in the context of Freetown, we discuss how Yoruba-based societies initially emerged in the mid-nineteenth century and the coming into being of Odelays after the Second World War when migration to the capital gathered momentum. This discussion is followed by three examples of the negotiated characteristic of order-making in Foulah Town on Freetown's margins where Firestone operates. These examples provide insight into Firestone's various roles as gatekeeper to the margins, engaging in community policing initiated by the SLP and in shaping electoral processes at the national level.

Secret societies: a total social phenomenon across the rural–urban divide

As an uneven, yet tightly structured landscape of institutional formations, secret societies in Sierra Leone constitute central sites of order-making in urban and rural space. 'Knowing the secret' gives access to resources and decision-making and the authority to claim a stake in the enforcement of local order. However, their historical origin, practices and the environments in which they operate differ significantly across the rural–urban divide. Unlike the Odelays, Poro/Yoruba-based societies overlap more or less stringently with ethnic and religious identities (Albrecht 2012; King 2012). Yet, there are substantial similarities as well, including how sodalities utilise resources based on secrecy of esoteric–medicinal powers.

All secret societies have the quality of being a 'total social phenomenon' in common (Durkheim 1915; Evans-Pritchard 1940, 1956). As such, their effects are not restricted to the field of security and justice, which are the focus of this book, but cut across the economic, political and ideational dimensions of social life. For instance, Firestone runs a school and a community centre, which points to the fundamentally decentred nature of service delivery in Freetown and social order in Sierra Leone more broadly. By setting up boundaries between members and non-members, secret societies regulate who can, and who cannot, access resources, whether it is land for mining and farming or voters in the run-up to elections.

For members of urban Odelays and the rural Poro alike, 'knowing the secret' is vital, not for what it is, *per se*, or for the content it guards, but for the authority and rights to participate in social life that initiation carries with it (see Bellman 1984: 17; Simmel 1950). Commonly, the secret revolves around knowledge of esoteric medicine, which protects a sodality as a whole, the masquerades of the Freetown-based societies, which we return to in the following section, and individual members. It is the ability of select members to use these powers that lays the foundation of esoteric–medicinal mysticism, a distinguishing characteristic of the secret society, which in turn projects the sodality's relative authority.[2]

The bottom line is that endowing some and not others with the secrets of the Poro, Agugu, Gelede or Firestone becomes an instrument in the struggle over monopolising order-making and an important marker of inclusion and exclusion in decision-making over scarce resources.

Yoruba-based societies in the city: Agugu, Hunter, Odelay

Broadly speaking, Freetown's secret societies can be divided into old and new societies. Those that are considered old are on the one hand the Freemasons (also called Masonic Lodges, Masons or Lodges), which have an international base, and on the other hand the Yoruba-based secret societies, e.g. the Agugu and Hunters, which emerged within processes of creolisation in Freetown and are founded on esoteric–medicinal mysticism.

Yoruba-based societies emerged when Freetown became the settlement of ex-slaves and intended slaves (Recaptives) of the trans-Atlantic slave trade in the nineteenth century. The Agugu is the oldest, formed around 1850 (Peterson 1969: 267), and was created in an attempt by members of the nascent Freetown community to have a secret society of their own with African roots.

This was done to reconnect with a perceived 'African essence' in an unfamiliar urban setting that was dominated by Krios, the identity shaped around resettled former slaves and to a large extent built on Christianity and British virtues. Cutting across ethnic and religious identities, Agugu and Hunters gained traction, because of what Peterson (1969: 266–267) refers to as their 'apparent efficacy' in bringing about urban integration.

A surge of migrants from Sierra Leone's interior led to urbanisation and overpopulation in Freetown, which produced poor economic and health conditions in the growing city. As the older secret societies progressively reinforced a sense of exclusiveness, an expansive and growing section of Freetown's populace found itself on the urban margins. The result was an experience of rootlessness, insecurity and exclusion of the newcomers in search of urban belonging.

Out of this quest grew the most important of Freetown's new societies, the Odelays, emerging in the post-World War II era and driven by a push for socio-urban integration (Nunley 1987: 60).[3] The Odelays' core membership consisted of what Abdullah (1998: 208) refers to as 'largely unemployed and unemployable youths, mostly male . . . who have one foot in what is generally referred to as the informal or underground economy'. As such, a motivating factor behind the emergence of Odelays may be captured by Giddens' (2001) notion of 'ontological security' in the sense that they safeguarded and stabilised the fluctuating and unstable context of Freetown (with the rapid growth of the capital during the civil war in the 1990s this sense of instability and transience has remained one of the city's strong characteristics).

Central to Freetown's Odelays is the relative open-endedness of the youth concept, which connotes socio-economic disadvantage rather than chronological age. Being 'a youth' is gender neutral and denotes someone who has not yet achieved social, economic or political adulthood (King 2007). The appeal of the Odelays is the social capital that arises from bonds within them, their functionality, oaths of secrecy, and inter-area networks. This is reinforced by the wide urban margins, combined with the inability of centrally governed institutions to accomplish what Mitchell (1991) refers to as 'the state effect'. Mitchell argues that while the state should not be considered an actual structure, it should nevertheless be viewed as the powerful, seemingly metaphysical effect of practices that make such structures appear to exist. In Freetown as well as rural areas of Sierra Leone, it is the absence of this effect that allows secret societies to generate authority right from the centre of marginality and from seeming powerlessness.

A key element of a Yoruba-based society's generation of authority is its public display in masquerades where the devil[4] appears, giving public visibility and materiality to the spirit of the secret society. The masquerade embodies the society's esoteric–medicinal foundation, and is thus a bridge between visible and invisible powers. Agugu and Hunters conduct masquerades any time that their members choose to do so, while Odelays only perform at specific times of the year. There are two reasons for this. First, the older societies are generally considered more powerful and, second, only members can participate in their performances, which limits the crowds that gather around their masquerades.

Unlike Agugu and Hunters, anyone can take part in Odelays' public performances. Their followers are a mix of members and non-members, with the former being vastly outnumbered by the latter. Furthermore, Odelays accept cross-membership with other Odelays, Agugu, Hunters and Jollays (the latter are juvenile organisations of Odelays, and are not considered fully part of a secret society). Their public performances are open to men, women and children alike. Most importantly, a measure of an Odelay's power to negotiate access to urban and national resources is the number of followers and onlookers that it produces during its masquerade. Therefore, the Odelays mobilise widely among their members, sympathisers, associates and residents in the area where their headquarters are located. Turn-out can be as high as 20,000 people, and numbers are not only a source of members' pride; they also consolidate the powers of the Odelay in Freetown's secret society landscape.

Medicine, as it relates to secret societies generally, refers to the system of esoteric ability that all secret societies across the rural–urban divide claim a stake in. Members of the Hunters, Agugu and Odelays all call their secret societies 'Awo' (a Yoruba word that roughly means medicine power). Even though many members of those older sodalities do not consider Odelays to be proper secret societies, the shared use of Awo is an indication of the nature of the contested space that urban societies occupy, operate and collaborate in.

Firestone Secret Society

Firestone, the main focus of the remainder of the chapter, is one of the dominant Odelays in Foulah Town, an area of approximately 8 square kilometres. It claims among other identities that it is a secret society with esoteric–medicinal powers. It communicates its secret society dimensions as Firestone Secret Society (or Mao Mao Society) and amalgamates its secret and non-secret dimensions in Firestone Youth Development and Cultural Association (FYDCA). Apart from the Mao Mao Society and FYDCA, the sodality encompasses two additional components, the Firestone Lantern Group[5] and the Women's Wing.

Before the establishment of Foulah Town, Freetown, especially its central part, was predominantly a Krio area. According to Peterson, Foulah Town was established in 1819 by immigrant traders of the Fula ethnic group (Fulbe, Fulani and Peul in other parts of Africa). In the 1890s, Foulah Town became populated predominantly by Moslem Yoruba (Peterson 1969: 164).

According to Peterson (1969: 109), Foulah Town was established on the fringes of Freetown, yet the community appears to have settled in an area where a community of Christian Krios already existed. Christian missionaries found secret society practices in Freetown intolerable. Indeed, one Reverend Beale at one point attacked a dancing Agugu devil in Pademba Road, one of Freetown's main roads. However, '[d]espite missionary endeavours', Fyfe (1962: 351) notes, the parish including Foulah Town was still the centre of 'non-Christian practices' of Yoruba-based and Bondo societies. There were de facto and, at times, active coexistence and interaction between religious and non-religious groups in Foulah Town. Mosques were built just yards away from churches, while Hunters and Agugu established a foothold in the same area. Until the end of the 1970s Hunters had divine and thanksgiving services in Krio churches.

Why did people in Freetown embrace Odelays such as Firestone as altern-atives to older Yoruba-based societies? Cohen (1981: 110) observes that membership of Masonic Lodges, in particular, was prohibitively expensive, synonymous with high status in Freetown, and commonly based on nomination by relatives and friends who were already initiated. Limitations to the appeal of the older Yoruba-based societies centred on religion, with Hunters being mainly Christian though open to women, while Agugu tended to be Moslem and male-exclusive, which they still are. Odelays grew out of these processes of inclusion and exclusion of marginalised urban youth and provided an institutionalised mechanism for urban integration.

Like other Odelays, Freetown residents generally regard Firestone members as secret society rejects. They live on the city's geopolitical and socio-economic margins, and many of them have not succeeded in gaining access to the older urban sodalities. At the same time, the margins are not inert. Via Odelays such as Firestone, members interact with centres of power and provide the means to engage with those centres. This does not take away the relative marginality of Firestone, but through Firestone's gatekeeper function marginality has strategic value. Membership becomes a route to building up relations with representatives of the central government from a position of power and a means to expose the limits of the central government's reach.

As a total social phenomenon, Firestone engages in everyday policing of Foulah Town, investigating crimes and apprehending criminals. As explored in more detail below, this kind of policing is at times done in support of the SLP, but never by the police alone. Indeed, SLP activity requires the collaboration of Odelay members to make up for its limited capacity and legitimacy to provide security on the urban margins. If a Firestone member commits a crime against another member or the organisation, the perpetrator is punished according to secret society rules and regulations. At times, this involves corporal punishment. Importantly, members subject to the Firestone justice system do not have access to an appeal system outside the physical and symbolic bounds of the sodality. No one else protects them and while legislation produced by the state is recognised by Firestone members, the capacity of the police to perform its con-stitutionally prescribed duties on the margins is limited.

Firestone's capacity to make order

Having shed light on some of the dimensions of Firestone as part of Sierra Leone's decentred governance system, what follow are three examples of how the central government and the urban margins engage one another in order-making. The cases explore the role that Firestone members play in making order through policing, including how that role is played out vis-à-vis politicians, electoral politics and in relations of patronage. Overall, the three examples emphasize the main argument of the chapter, which is that Firestone membership on the urban margins provides the means to engage with the central government from a position of authority and power.

The first case provides insight into the need of national politicians all the way to State House to engage an organisation such as Firestone and co-opt its leadership and members to access votes during general elections. In doing so, and by visiting the Firestone area in Foulah Town, politicians comply with the rules and regulations of Firestone, including its security apparatus. The second case revolves around the SLP's own community policing model that centres on Local Policing Partnership Boards (LPPBs). It shows that only by engaging Firestone members, and accessing their close-knit network of members, can community policing as a SLP-led initiative operate effectively in Foulah Town. The third case exemplifies this latter point, where a case of theft, involving a high-ranking politician was only properly investigated and resolved by engaging Firestone members. But it was also the case that the victim's high status prompted Firestone to dedicate time to the case, as such showing how politics and patronage shape policing responses on the urban margins.

National politics and elections on the urban margins

In 2007, presidential and general elections were held in Sierra Leone. The country's President during the previous decade, Ahmad Tejan Kabbah of the Sierra Leone People's Party (SLPP), had served two terms. Therefore, as prescribed by Sierra Leone's Constitution, Kabbah was not eligible for re-election. Because Freetown is the seat of political power, election campaigns in its constituencies are intense, and major parties and politicians make an extra effort to win a majority of votes. One of the means by which politicians canvass votes is by co-opting the members of Odelays. Politicians seek to advance their chances with the socio-economically disadvantaged in Freetown – the majority of the urban electorate – by gaining the support, just short of an endorsement, from one or more of the four main Odelays: Paddle, Firestone, Civili Rule and Rainbow (especially the first two).

One high-ranking politician of the ruling party understood that sections of the Firestone organisation had been supportive of the one-party government led by the All People's Congress (APC) that ruled Sierra Leone up until Sierra Leone's civil war broke out in 1991. However, in the new millennium, and following the return of multiparty democracy in 1996, Firestone became a more open forum for political competition. In addition, under President Kabbah's leadership, the SLPP engaged Firestone members in various state-sponsored programmes, including disarmament, demobilisation and reintegration as well as the development of a youth agenda. Through the National Commission for Social Action (NACSA), the SLPP government had also been one of the major funding agencies of the Firestone School.

Nevertheless, after ten years in power, the SLPP was struggling to maintain a hold on seats in Freetown and elsewhere. As it was masquerade season, the aforementioned high-ranking SLPP politician therefore decided to pay Firestone a visit to cultivate the party's Odelay-based urban support. Earlier that day in mid 2007, he had been on his way to campaign in his party's stronghold of Bo – the second largest town in the southern part of Sierra Leone – but at the last minute changed his mind and chose, as one informant put it, 'to pay the devil a visit'. As we shall see, the politician's visit to Firestone illustrates the negotiated nature of authority to make order and the simultaneous inclusion and exclusion of representatives of the state.

The Firestone executive and the politician arranged the visit between them. The latter's convoy of heavily armed bodyguards drove up the steep road of Owen Street in a fleet of about seven black jeeps. The vehicles were parked in the area just before Firestone's walled estate. As security precaution and protocol demanded, the soldiers, police personnel and other bodyguards stepped out of their jeeps, and opened the door for the politician. The Firestone executive also reached out to greet him. This was where representatives of the central government met Firestone for the day, with the state being in control.

Immediately before the politician and his retinue went through Firestone's first gate, Firestone members, including the most powerful esoteric–medicinal expert, told the politician that within the Firestone area, Firestone Awo[6] would protect him. The police personnel, the military and other bodyguards who escorted the politician were, according to the Firestone executive, not needed in their domain where state-sanctioned security was ineffectual and powerless. Perhaps the retinue wanted the visit to go ahead, whatever the conditions. Perhaps the uniformed personnel, representing the state, recognised the difficulty of getting the group of possibly non-secret society members protecting the politician into an esoteric-medicinal sphere. Whatever may have been the case, the visitors agreed to the terms, and sent only the politician and the group around him.

This was the state's outer limit and the politician and his entourage had entered a domain where the security that uniformed personnel could provide no longer applied. The most-reputed men in Firestone's esoteric–medicinal sphere served as the bodyguards within the inner sancta of the Odelay. During their walk, the visitors were shown the Firestone School, which was built with government support, the church/community centre, the tin tenements and the 'Firestone Parliament' where members sit and debate social, economic and political matters. Richardson (1988: 209) notes that '[i]nteractionally, status differentials are power differentials'. In this and similar cases of interaction between representatives of the state and Firestone members, it was evident that with the authority they held in Foulah Town during this period of elections and as gatekeepers of a significant number of voters, they were able to set the rules of the engagement. This explicitly included who was in charge of security.

The high-ranking politician's visit to the school on this occasion marks a curious return that deserves emphasis. He had been the designated 'Chief Unveiler' of the Firestone School when it was completed by the NACSA in 2004. It was he who had cut the ribbon and formally handed over the school to Firestone. At that time, in 2004, the politician had been escorted by the military and his bodyguards; their security duties had been countenanced by the secret society because the presentation of the gift of the school had to be reciprocated. In short, the politician was making a gift that Firestone wanted – just as Firestone held something in 2007 that the politician desired. On his second visit, the tables had turned, so to speak.

During the 2004 visit, representatives of the state had met the secret society in the zone between the first and second gates. The boundaries had been strategically shifted to accommodate the central government and its security apparatus, because through NACSA it had helped to provide a vital social service. The unveiling of the school constituted a transition of a part state-funded project that was handed over to Firestone to manage on behalf of the community in Foulah Town.

When the high-ranking politician returned in 2007 in need of the secret society's support for his party and its presidential candidate, Firestone deemed it unnecessary for him to have Firestone bodyguards. He was coming to a home of sorts, it was argued. While this was certainly part of the explanation, the politician's visit also exposes how the authority to make order was not one of vertical encompassment – of a state and its representatives standing above, while at the same time containing its localities. This was Firestone land where a multitude of orders applied, and where authority was formally based in a esoteric–medicinal rationale; a matter of power in action and interaction. Arens and Karp (1989: xvii) explain the practical consequences of power based on esoteric knowledge, stating that societal members assert their authority 'in the interaction between natural, social and supernatural realms'. As such, Firestone was manifesting its order-making powers vis-à-vis the political leadership outside Foulah Town by reference to the esoteric–medicinal foundation of Firestone's authority.

The high-ranking politician's second visit to Firestone in Foulah Town shows what the localisation of authority means in practice. Authority cannot by definition be seen as a hierarchical relationship between a centre that sets the rules of the game and a periphery that follows or seeks to bypass those rules from a position of inferiority. Sometimes the urban margins *are* the centres of power. Like 'the social', authority is continuously reproduced through interaction, and can be analysed by taking into account what Westwood (2002: 19) refers to as the 'fluidity and ubiquity of power'. Authority, then, does not always mean conceiving order as the enactment of a hierarchy of consolidated positions. On Freetown's margins Odelays such as Firestone are the gatekeepers of resources – in this case voters for the general elections that took place on 11 August 2007 – while monopolising authority to make order, centred on esoteric–medicinal power.[7]

Having set the scene of how the authority to make order is in the hands of Firestone during extraordinary events – which a visit from one of the country's highest-ranking politicians is – the next section explores its role in everyday policing.

Community policing and Firestone

For almost two decades, Sierra Leone received considerable international support to broad-based security sector reform of the military, intelligence services and the police (Albrecht 2010; Albrecht and Jackson 2009, 2010; Jackson and Albrecht 2011; Albrecht *et al.* 2014). Noting the bureaucratic collapse that Sierra Leone experienced during the 1990s, this meant that as the SLP was resurrected, policing was defined by the ability of officers to use force according to international advisers and SLP officers alike. It was also evident that this ability had to be combined with the police's skills to negotiate access to areas where they had not been present for more than a decade.

Negotiations were shaped around efforts to rebuild trust between the police and the general public, based on a concept of 'policing by consensus'. As noted by Brima Acha Kamara who became Inspector-General of Police after the war ended in 2002:

> There were other forces, warring factions, RUF [Revolutionary United Front] combatants, CDF [Civil Defence Force], competition about who should really be in charge of internal security. We were not able to flex our muscle, and were ultimately doing *policing by consensus.*
> (Brima Acha Kamara quoted in Albrecht 2012: 184)

Kamara was describing policing in the immediate aftermath of war. Yet, in his assertion also lay the rationale in the years to come, and the SLP's new ethos of Local Needs Policing, which was introduced in the late 1990s (Albrecht *et al.* 2013: 28). LPPBs became one of the main institutional expressions of that ethos, and were established to ensure community involvement in apprehending criminals, preventing crimes and setting police priorities.

Formally, LPPBs are chaired by the Local Unit Commander and other officers from the police division, primarily those in charge of operations. In addition, a number of community members are represented, including teachers, youth representatives and religious organisations, among others. In practice, there is a significant difference between how this model was implemented in Freetown, the provinces, and specifically the places in the centre of the capital, which constitute the 'secret society belt', including the Magazine, Foulah Town and Fourah Bay.

The LPPBs in this 'belt' were established in 2008 and apart from incorporating police officers and a cross-section of community leaders into the LPPBs' rank and file, they included senior executive members of the major secret societies, in particular Paddle and Firestone. Unlike older secret societies, Odelays found it easier to incorporate this security and justice function into their line of activities, because Firestone regulations accommodate the engagement of non-secret society dimensions. Older secret societies thrive on being exclusively secret societal as it is on such consistency and assumed transcendence that they draw their mystique.

In a speech held in 2008, the Inspector-General of Police pointed out that areas of central Freetown where Odelays have a strong foothold had some of the highest crime rates in the entire country. As a Firestone member of the LPPB noted, not only was theft, including house-breaking and pick-pocketing, a common occurrence in those areas, but they had also been notorious for violence and killings.

For more than thirty years the police had not been able to bring crime rates down in those areas, and as such the problem predated the civil war in Sierra Leone, which began in 1991. In one among other attempts to reverse this trend, the SLP in those areas had adopted the version of LPPBs that had been used elsewhere in the country. However, the model was not effective, because those LPPB members, such as religious leaders and teachers, did not have the networks to identify and access criminals or they feared entering specific areas of the centre of Freetown due to safety concerns. In fact, the area around Freetown's Eastern Police Station, the busiest part of the capital, was notorious for daylight robberies, which also took place when earlier versions of the LPPB had been in operation. According to four interviewed police officers, it was the incorporation of Odelays into the LPPB that made it more effective in dealing with criminal offences.

Odelays, and Firestone in particular, encompass expansive networks of youth, and for this reason the police saw it as necessary to co-opt rather than challenge the sodalities. Indeed, the SLP was on the one hand keen to present relations with Firestone as an example of why criminal activity was not worth the effort and on the other hand that good citizens could emerge from former strongholds of crime. The SLP therefore actively sought to incorporate the organisation into the rank and file of the LPPB.

As part of the LPPB, Firestone members could use their wide-ranging vertical and horizontal networks across new and old urban secret societies to access information and identify criminals. However, they get the most important information from fellow secret society members who are certain that their identities will be kept a secret no matter the information they provide.

Confidentiality is ensured through the oath of secrecy that is taken as a requirement to become a secret society member, and as such loyalty to the Odelay ranks above loyalty to the state and its laws.[8]

In 2008–2009, one executive LPPB member in Foulah Town was also an executive member in the Paddle Odelay. Firestone had a total of five members in the executive of the LPPB, including the position of Secretary-General (third in rank after the LPPB Chairman and Vice Chairman). A central executive member of Firestone's Women's Wing was also a LPPB executive member. Added to this, Firestone created a branch of the LPPB in the Firestone–Foulah Town joint area, where male and female members and members of associated organisations such as the older Agugu and other Odelays were present.[9]

Informants noted that collaboration between the police and the LPPB of the Eastern Police Station resulted in the apprehension of numerous criminals, including thieves, frauds, arsonists and even killers. As such, Odelays were an important expression of boundary-making between the SLP and the local population that often fears or distrusts the police. Importantly, some of the criminals operating in Foulah Town did not live there, but were staying on the outskirts of Freetown where there was often less clarity about those who belonged to the areas and those who were newcomers (e.g. in Waterloo). One known criminal in the secret society belt had been living about 20 kilometres away from Foulah Town, and he was captured through the collaborative effort between Odelays of the LPPB in the division of the Eastern Police Station and older urban societies.

Similarly, it was the network of intelligence that secret societies constitute that led to the capture of an alleged killer of a young man in the Firestone area in December 2008. The police had initially characterised it as 'a crime against the state', and had therefore treated the investigation as a police matter. However, after more than a week of investigation proved futile, it was the Firestone–Foulah Town LPPB that drew on its networks to investigate and resolve the matter. In sum, setting up of the LPPBs confirms the notion of a state attempting to co-opt the urban margins. However, from the perspective of the urban margins and those who live there, the LPPBs had the opposite effect as well, namely to confirm the margins as the centre of power. In the final section of the chapter, we go into more detail on how politics and policing are intertwined by exploring one case of theft of a valued item, a mobile phone, from a member of state.

Political patronage and protection

On 26 April 2008, the eve of Sierra Leone's Independence Anniversary when lantern masquerades normally take place, a major government official with the rank of Minister was having a drink in a popular bar in Foulah Town (we will refer to him as 'the Honourable' in the following). The bar was located at a point where all the lanterns would pass. From there he could enjoy the relaxed atmosphere of the evening and at the same time see all the lanterns, while giving money to those of his friends and acquaintances who took part in the masquerades. However, it would soon become evident that the Honourable made the mistake of feeling too safe that night in an area that was notorious for robbery, pick-pocketing and bag-snatching. At one point, he received what seemed to be a very important call that kept him talking until the lantern of his Odelay passed by.

The Honourable divided his attention between continuing the seemingly important call, acknowledging the members of his lantern club and at the same time giving them money. It was at this point of intense activity that the majority of followers of the lanterns reached the Honourable's position, and somebody snatched the mobile phone from him. The thief disappeared into the crowd. The Honourable followed the crowd in a bid to get his phone back, but did not succeed. He reported the matter to the SLP, which said that they would carry out a 'thorough investigation' to recover the phone. The police in the area saw the matter as particularly pertinent, because the Honourable lived close to the police station; indeed, he had always been financially supportive of the police.[10]

Two days went by and the police could not find useful leads on who the thief was or where the phone could be found. In a show of having given up, a senior police officer told the Honourable that he should not have used the phone 'in the night, especially when those bad boys are around in large numbers'. However, the Honourable insisted that finding his phone was vital and bemoaned the loss of his important international and local contacts that were stored in the SIM card. In an articulation of peripheral authority by the centre, the police suggested to the Honourable that he use the networks of his Odelay members to track the thief and the phone. After some thought, the Honourable consented and later explained the problem to one high-ranking member of Firestone. The latter used his contacts to gain insight into the patterns of petty thieves who operated during the night where the phone was stolen. Through his investigation, he got on to the mobile phone thief and reportedly told him:

— 'Man, you made a very big mistake. Do you know whose phone you snatched on Lantern Night?'
— 'No,' the thief replied.
— 'You ought to be ashamed of yourself. Did you not recognise that that man was the major youth sponsor in this area? Don't you know that that was the man who helped pay for a lawyer for "Area Father"[11] when he had his court case?'

The thief reportedly became remorseful, saying that he regretted his actions. However, he had already sold the phone for 200,000 leones (about US$40) and had spent approximately 60,000 leones of that money. To reclaim the phone from the buyer, the thief requested that the Honourable give him the 60,000 leones and an additional amount as transport fare to, in street speak, 'redeem' the phone. The Honourable gave the thief 150,000 leones; the thief got the phone back from the person who bought it and gave it to the go-between; he sent his apologies to the Honourable, and promised to 'safeguard his interests in the future'.

As the case was being resolved, the thief was not handed over to the police. Resolution took place on the margins where police powers and skills had limited effect. It was the urban marginal secret societies and the networks they encompass that helped to trace the thief and reclaim the phone. How the phone was redeemed was based on the trust and oath of secrecy of Firestone, which protected the thief while at the same time leading to resolution of the matter. There is also little doubt that the political office of the victim, a Minister, was important in mobilising both the SLP and Firestone. In sum, the case of theft presented in this section provides insight into the networked nature of policing and the effectiveness of order-making on the margins, but it also shows that political interest and patronage were important elements in its resolution.

Aretxaga (2003: 395, 398) believes that the state's traditional role of regulating education and security, for example, has been substituted by private institutions. Odelays are not private institutions in this sense, because they did not emerge as a consequence of centrally governed institutions withdrawing from delivering public services. In short, the state never held a monopoly on service delivery in Sierra Leone. Odelays emerged in a context where the involvement of a multitude of actors in order-making has been and remains a historical mainstay. Firestone built a school for the community. In concert with other secret societies and state representatives, specifically the SLP, its members prevent and resolve crimes, for instance, to redeem the mobile phone of an important state official when the state apparatus failed to do so. As such, Firestone's role reflects a state formation process that has produced large margins that the centre and its representatives cannot, have not or will not master directly (see Albrecht and Buur 2009: 397; Das and Poole 2004).

Conclusion

A particular variety of Freetown's Yoruba-based secret societies, Odelays, emerged in the wake of post-Second World War urbanisation, and the experience of rootlessness and insecurity of newcomers. This chapter explores Firestone, a dominant Odelay in Freetown, where the secret like in many other of Sierra Leone's sodalities revolves around esoteric–medicinal mysticism. As a socially integrative body, Firestone encompasses a wide variety of functions, including the provision of security and justice. In different empirical cases, the chapter shows how Firestone becomes a vehicle for poor people on the urban margins to engage with the central government and a route to building up relations with state representatives from a position of power.

The chapter provides insight into the multitude of actors involved in order-making on Freetown's urban margins. On the one hand, it shows the negotiated and disaggregated nature of who can lay claim to the means of order-making, and the physical and symbolic boundaries that are established between different actors in these processes of inclusion and exclusion. On the other hand, it provides insight into how security and its provision become a concrete political expression and manifestation of power. Policing, politics and order-making have thus become inseparable, because how security is provided, to whom it is provided and why it is provided are integrally linked factors.

At the heart of interaction between Firestone and state representatives lies contestations and collaborations between a small centre and wide margins. At play is boundary-work. It is a process that demarcates Firestone's territoriality and produces separation between insiders and outsiders, that is, those who are furnished with the secret and those who are not. Overall, this plays into how power works in the sense that it derives from various sources, feeding into different claims to authority and forms of order-making.

This leads to the final point of this chapter, which revolves around the question of legitimacy. The margins where Odelays are located and emanate from are in the capital, Freetown, where the state might best be described as 'absent present' (see Goldstein 2012: 83; King 2012: 157, 251). The government garners legitimacy, because it was voted into office, including by those who inhabit the margins. However, because the state effect has been limited in these areas, the state and its representatives have comparably limited legitimacy. Yet, even if representatives of the state do not consistently enforce the law or hold the authority to do so, they remain an important partner, not least with respect to patronage.

Notes

1 There are close to 170 Odelays in Freetown.
2 The notion of mystique is a dialectical resource as mastery of the medicine begets mystique.
3 Modelled on the Agugu and Hunters, Odelay is a cross between the two. In fact, Odelay means 'small ode', where 'ode' is the name of the Hunters' masquerade and 'lay' is a diminutive suffix in the Yoruba argot that typifies Freetown's secret societies.
4 Nunley (1987: xv), writing about the aesthetics of Freetown's marginal secret societies, points out that the 'devil' characterisation goes back to early missionary activities in Sierra Leone. Christian missionaries presented masquerades to Christians as symbols of Satan, and Odelays as an antithesis to the Christian God, thus discouraging their congregations from becoming members of the urban sodalities. Secret societies have since used this negative appellation to their advantage to generate fear among non-members. The term 'devil' is now also used to mean the secret societies themselves. The right to use the word 'devil' is contested between old and new urban secret societies. The former claim that they have the real devils and that those of the latter are mere imitations – a fact that the old urban secret

societies believe is confirmed when the Odelays fuse non-members and members during their public performances, and include women in their membership.

5 'Lanterns' refer to displays of effigies of historical figures or paper-covered figures performing topical issues in the country's social, political or economic development. Nunley (1985: 45–48) describes them further:

> Mounted on wheeled platforms, they were made from timber, sticks, raffia pith, and cane, and covered with various combinations of paper, cloth, and rice bags. All but a few were lit by bulbs strung around the outside of the frame and wired to a generator hidden below. Just a handful of floats had bulbs fitted internally, like the candles which illuminated floats in the past and which gave rise to their Krio name of lantans.

Previously, lantern parades were organised at the culmination of the Moslem holy month of the Ramadan (Nunley 1985: 45). Now, the day allotted to them is on the eve of Sierra Leone's Independence Day, 26 April.

6 This is a Yoruba term for esoteric knowledge of medicinal powers. Earlier the term only referred to the Agugu and Hunters, but now it is also used to describe the powers that marginal urban secret societies such as Odelays lay claim to.
7 SLPP lost elections to the APC in 2007 and again in 2012.
8 Spiritually, members draw on the esoteric–medicinal powers of the Odelay before searching particularly dangerous areas.
9 Boys' specific organisations that are below the level of Odelays.
10 Due to limited funding provided by the central government, it is common that private and public individuals support the police financially (and sometimes logistically) (Horn et al. 2011: 37).
11 An alias for a well-known self-professed reformed criminal in Foulah Town.

References

Abdullah, I., 1998. 'Bushpath to Destruction: The Origin and Character of the Revolutionary United Front (RUF/SL)'. *Journal of Modern African Studies*, 36:2, 202–235.
Abdullah, I., 2002. 'Youth Culture and Rebellion: Understanding Sierra Leone's Wasted Decade'. *Critical Arts*, 16:2, 19–37.
Albrecht, P., 2010. *Transforming Internal Security in Sierra Leone – Sierra Leone Police and Broader Justice Sector Reform*, DIIS Report 2010:07, Copenhagen: DIIS.
Albrecht, P., 2012. 'Foundational Hybridity and its Reproduction: Security Sector Reform in Sierra Leone', PhD Series, 33.2012, Doctoral School of Organisation and Management Studies, Copenhagen: Copenhagen Business School.
Albrecht, P., 2013. *Local Actors and Service Delivery in Fragile Situations*, DIIS Report 2013:24, Copenhagen: Danish Institute for International Studies.
Albrecht, P. and Buur, L., 2009. 'An Uneasy Marriage: Non-State Actors and Police Reform'. *Policing and Society*, 19:4, 390–405.
Albrecht, P. and Jackson, P., 2009. *Security System Transformation in Sierra Leone, 1997–2007*, Global Facilitation Network for Security Sector Reform and International Alert, Birmingham: University of Birmingham.
Albrecht, P. and Jackson, P. (eds), 2010. *Security Sector Reform in Sierra Leone: Views from the Frontline*, Berlin: DCAF/LIT Verlag.
Albrecht, P., Garber, O. and Gibson, A., 2013. *Democratizing Security: Local Policing Partnership Boards in Sierra Leone*, Freetown: Access to Security and Justice Programme (available upon request from authors).

Albrecht, P., Garber, O., Gibson, A. and Thomas, S. 2014. *Community Policing in Sierra Leone – Local Policing Partnership Boards*, DIIS Report 2014:16, Copenhagen: DIIS.

Arens, W. and Karp, I., 1989 [1984]. *Creativity of Power*, Washington, DC: Smithsonian Institution Press.

Aretxaga, B., 2003. 'Maddening States'. *Annual Review of Anthropology*, 32, 393–410.

Bellman, B.L., 1984. *The Language of Secrecy: Symbols and Metaphor in Poro Ritual*, Brunswick, NJ: Rutgers University Press.

Cohen, A., 1981. *The Politics of Elite Culture: Dramaturgy of Power in a Modern African Society*, Berkeley and Los Angeles, CA: University of California Press.

Das, V. and Poole, D., 2004. 'The State and its Margins', in V. Das and D. Poole (eds), *Anthropology at the Margins of the State*, New Delhi: Oxford University Press, 3–34.

Durkheim, E., 1915. *The Elementary Forms of the Religious Life*, New York: Free Press.

Evans-Pritchard, E. E., 1940. *The Nuer*, Oxford: Oxford University Press.

Evans-Pritchard, E. E., 1956. *Nuer Religion*, Oxford: Clarendon.

Fyfe, C., 1993 [1962]. *A History of Sierra Leone*, Oxford: Oxford University Press.

Giddens, A., 2001. *Modernity and Self-Identity: Self and Society in the Late Modern Age*, Cambridge: Polity Press.

Goldstein, D. M., 2012. *Outlawed: Between Security and Rights in a Bolivian City*, Durham and London: Duke University Press.

Hansen, T. B. and Stepputat, F., 2001. 'Introduction: State of Imagination', in T. B. Hansen and F. Stepputat (eds), *States of Imagination. Ethnographic Explorations of the Post Colonial State*, London: Duke University Press, 1–38.

Hansen, T. B. and Stepputat, F., 2005. 'Introduction', in T. B. Hansen and F. Stepputat (eds), *Sovereign Bodies: Citizens, Migrants, and States in the Postcolonial World*, Princeton University Press, 1–36.

Hansen, T. B. and Stepputat, F., 2006. 'Sovereignty Revisited'. *Annual Review of Anthropology*, 35, 295–315.

Horn, A., Gordon, M. and Albrecht, P., 2011. *Sierra Leone Police: Review of Capabilities*. Unpublished.

Jackson, P. and Albrecht, P., 2011. *Reconstructing Security after Conflict: Security Sector Reform in Sierra Leone*, London: Palgrave Macmillan.

King, N., 2007. *Conflict as Integration: Youth Aspiration to Personhood in the Teleology of Sierra Leone's 'Senseless War'*, Uppsala: Nordic Africa Institute.

King, N., 2012. 'Contested Spaces in Post-War Society: The "Devil Business" in Freetown, Sierra Leone', PhD dissertation, der Philosophischen Fakultät, Martin-Luther Universität, Halle-Wittenberg.

Lund, C., 2002. 'Negotiating Property Institutions: On the Symbiosis of Property and Authority in Africa', in K. Juul and C. Lund (eds), *Negotiating Property in Africa*, Portsmouth: Heinemann, 11–43.

Lund, C., 2006. 'Twilight Institutions: Public Authority and Local Politics in Africa'. *Development and Change*, 37:4, 685–705.

Lund, C., 2008. *Local Politics and the Dynamics of Property in Africa*, Cambridge: Cambridge University Press.

Mitchell, T., 1991. 'The Limits of the State: Beyond Statist Approaches and their Critics'. *American Political Science Review*, 85:1, 77–96.

Nunley, J. W., 1985. 'The Lantern Festival in Sierra Leone', *African Arts*, 18:2, 45–48.

Nunley, J. W., 1987. *Moving with the Face of the Devil*, Chicago, IL: University of Illinois Press.

Peterson, J., 1969. *Province of Freedom: A History of Sierra Leone, 1787–1870*, London: Faber & Faber.

Richardson, L., 1988. 'Secrecy and Status: The Social Construction of Forbidden Relationships'. *American Sociological Review*, 53:2, 209–219.

Sharma, A. and Gupta, A., 2006. 'Introduction: Rethinking Theories of the State in an Age of Globalization', in A. Sharma and A. Gupta (eds), *The Anthropology of the State: A Reader*, Oxford: Blackwell, 1–42.

Simmel, G., 1950. 'The Secret and the Secret Society', in K. H. Wolff (ed.), *The Sociology of Georg Simmel*, New York: Free Press of Glencoe, 307–376s.

Westwood, S., 2002. *Power and the Social*, London: Routledge.

Index